Goodbye, Mr. Wonderful

Goodbye, Mr. Wonderful

Alcoholism, Addiction, and Early Recovery

Chris McCully

Jessica Kingsley Publishers
London and Philadelphia

First published in 2004
by Jessica Kingsley Publishers
116 Pentonville Road
London N1 9JB, UK
and
400 Market Street, Suite 400
Philadelphia, PA 19106, USA

www.jkp.com

Copyright © Chris McCully 2004
Printed digitally since 2009

Library of Congress Cataloging in Publication Data

McCully, C. B.
  Goodbye, Mr. Wonderful : alcoholism, addiction and early recovery / Chris McCully.-- 1st American ed.
    p. cm.
  Includes bibliographical references and index.
  ISBN 1-84310-265-X (pbk.)
  1. McCully, C. B.--Diaries. 2. Alcoholics--Biography. 3. Alcoholics--Rehabilitation. I. Title.
  HV5068.M36 2004
  362.292'092--dc22

                                    2004011287

British Library Cataloguing in Publication Data
A CIP catalogue record for this book is available from the British Library

ISBN 978 1 84310 265 6

To my friends in and out of recovery.
Their name is Legion.

Contents

Acknowledgements

There are two kinds of acknowledgement I need to make – the first, chiefly personal; the second, textual. Of the first kind, I would say that an extended family, and a number of friends and fellow addicts, read drafts of the material in this book. These people gave unstintingly of their time, and their love, in order to read, and to criticize, what is – what had to be – a very frank piece of writing. Without exception, their comments were clear, helpful, and constructive. I have acted on those comments, but at the same time have been surprised at how little of the original manuscript I have had to change. Some given names have been altered – they had to be, in order to protect the sensitivities of those who, in different ways it may be, are surviving alcoholism – and some entries have been very lightly modified, again in order to accommodate others' sensitivities. In preparing the text for final publication, however, I'm above all grateful for the time and trouble so many people have taken in advising me about things I might consider changing, or adding or deleting from successive versions of the manuscripts. I'm also grateful for the delicacy with which people have sought to clarify my thinking about the very real ethical issues surrounding anonymity, autobiographical styles of writing, and personal disclosure. That delicacy eventually taught me that although this *testimony* is indeed mine, and appears under my own name, the *story* is in all truth and conscience the story of alcoholism. There are many testimonies – perhaps millions – to the same story, the same banal, terrifying narrative of addiction. It helped me at the time of writing, and it helps me now, to see my own experiences as generically similar to the unwritten testimonies of other addicts, and of their families and friends. If this testimony helps anyone think about that wider story with more insight, humour, rigour, and compassion, then it will have served one of its main purposes, and I will be glad.

I have explicit textual acknowledgements to make. The first is to my former colleague Ken Lincoln, of the Department of English at the University of California, Los Angeles (UCLA), who so generously has allowed me to reprint two extensive excerpts from his book *The Good Red Road: Passages into Native America*. Full bibliographic details of this masterpiece appear in the section detailing 'Some reading' that closes the present work. Second, Journal entry 49 of the present text appeared as the essay 'On neither writing nor revising' in *PNReview 28*, Number 5, May–June 2002. I am very grateful to the editor of *PNReview*, Michael Schmidt, for allowing the same work to appear again here, in its first context.

The poem found on p.175 first appeared in *The Country of Perhaps* (Manchester: Carcanet, 2002), and I'm again grateful to Michael Schmidt for allowing me to reprint this here, only adding my further thanks for his many acts of support and kindness over what are now two decades. The poem found on p.177 was, to my great surprise, among the prize-winners in the 2004 Academi Cardiff International Poetry Competition, and I'm grateful to the Welsh Academy, the Welsh National Literature Promotion Agency and Society of Writers, and the judges and organisers of the competition, for permission to reprint the poem in this book. I further acknowledge Harvard University Press, for permission to reprint small excerpts in Appendix 3 from Robert N. Proctor, *Racial Hygiene: Medicine Under the Nazis* (Cambridge, Mass.: Harvard University Press, Copyright © 1986 by the President and Fellows of Harvard College). I extend my thanks, too, to Jacqui Thornton and *The Sun* newspaper, for allowing me permission to use material first published in *The Sun*, 13 June 2003, as Appendix 1. Finally, I offer warm gratitude to Online Recovery Services for graciously allowing me to reproduce *The Johns Hopkins Test for Alcoholism* and *Did You Grow Up with a Problem Drinker* from their website, *www.recovery.org.*

My final acknowledgement is both personal and textual. It is to Monika. Her contributions to parts of this text were so extensive that Appendix 3 here – which says a little about how alcoholism was viewed under National Socialism in the Germany of the 1930s and 1940s – appears under our joint names. Here, I offer her, again, my gratitude. She already knows that in the wilderness of choices I am trying to live, in the connections I'm trying to make, and in the recovery I am trying, today, to sustain, she has my love.

Chris McCully
Amstelveen, May 2004

About this book

At the end of 1999, over a month-long period that included Old Millennium Night, and after three years of trying, and failing, to maintain sobriety and recovery, I was hospitalized. 'Chronic alcoholic' was hand-written across the medical notes. 'Dr. McCully is a high-risk offender' was typed into my DVLA and criminal record. All therapeutic strategies had apparently failed. All my excuses, and even the excuses of others, were exhausted. Whatever was left of myself – or possibly, my Selves, including the persona I've called Mr. Wonderful – was shattered, poisoned, not to trust. Wherever I looked seemed to be full of chaos. The chaos, when I could bear to look out from the remnants of myself at the life I seemed to be inhabiting, felt nauseating, like vertigo. Nauseating, like fear, or self-disgust, or both. As it reached for the vodka, failure could barely manage to articulate 'Who am I?' Whoever this 'I' was, its only reality was an alibi. One marriage had collapsed. Relationships with family and close friends were in tatters. I couldn't work, and had only just managed – by luck, by the intervention of others – to hang on to my job. I didn't want to go fishing any more. My driving licence had been suspended after a serious conviction. I had sold the house, given away my dog. I was living in rented accommodation. I had lost nearly 30lbs in weight, and had razored off my hair. I was broke.

Those are some of the facts.

Another fact is that these kinds of squalid drama are shared by millions.

On 7 December 1999, I don't think I had very long to live. Perhaps I didn't altogether want to live. For the two previous years I'd slept – when I did sleep – with the means of self-destruction very close at hand.

That's a fact, too.

This book is a record of what happened, of what happened next, and what seemed to happen as the consequence of what happened next. If it's a record of anything, it's a record of early recovery, and of a mind and life trying somehow to cleanse itself, and to live again. To live again – not in the old way, but in the chosen, difficult way of recovery, and of freedom.

Today, I am sober, and in recovery. I could paraphrase, and almost with justice, the great words of Kazantzakis: I want for little. I fear almost nothing. And therefore, I am free. I also know that I have to be able to repeat those words tomorrow, and yet I can't live tomorrow today. I must *expect* nothing. I have enough to do, living recovery in the now-ness of Now. In that Now, which vanishes even as I write it, I realize that I'm only in recovery today. Therefore, today, with this realization and with that freedom, I'm living again.

You may think I wrote this merely for myself. That would be partly true. It helped, in the early months of recovery, to sit down with this simple discipline. If I was trying to overhear myself thinking, I was urgently trying to overhear myself *feeling*. Nevertheless, however clumsily, I was trying to write for others. I thought it might be useful if even the souls lost to themselves, and the ones who love the souls lost to themselves, could also overhear these pieces of recovered thinking.

In the bookstores, you'll find a whole literature related to recovery from alcoholism. A great deal of it is American in origin. A great deal of it is self-helpy sentimentalism. It doesn't tell you how it is, or how it feels, only how it might be, in a white, Protestant world filled with the good life, a lawn-sprinkler, and two cars in the driveway. This literature sounds as nonsensical to me as the tinklings of a perpetual Buddhist Christmas.

To an alcoholic attempting to dry out, and to live in recovery, I don't think such literature has a great deal to say. There are shining exceptions: you'll come across references to some of the literature I found most helpful at the end of the present text. In particular, Alcoholics Anonymous (AA) can provide a rich, thought-provoking, and relatively focused literature. The problem there is that to access the literature, and the resource that is AA, you have under normal circumstances to get to an AA meeting first. And getting to that first AA meeting is probably one of the most difficult things an alcoholic will ever have to do. Staying with such a programme is, if anything, even more difficult.

There was nothing in the bookshops – there seems still to be nothing – that provides the kind of structured overhearing I still need. I didn't want to hear the ill-written indulgence that was someone else's diary. I didn't want exhortation, nor did I need warning. I was at the end of warnings and exhortations. I wasn't quite smart enough to plough through medical textbooks detailing the aetiology of Korsakoff's psychosis or Wernicke's syndrome (though I tried). I wasn't quite patient enough to master the psychological literature of dependency and addiction (though I tried). Above all, I needed something that I could read quickly, something I could browse, or excerpt, perhaps one sitting at a time. Something that shared loneliness. Something that could function as a kind of way-mark on whatever kind of journey it was that I was undertaking.

And so I shared my own loneliness, in the way that I could.

In what follows, you'll find dated records (the Journal entries) of how it was – of how it was to *feel* how it was – in the early months of recovery. Most such records are around 750–1000 words long, and each is short enough to be read at one sitting. They don't try to 'explain', nor – I hope – do they patronize, largely because it's very difficult to patronize oneself. If they do exhort, the only person they're exhorting is me. There were certain fundamentals of recovery I often had to remind myself to remember, and to put into practice.

Whoever may read this is free to read the Journal entries one at a time, or browse them sequentially. You can even read them backwards. They don't provide, thank goodness, a diary-type narrative, although the earliest entries were written in hospital, and the later ones detail how it felt a year, two years on. But although there is a form of chronology at work, the entries build to no particular climax. Nor will you find specific details of love affairs, bank accounts, personalities. All you will find is a kind of record that gently insists on itself, encoding a kind of truth merely by being there.

Interspersed with the dated records (and in one instance, within a record), you'll find sections of italicized text. These were largely written retrospectively, in 2002, though some pieces of retrospective were written in 2003, at the revision stage of manuscript preparation. Reading through the original manuscript, I'd found – as one or two kind readers had found – that some additional material on *circumstance*, rather than on the veracities of 'how it felt', would help both to ground and to contextualize the dated records. And so, visiting myself again, but recalling some more circumstantial details of 'how it was', I provided this.

I also provided an index. There are practical things that an alcoholic, and the remaining family of an alcoholic, needs to know about – about the likelihood of diabetes, for instance, or about craving for sugar, or about what to do when sleep won't come. For those using this book who may be in the chaos of the final, impossible encounters with alcohol, I recommend turning to the index first.

December 1999

1.   11 December 1999

I don't know whether you want the good news or the bad news. The good news is that there's a rehabilitation clinic that specializes in people whose lives have been invaded. The guest – alcohol, booze, hooch to his American relations – was of course welcome at first. Soon he began vomiting on the curtains, breaking the chairs, seducing and insulting the friends who came less and less often to dinner, and ended by dry-retching into the kitchen sink, onto the carpet, and over the unpaid bills. The bad news is that the same clinic has no bar tariff, and the wine waiters have gone on strike. Permanently.

I'll spare you the shame, the guilt, the remorse, although like most alcoholics I am expert in virtually nothing but shame, guilt, remorse. What I won't spare you, and can't spare myself, is the fear. This is a treatment programme. Today, an endless Sunday of post-withdrawal symptoms – shakings, agitation, nameless fears, and a doughnut that was difficult to keep down – today is my second day. I've been diagnosed, admitted, prodded and poked by registrars with kind hands and knowing eyes. I've been watched every half hour, even through the night, for the typical symptoms of the drunk in withdrawal, which include black-outs, hallucinations, uncontrollable shakings of hands and body, and clean sheets laundered in sweat, urine, and a handful of purple shit for good measure. But in truth this withdrawal, massaged by Librium, is no worse, and in fact a great deal better, than those of the two detox. treatments of 1997 and 1998. No millennial birds have wheeled about the horizon, or squinted critically from a corner of the bookcase. I've still been able to stand up to piss. I haven't fouled myself, or had to crawl. I've even been able to eat. But there's still fear, and the fear is that this time it will have to work, that this time there's a programme, and that this time I'm going to have to tell the bloody awful truth.

One truth is that I was drunk, or at least disastrously hungover, at work, which is the immediate reason for the lack of wine waiters. After a squalidly Olympian weekend of champagne, vodka, red wine, and whatever else I can't remember, I stood at 8.30 on Monday morning in a portal sipping an unshaven cup of coffee and attempting not to retch into the nearest waste bin. Speech and I were strangers, largely because my lips couldn't be encouraged to work. 'Hangover? Huh,' you shrug, remembering the days of Alka-Seltzer and fresh air, hot-and-cold showers, pints of water. No, this wasn't a hangover as perhaps you understand it. This is, was, toxicity of a different kind. It's tuning-fork, uncontrollable shakings of hands, fingers. It's numbness in the top of the left foot, muscle weakness in the left hand. Two years ago, I'd been told that the numbness was due to neural damage, and was at least partly irreversible. This can't be fixed by Alka-Seltzer or the ironically named Resolve. And so I stood, nervously eyeing the waste bin, sipping coffee and trying not to throw up. 'I hope no one notices.' Abandon Hope, All Ye Who... But wherever Here was, everyone had abandoned it, and most had run a mile.

Notice it? Several hours later, someone did. You've heard, of course, of that old wives' and sailors' remedy, the Hair of the Dog ('Better still,' Cyril Connolly once remarked, 'the Hair of the Dog, including its skin'). At lunchtime the same day, after a wilderness of non-teaching that was merely aiming gratefully at anything or anywhere that could get me to the next beer, I had the fabled, the luminary Hair of the Dog, which had strangely metamorphosed into two bottles of something that tasted disgusting but had bubbles in it.

Some statistics may help. A human liver can only handle 1 ounce of alcohol an hour – about a can of normal-strength beer, or a pub measure of spirits. Whatever you do, that's the deal. No faster; no slower. If, then, you drink two six-packs and three pints over the course of an evening, it will be at least sixteen hours before all the alcohol has vacated your system, through sweat and urine. The chance is that you'll be drunk well into the following day. And at lunchtime? Another couple of pints, another large vodka-and-tonic, even a couple of apparently well-mannered spritzers, and you'll merely top up the alcohol already present. It would be highly unlikely that you'd stand a cat's chance in hell of passing a breath-test. Technically, you'd still be pissed. And that is the Hair of the Dog, the cat's chance in hell, and any other creature you may care to think of. Pink mouse? Puce vulture? Who cares?

I don't know if you've ever attended a lecture given by a drunken dog, as in Hair Of, but it's not pretty, it's not cogent, and it's certainly not worth attending the twenty-two minutes of shuffling, embarrassed silence that I can still hear as I write this.

There were complaints, there were procedures, there was shame. There was also a love, a care, and a support so potent and rapid that it stings my eyes now in the way that bar-smoke and tequila never did or could. And this brings me not full-circle, whatever bit of Dante this may be, but to the soft-drinks dispenser, the careful hands of consultants, the Librium, and the nurses. The treatment continues tomorrow, after I've written up tonight's Drinking Diary. Perhaps we'll have to model champagne glasses out of Plasticene, perhaps thread olives onto pipe-cleaners. I don't really know. What I do know, dear bloody page, is that I'd sell all the kindness, love, and professional support in the world for a large glass of something or other, preferably chilled. In this case, we'd better call it Hope.

2.   12 December 1999

I've tried to find euphemisms. 'Hospital' sounds too general: there's no obstetric ward or gastro-enteric acuteness here; no departments of neurology, urology, or quaintly named Centres for the treatment of painfully intimate diseases. I reach for the word 'Clinic'. This always makes me think of Elizabeth Taylor, and something in ambulance-pink. Then I reach for words approaching the truth, and know that this is an acute facility for psychiatric illness. It specializes in loss, dislocation; in diagnosis, treatment, therapy. It doesn't necessarily specialize in 'cure'. Given the kindness and care of the staff here, this sounds brutally hard; but certainly, for addiction, there's no cure. There is no cure. The best that can be hoped for is long-range, long-term management.

Therapy. 'Will I have to model things in sand?' I thought. 'Will I have to make Play-Dough models of my deepest Fears?' Will Tuesday afternoon be Painting Therapy, Thursday Reflexology, Friday something arcane to do with crystals? And, for God's sake, will I have to talk – or still worse, Emote – about my precious so-called bloody Feelings?

It hasn't been quite like that. It's been tough, moving, structured, and punctuated by a thousand cigarettes. Cigarettes function as a black-market currency here, a lesser addictive evil still tolerated in the Smoking Lounges by overflowing ashtrays, and mute benedictions of the broken heart. And strangely, among the tears, the unbearable testimonies of the dispossessed and the fucked-over, the fractured stories of lives and ruin, there too has been laughter, realism, and a humour so black it's almost vivid. A vivid darkness: the lived, half-lived, almost dead night of the hour-before-dawn wilderness. And somewhere in the laughter, among the shrewd, difficult witness, there's been a glimpse of a future.

No one recovers from alcoholism. One thing I hadn't realized was that if a drinker of twenty years' standing is abstinent for another five, and then begins to drink again, the cumulative effect of his or her drinking is twenty-five years. You pick up exactly where you left off. There are no interims, and no let-ups. A dry alcoholic – or better, an alcoholic in active recovery – may more truly be said to be 'in remission' than anything else. Resume drinking, and the damage continues as if you'd never stopped. It may even accelerate. It probably will.

For years – for the years of lies, broken promises, of vows to reform; for the years of self-neglect and hurt – I'd utterly rejected the idea that alcoholism was an illness. 'If alcoholism's an illness,' I thought, 'then it's a strange kind of illness, because you can choose to get well.' To me, as to many, an alcoholic was the sleeper in the doorway, the tramp on the street, the mumbler to itself among the torn cardboard voices of a former life. He's the man holding a cup of stale coins in the subway. He's someone Other, hopeless, morally degenerate, beyond help.

It's no good saying to me, or to yourself, 'This man is sick' if by *sick* you mean sick in the head and therefore outcast, soiled, an unlucky and uncomfortably close piece of unclean bad luck. No. This man, this woman, is ill. They are suffering now, they have been suffering, from a disease. You can no more choose to recover – you can certainly not choose on your own – than you could choose on your own to recover from cancer, polio, or AIDS. Surely, you can have the will to choose, but this doesn't alter the fact that alcoholism itself is often (though not inevitably) gradual, but always unchosen. You can no more choose not to be an alcoholic than you can choose not to have a broken leg. Alcoholics don't drink because they like it; they drink because they have to. Drink moved in to their lives and slowly, imperceptibly, embarrassingly, took the life over. And all the constituents of the life: the friends, the money, the partner, the car, the licence, the house, and the job.

Alcoholism hasn't always been seen as a disease. It's been seen merely as drunkenness, or moral degeneracy (there are many who still hold this view), as a pattern of learned behaviour, as a form of self-medication. But since the mid-twentieth century there have been signs that alcoholism is aetiologically recognizable as a disease. In 1968, for example, the American Psychiatric Association defined alcoholism as '[a] category for patients whose alcohol intake is great enough to damage their physical health, or their personal or social functioning, or when it has become a prerequisite to normal functioning'. In 1977, the American Medical Association stated: 'Alcoholism is an illness characterized by significant impairment... Impairment may involve physiological, psychological, or social dysfunction.' By 1993, and emphasizing that the word *disease* means 'involuntary disability', the American Society of Addiction Medicine nailed the illness as follows:

> Alcoholism is a *primary*, chronic *disease* with genetic, psychological and environmental factors influencing its development and manifestations. The disease is *often progressive* and *fatal*. It is characterized by continuous or periodic: *impaired control over* drinking, preoccupation with the drug alcohol, use of alcohol despite *adverse consequences*, and distortions in thinking, most notably *denial*...

I looked round at the Smoking Lounge this afternoon, while denying my own denial. Somewhere on an ash-stained table, someone, perhaps a visitor from a forgotten yesterday, had been modelling figures out of jars of Play-Dough.

The Hospital

T hose are the only two entries I wrote while I was in hospital. I re-read them, and I can taste the nervousness, and the fear. It shows itself in attempts at jokes ('...the wine-waiters have gone on strike. Permanently' – a joke I stole from the therapist whose intervention, in December 1999, helped to save a life); it shows in the cracks about Play-Dough, the unease about 'therapy' or 'feelings'. Behind everything I was, including the everything I wrote, there was the everything that was fear.

The fear attempted to disguise itself as scoffing. Fear often does.

I was lucky. After a preliminary phone-call – someone had told me almost in passing of the existence of the place, and I found the number through Directory Enquiries – I was asked to get myself in person to the hospital, where an initial interview would be carried out. It was hard, making that phone-call. In truth, I had made the same call twice – once, a month before, and the second time on 6 December. First time round, and knowing of the expertise and the expense that was facing me, I put down the phone, cried poverty, cried reform, and poured myself, shaking again with withdrawal from the last time, and the time before that, towards another glass of something or other. Second time round, and as the disciplinary procedures were being put in place at work, there seemed to be nowhere left to go. Subterfuge, alibi, the pretence at a normal life, the sham of trying to appear sober: it was all, every bit of it, about to be found out. And yet, after this second phone-call, and a promise to come 'tomorrow', I opened a bottle of red wine, and knew it would be my last. How did I *know? I just knew. I was exhausted with myself. The life I'd been trying to lead was exhausted. I'd come to the end of something, the edge of something. Though I was still shaking, and in the beginnings of withdrawal, I felt something like a sick calm.*

I just knew.

Unbidden, a phrase came into my head and stayed there. 'It's over.' I knew it was over. I knew too that more than alcohol was over. And beyond that, I understood that everything was going to have to change – though I recoiled from that thought. It was too big to think about, and I didn't know how I could do it, when the time for changing came.

When the unreliable promise that was 'tomorrow' arrived, the same calm persisted in the taxi. 'It's over.' And before the interview, in some barely known state of calm anxiety, I still knew that something was over.

I was asked to wait in the lobby of the hospital. It seemed like a hotel. It was very quiet – the plush quiet that comes with money, carpets, cutlery, and with people having the time to do their jobs. I remember thinking that this was exactly the kind of up-market place that would never admit someone like me. It seemed too peaceful, too structured, too... clean.

At this distance, I recognize the very cleanliness and quiet of the place as part of a therapeutic strategy. Most drunks, after all, eventually know nothing but chaos. Chaos and dirt, inside and out. That's the nature of the landscape they come to inhabit. And certainly, I didn't actually feel I was worth any more than the chaos and the dirt. In my own rented house, there was still the stain of a pile of pathetically thin, vinous, vomit somewhere on top of the landing stairs. I hadn't bothered to clean it up properly, because the smell of household detergent made me want to retch. Or perhaps it was the smell of my drinking self that made me want to retch.

As I was waiting in that lobby – piles of glossy magazines lay on a table, there was the chink of cutlery from the dining-room – even the staff who passed smiled at me, gently.

I hadn't been smiled at properly in a long time.

I was interviewed. The interviewer was an alcoholic five years into recovery. How much did I drink? What symptoms of withdrawal had I had? What sort of criminal record did I have? What had I lost?

Half-way through this interview, and because I felt strangely... visible, I began to cry. I was a professional man, I had travelled around the world, I had lectured in important places, I had... I was...

I was nothing. Whatever I was, whatever job I had, however much or little money I had in the bank, wherever the honest and dishonest hopes and dreams had gone, I just felt dirty, ashamed, sick, small, and lost. A piece of nothing. Crying.

And still, I just knew. It was over. Somewhere in the piece of nothing, some fragment, some remnant, knew.

When my interviewer kept wearing the same encouraging smile – it was almost an invitation – I knew he would recommend that I was admitted. 'Today,' he said. 'Not tomorrow or the day after tomorrow. And not next week. Now.'

There was nowhere for the posturing and the excuses to go.

I still had no idea who would pay for the treatment. No one close to me had the kind of money this sort of intervention would need. Kindly, efficiently, without any fuss, my interviewer made some phone-calls.

I was quite incapable of saving my own life. But I acknowledge now, and will acknowledge until the day breath finally stops, that it was my employers who finally, critically, stepped in. By some unprecedented process, they constructed an interest-free loan there and then. It wasn't a small sum. But their exact words, reported calmly to the sobbing piece of nothing that sat by the interviewer's desk, were that such a course of action was 'cheap at the price'.

The sobs racked and lurched until they came from my roots. If I continued to number and name them, they would be endless, and be called Gratitude.

'WILL I HAVE to Emote about my precious so-called bloody Feelings?' I sneered, to whomever in an audience of zero might have been listening.

I had to do a great deal worse, along with the rest of the small group of drunks and junkies who had inherited each other. I did not just have to 'emote': I had to think, *with precision, with clarity, and then with articulacy, about exactly the feelings I professed to despise. About the feelings I did despise.*

Treatment was at least tripartite. The medical, the physical side of things was looked after by a team of nurses headed by one resident houseman. There was access to a psychiatrist. The psychology of addiction was handled by a team of counsellors and therapists. And further, not least important, the kitchen provided well-cooked, nourishing food. Why, they would even cook you up what perhaps you fancied, within limits: don't fancy the risotto? Then how about a couple of softly poached eggs? Ice cream? What flavour?

Everything, absolutely all of it, was designed carefully, down to the poached egg and the soft-drinks dispensers in the dining-room. You didn't feel like a freak, a nomad, a shambles of a bar-room tourist with no future. You started to feel less like a dirty, wiped-out drunk.

Each day had an equally careful structure. Central to each day were meetings with a group of fellow addicts who, like you, had completed what was unpromisingly called a 'Feelings Diary' for the previous day. These diary entries were shared, commented on, criticized. And formed one of the foundations for the work of the skilled team of therapists (all of them recovering addicts).

What's a 'Feelings Diary'? I have a photocopy in front of me as I write.

(i)   *I feel that today I experienced*
      A very good day / A good day / A bad day / An indifferent day (please tick)

(ii) *This was because I felt*

(iii) *Today I enjoyed*

(iv) *Today I did not enjoy*

(v)   *Today I learned*

(vi) *Today I have made progress in the following areas*

(vii) *I am aware that I need to make progress in the following areas*

(viii) *I intend to make progress by*

(ix) *Give a specific example of how you have practised Steps 1, 2, and 3 today*

The therapeutic strategy was effectively a guided introduction to the first four steps of the 12-step programme of AA. Yet it was also much more. It was sustained by the absolute conviction that addicts – even those who are critically ill at the point of admission – can get well. It depended on honesty, openness, and willingness to recover. Its group-work was a re-introduction to the pressures and responsibilities of living as part of a society, however small. The emphasis on 'feelings' was a democratic emphasis which acknowledged that no one, whatever their position in life, whatever their income, however powerful their connections, is exempt from the condition that is alcoholism (or other addiction). This emphasis on feelings also stressed that addictive patterns, once they became uncontrollable, summed up to nothing less than a disease of the emotions.

I SEE – I saw even at the time – how lucky I was. I wish, beyond hope, that everyone had access to such treatment. By the end of 1999, I knew at first hand the difference between the hospital's meticulous, experienced, and well-planned care, and the strategy of the NHS. I had been detoxed twice at home, both times by skilled and patient community nurses. And yet in those earlier circumstances, surrounded by love and goodwill (had I chosen to admit it), pumped up with Librium and grief, I had not learnt, perhaps because I'd not been told, about the disease that could centre on much-despised 'feelings'. I didn't want to feel. I wanted to go back to being a Success, quickly. I wanted the shortcut to sobriety. I wanted to be cured. I still wanted the girl, the money, the travel, the spotlight. I wanted... I wanted... I can still hear the masquerade that was then a set of passionate and disastrous attachments, includ-ing the attachment that was a relationship with ethanol. I don't think, deep down, I wanted to get well. I just wanted to get technically sober, then go back to living the old, bad, unlived life.

No one had explained to me the difference between sobriety and recovery. It seems obvious now. It didn't seem obvious then.

Under the NHS, and because funds for the treatment of addiction (particularly alcoholism) are limited, it's perilously difficult to get treatment for acute alcoholism in the first place. If you are lucky enough to get it (and I was), then there's often a waiting list of many months. That is, if you are able to get onto a waiting list. To get that far, you first have to be referred by a GP, and many general practices will not accept alcoholics as new patients – precisely because alcoholics are difficult to treat, because they can waste resources, because there is no cure...

It's more than a vicious spiral. For many alcoholics, it may turn out to be a lethal one. But in this context the treatment strategy of the NHS seems to operate on the unspoken belief of its bureaucrats and fund-holders that we are 'just', we are 'only', alcoholics.

There are many millions who are 'only' alcoholics. There are many millions more who are only their families. They are exactly like me, with the same rights to dignity, and freedom, and treatment.

They didn't, finally, choose their condition. Somehow, out of some insanity of need, some ultimate disaster of desire, some set of faces that couldn't bear to be called chaos, their condition chose them.

They could easily be you.

And therefore, they have the same rights to be smiled at. Gently.

AND SO, IN *a community of drunks, I began to feel, and began to acknowledge how it was to feel. For days, and despite the sobbing of Day 1, I tried to pretend I wasn't grieved, wasn't sick. I stuck a persona in place – the sneering, the sarcasm, the attempts at jokes. I was Mr. Hail-Fellow-Well-Met. I was the remains of Mr. Wonderful.*

I was another sham. If I give myself some little credit, it is for admitting the fact that the sham couldn't last long, that I would have to get real, stop indulging the self-ishness of personae and fantasy, and start afresh at some old, warm, human place that included my own authenticity. Whatever that was.

But I give myself no particular credit for this recognition even now. I had to be helped towards it, by two painstaking, and very different, therapists. I thought I was smart? They kept asking me how clever I was, if all the cleverness I was had brought me to a mental institution on the brink of Millennium Eve.

They didn't break me – they didn't break the part of me that just knew – but they turned me. I don't know of another verb that would be more accurate. They turned me, somewhere in that first week. They turned me so I started on a new and different kind of journey.

There was no more false humour after that.

BUT THERE WAS *humour, black humour, real humour. Somewhere in week 3 of my own treatment, the well-known international teetotaller Boris Yeltsin, President of All the Russias (or what was left of them), stepped down from the demands of continual sobriety, and retired, smelling vaguely of something medicinal, in the general direction of a dacha in the woods outside Moscow.*

The following morning, a small group of us completed the Daily Feelings Diary of a new inmate. It went something like this:

Name: **Boris**

(i)   I feel that today I experienced
        A very good day / A good day / A bad day / An indifferent day (please
        tick)
        (We ticked **An indifferent day**)

(ii)   This was because I felt
        We filled in the words **Apprehensive; and resigned**

(iii)   Today I enjoyed
        My secretary

(iv)   Today I did not enjoy
        Putin's speeches

(v)   Today I learned
        I am no longer President of Russia

(vi)   Today I have made progress in the following areas
        Chechnya

(vii)   I am aware that I need to make progress in the following areas
        Georgia; Lithuania; Latvia; Estonia; the Ukraine...

(viii) I intend to make progress by
        The sword that is mightier than the pen

(ix)   Give a specific example of how you have practised Steps 1, 2, and 3
        today
        Shakily, on the Aeroflot steps

This masterpiece of schoolboy banality we handed in along with our own A4 sheets.

There was a long silence in the office the therapists shared that morning. Were they discussing important aspects of individual or group dynamics? Had the nurses' reports shown up some unsupervised nocturnal behaviour even more worrisome and aberrant than usual? Had someone died? Had someone relapsed?

Eventually, the chap whom we'd all identified as the most serious, most challenging, most confrontational, and most 'difficult' of the therapists emerged from the office. His face was wet with tears.

He was still laughing.

I JUST KNEW.

And so it all changed, because it all had to change.

But things only changed slowly. And some things – small things – didn't change that much, while other things didn't change at all.

If, beyond gratitude, I had to sum up these fragile, life-saving experiences, I would do so in two words:

After-care. Authenticity.

February to March 2000

3.   24 February 2000

There are alcoholics who slip gradually into the disastrous nurture of this illness: 'heavy drinking' insensibly becomes critical drinking, morning drinking, secret drinking, hangover drinking. And then there are those alcoholics – and they're many – who've never drunk 'normally'. I'm one. If I look back to my first serious drink, it was my first drunk. It presaged a pattern. Or perhaps the addictive pattern was present, even then, and was merely waiting to be triggered by time, dislocation, and opportunity.

It was the day my mother was taken into hospital. My callous sixteen-year-old self knew beforehand, and surely, that something was amiss, but didn't, or wouldn't, realize how badly awry. The first I knew of my mother's vanishing was a sealed note on the kitchen table. It said, in true Alan Bennett fashion, that I wasn't to worry and that there was a flan in the fridge.

I ate most of the flan (real men didn't eat quiche, even in 1974), then called a friend to ask whether he wanted to go out for the evening. I didn't mention my mother, the note, the absence, the loneliness, or the panic. Real men didn't do that, either. We arranged to go out that evening to a tawdry nightclub called, I think, Annabel's, much favoured by awful teenagers and lurid lagers.

Meanwhile, one of my mother's friends arrived. We drove to the hospital, mute and shattered as failed conspirators, and were eventually admitted to the ward. Elderly women were wandering around. I seem to remember someone playing with string, though it could have been someone frantically knitting. My mother barely recognized me. I had disappeared. She had, temporarily, disappeared. Perhaps it was the straightness of my face, or the stiffness of its upper lip. Perhaps it was the fact that I was unable to talk through the silent, screaming tears. Outside, I collapsed.

Deposited home, I splashed on some awful aftershave and poured myself into something like a flowered shirt and crushed-velvet loon pants. I had style, man – so much style that it courted the mirror for oblivion. Then I was driven towards it in an ageing Ford Escort. Sod the flan – and everything else.

One beer is fine when you're sixteen. Two beers feels better. Three beers, and you're keeping up with the boys. Four, and you start to feel light-headed among the drapes and postures of a darkened club somewhere in the West Riding of Yorkshire. You could, after all, easily pass for James Dean, who was also, and regularly, known to find patterns in the singing carpets of after-hours Keighley. Five beers, and you're ready for anything – heaving nicely into a passing wastepaper-basket, for example; touching up a sequin; or...

Gathering all dignity with immense sang-froid, I was the sole entrant in a Yard-of-Ale competition, for which the prize was a bottle of Charlie perfume. 'You can gi' it t' girlfriend,' said the DJ, whose faux Brooklynese failed to conceal the fact he'd been born in Halifax. Of course I could, despite the slight technical problem posed by my permanently mislaying whatever girlfriend I might never have had. A cheering, jeering crowd of scents and breaths mugged me on as I tipped a hunting-horn full of John Smith's Best down my shirt, my trousers, and my life. It was just past midnight, and the turntable was, unforgettably, playing 'Unforgettable'. I've never been able to stomach the smell of Charlie since. Ten minutes later and I was outside in the car-park, vomiting over the Escort's bonnet and feeling like a man. Then I passed out. The mirror promised oblivion, and here it was.

The problem with a drunk's oblivion is that it doesn't last. I think it was Kingsley Amis who wrote (I'm paraphrasing from memory) that a hangover had two components, the physical and the metaphysical, and of the two, the second was infinitely worse, compounded as it is of guilts, shames, remorse, and debts. Unsteadily I took the guilts, shames, remorse, and debts to a spoonful of Epsom salts, a phone-call to the hospital and a kind sister. Did I know then that a quarter of a century later I'd take very much the same metaphysical equipment to an early-morning consultation with Dr. Vodka, just to quell the shakes as my body vibrated like a piano-string and my mouth retched dryly into yesterday's tea-leaves? Perhaps not, but the drinker inside me had discovered how to swallow a crisis and turn it into an upper lip that was still stiff even after it had thrown up into the gutter. And even then, I hoped no one would notice, just as much as I needed someone to tell.

4.   24 February 2000

Therapeutic strategies for alcoholism vary widely. There's widespread ignorance of this... If you jib at the term 'disease', let's simply call it a...'condition', even among the medical professions and the professions that are called, with some justice, caring. Several doctors of my consulting acquaintance seem to have an aversion to recommending any form of treatment to someone they suspect may be merely a form of hysterical and self-obsessed shirker who needs to pull themselves together. Others fail to spot early signs of the onset of alcohol-related illnesses: persistent diarrhoea, for example, was in my case diagnosed as a mild case of irritable bowel syndrome and a partiality for extra-strong mints. Others try a form of reciprocal jocularity. 'Listen, Chris,' said one smiling and exasperated bow-tie to the consulting-room wall, 'why don't you just get pissed at the weekend like everyone else?' Others will nod knowledgeably, as if the condition sitting in front of them is common (which it is) and can be treated by tranquillizers or anti-depressants (which it can't). Several weeks of side-effects later, and your anti-depressants will have kicked in, but you'll neutralize whatever effect they may have had by drinking down another one for the road, the alley, and (make mine a double) the gutter.

More specific alcohol strategies include the adoption of Controlled Drinking, and/or the prescription of drugs such as Antabuse, which theoretically makes any consumption of ethanol hazardous to the point of being fatal.

During the first detox., Controlled Drinking was considered as an option by the Community Alcohol Team whose patience and expertise brought me through the hallucinations and the shakes. Eventually, beyond the first detox. and into the second, Controlled Drinking was abandoned, but not before I'd given it a fairly extensive trial. It didn't work for me as a recuperative tactic, and frankly, if you're an alcoholic I don't think it can. You might go a few weeks or months on a couple of large G&Ts a day, but if I were a betting man (and yes, of course I am, I'm an addict) I'd lay odds that if you're an alcoholic you'd be pissed again within half a year. Not only that, you'd be pissed more permanently, and your life would be even more ruined than it was the time before the time-before-that.

To an alcoholic, Controlled Drinking is Nirvana, it's paradise, it's Dante, and it's Never-Never Land. It's the dream of drinking normally, responsibly. It's sober, judicious drinking. It's a dream that will break your heart, and the hearts of all the people you care about. You can of course kid yourself. 'This time it'll be different.' And it may appear to be. Tomorrow I could go out for dinner, have a couple of glasses of wine, drive home, and have six-times-a-night sex while being effortlessly charming (simultaneously playing chess…and Chopin). The following day, I would have two glasses of wine with dinner and end up half an abandoned week later in a field somewhere. I have lost control over the use of alcohol, and if you're an alcoholic, so have you. You're utterly unpredictable, and no one wants to lay odds any longer. Try Controlled Drinking for a few days, weeks, or months, and you'll soon see why.

Antabuse is still widely prescribed. It works by stopping the metabolism of alcohol, whose constituent parts are, in any normal human, broken down first, and primarily, by the liver into acetaldehyde; then into acetic acid; then into carbon dioxide and water. Antabuse (disulfiram) stops the process at the acetaldehyde stage. Acetaldehyde, which is highly toxic, then accumulates in the body. If you drink while taking Antabuse, the theory runs, you suffer 'antabuse reactions' – flushing, palpitations, and sweating – as acetaldehyde builds up in the system before slowly dissipating in sweat and urine.

I've known several people who've used and abused Antabuse. We're still alive, though one of us is still alive only via Intensive Care. All of us drank while on the 'anti-alcohol' drug. My guess – educated, but hardly inspired – is that this is because an alcoholic's normative reaction to almost anything is to drink. We're programmed to drink; we've programmed ourselves to drink; we drink. If we choose to drink, nothing will stop the choice, not even the threat of death. We've swallowed the threat of death before now, just as we've swallowed threats, entreaties, bankruptcies, jails, institutions, sanity, and pride. Meanwhile, the society of which we're a part (from which we're apart) looks on, having criminalized heroin, and even its caring professions still have a great deal to learn.

5.   25 February 2000

Recovery isn't easy. Today, Friday, has been a bad day, and I don't know quite why. Nothing unusual has happened. The early morning mute yell of horror is still the same mute yell of horror. The mirror tells its commonplace story of post-marital middle age. The birds go somewhere about their business. Business goes about its business, and computer hums to computer out of money and need. The world still turns in the grip of celestial mechanics. And today I was close to a drink.

I had sober periods before finally throwing in the towel (despite not being able to see the ring at the time). For weeks, or months, I'd grit my teeth, ignore the blandishments of Dr. Vodka, get on with my work, and be thoroughly miserable. It's hard to smile properly when you're gritting your teeth; it's worse when you're grinding them. And I thought this was recovery. It wasn't. It was mere sobriety. Even the jokes had turned brittle, as if something were waiting to break.

In the trade, there's a phrase for this I rather like: 'white-knuckle sobriety'. You clench the dry spell in two dry fists, and lock your mind into an empty glass. In some ways this is great. I admire any alcoholic who can stop drinking for a day, let alone for tomorrow or through next year. You'll feel better, physically, within a week. Within two weeks, you might even be beginning to eat properly. Within three weeks, you'll begin to wonder what the fuss was about. But you'll still be white-knuckled, and no wonder: sometime, and soon, you're about to have the fight of your life, and all the shit will be beaten out of you. Mere sobriety is no defence against alcohol: Dr. Vodka is, as the AA phrase has it, a cunning, baffling, and powerful opponent and, as you've proved a hundred and a thousand times, she will always win.

Mere sobriety is something you do on your own. Sobriety is to recovery what masturbation is to intercourse. Recovery is something you do with and through other people. It isn't so much something you achieve, as something in which you're included.

The single biggest and most important difference between sobriety and recovery in this life has been the phone. For most of the previous telephonic years, I'd used the telephone with a certain amount of distaste. It was a weapon loaded with diffidence and distance, only to be used to confirm plans or avert the avarice of double-glazing salespersons. There are also residual memories of just how much I hated answering the phone when I was a child. It was, then, like connecting with an adult language I didn't know, and couldn't be fluent in. And so I felt clumsy, and at a loss. But these days, the phone is full of warmth. It makes me smile, to think that in the Caesar-salad days of marriage and career, the phone held editors and invitations, dinner-parties, and the siren sibilance of Success. These days, the answer-button brings on line alcoholics and fellow addicts. Between addicts and editors, I know which I usually prefer. This isn't to say that the phone fills up with tired platitudes of recovery metaphysics, the dubious revelations of self-discovery, the cracked voices of self-obsessed indulgence. It's actually full of humour and recognition, of bad jokes, of encouragement, weariness, the messiness of being human. I've come to depend on the presence of these voices, and for a man who's always prided himself on non-dependence ('of course I can do it, now leave me alone') this is the gentlest and most lasting form of a kind of luck.

Which brings me to today's bad day. Fractured in ways I couldn't or wouldn't understand, coming off the perilous allure of a bad night that had seen me pacing round the house as in the old drinking days, unable to keep down a mouthful of food, ash from endless cigarettes building up on the keyboard, I phoned a friend who's also in recovery.

'Have you wanted to drink on it?' Yes, I had, I said, then added that I felt I was way off any kind of recovery.

'But you haven't had a drink,' he said, 'and it's only when you recognize you're off-programme that you're actually on track. Now get some bloody food down your neck, drink something sweet, and I'll pick you up for lunch in twenty minutes. Put the kettle on.'

Sometimes it needs someone else to tell you you've been worrying for nothing, and that all the dispersed fragments of worth and insight amount, in truth, to a life that's flawed, vulnerable, honest, and funny. I put the kettle on, and didn't immediately feel better, though I knew I would, and that the day would pass as it must. And so it has: not great, but bearable, and with an attempt at a smile. I might not be a better person than I was at five this morning, but I'm more coherent, less scattered, and still in recovery. Sobriety takes balls, surely, but recovery means, among other things, the telephone's crackling love.

6.   25 February 2000

In the early stages of alcoholic recovery the advice others give, and more importantly, the advice you give yourself, ranges from the banal ('Don't pick up a drink today') to the surprising ('Give yourself a foot massage with an implausible Japanese essential oil…'). Of course you'll use the phone. Maybe you'll hit some AA meetings. Naturally you'll continue with some significant and educative reading. But of all the words of wisdom, none is more useful than the acronym HALT. This mnemonic brings with it a whole package of practical recovery Don'ts, and they're quite simple. Don't allow yourself to become (a) Hungry, (b) Angry, (c) Lonely, or (d) Tired.

Any one of these Four Pissed Horsemen of the Apocalypse – named, let me repeat, Hunger, Anger, Loneliness, or Tiredness – threatens recovery. The presence of any simultaneous two makes recovery unlikely. Any malevolent combination of three, and you're on your way to the bottom of the next glass, the one after that, and then to a small field in Shropshire, probably via the local nick.

Avoiding hunger is necessary because for years your body was fooled by the calories in alcohol. Ethanol calories aren't calories that are nutritionally worthwhile, but they are calories, mostly carried in sugars. Typically, alcoholics and heavy drinkers either skimp increasingly on real food, or they're overweight but malnourished. It's a fact that someone can carry a beer-gut and still be suffering from malnutrition. It's another fact that in recovery, your body and brain seek nutrition, and therefore calories, from the source they've learned will never seem to fail them: booze. Therefore, by a fairly inescapable logic, in the alcoholic condition, hunger can lead to craving. Many alcoholics – I'm one of them – carry a bar of chocolate somewhere in their briefcase, or keep a fruit-bowl stocked on the desk. And although it's not my joke, I'll offer you this because I like it: *No one was ever arrested for Banana Driving.*

Anger and, its equivalent spread thinly, resentment are luxuries alcoholics can't afford. Strong emotions of any kind can function as alcoholic triggers. After all, for many of us, drinking swallowed down emotions, kept them invisible. We couldn't handle them, so we tried to obliterate them. In recovery, obliteration's not an option, and any incident, however apparently trivial, can flash up anger. The fact that there's a knot already in your shoelace; the blunted razor; the fact that the trash hasn't been emptied (again); the memo at work… Anger, anger, anger – momentary, lasting, bewildering, hurtful. Do anything (I tell myself). Walk away (I tell myself). Scream quietly at the wall. Take the dog out. Put an advert in the local paper saying you'd like to protest about, well, everything. But let the anger go. Let the longstanding resentment go. As AA's wise advice has it, 'accept the things you can't change'. It's difficult. It's not impossible.

Loneliness kills. If you live on your own – and as an alcoholic, you may well be as alone as I am – you have somehow to accept your own loneliness. It isn't easy. Keep other voices in the house: listen to the radio, read the paper. Use the telephone. Plan spare time so that it includes other people – a recovery meeting; charity work; coffee or lunch with work colleagues. Make the most of any invitation – people will always, and I mean always, be glad to see you sober, and in recovery. Learn to use the Internet from home or from a local library – and ask for help if you don't know how…

Or so I tell myself. You think this is easy for me to say? You have a job, you mutter at me accusingly; you still have some friends. Yes, and I gathered into crowds and was also alone, and I still fall asleep to the voices of a radio permanently tuned all night to the BBC World Service. If you want to know about late-breaking stuff from the Balkans, I'm an alcoholic, and I'm your man.

And then tiredness. Don't overwork, don't take on too much. You're an addict, and you'll probably want to show the world, the cook, the thief, and his lover that you're strong, capable, sparky, and full of stamina. Take it easy, and if you can't take it easy, learn. Learn anyhow: take a nap, or a long bath before trying to get some sleep; use lunchtimes to go swimming, and then rest afterwards; use ten minutes to be quietly by yourself in the middle of a working day.

Listen. I screwed up just as badly as you did, and probably worse. These are simply some of the things I do now, though I by no means get all of them right all of the time. And now, today, I don't give a nod to a tinker's horse about ambition, success, and all the furies of illusion. What I must have, and what I'll maintain, is some sense of balance, even if it's a balance that hangs by its fingernails off an acronym, HALT.

7.   1 March 2000

People often ask me whether I crave for a drink. That is, they don't ask me, but the tacit question's falling through their eyes as rapidly as a query would go spin-chink-chink in some malevolent mental slot machine. Perhaps people are too polite to ask directly (though I doubt it). Perhaps they worry about whether alcoholism's infectious. Perhaps they merely avoid my unspoken reply as if I'm some kind of unlucky place. Perhaps they actually prefer to watch me carefully out of the corner of their eyes for any hint of unsteadiness, slobbering, or incipient DTs. And perhaps, after all, they think they know best. But they wonder, and I can see them wondering. *Chink-chink.*

The truth is that I hardly ever crave booze, but I often think about it. Physical cravings tend to pass the further away you are from the last drink. In active alcoholism, all the systems of the body, even down to each cell, crave more ethanol as a relief from the stuff that went before. If the ailing physiology of the hangover doesn't get what it craves, the result is physical withdrawal: nausea, shaking, sweating, and all the rest. But I was lucky. What tests I had – interesting scans with medical implements whose smart results were shown on some kind of intestinal television, much to the mystification of the radiographer – indicated that the liver, while enlarged, was functioning relatively well. Spleen, intact. Pancreas, intact. 'How much were you drinking?' the radiographer asked, whose disappointed frown spoke disappointment that the usual suspects were in fact clean. I told him. 'Christ, you've been lucky.' And so I was, largely, with the result that physical cravings are a thing almost of the past. I don't shake, and don't sweat. The fine and savage agitation that's such a feature of withdrawal is no more. I can sleep at nights, even if I do wake up stricken by panic after dreaming booze.

But I do think about the stuff, often. I think about it at what used to be critical moments in the structure of the days and weeks: when I'm walking home from work after a hard and long day; when I'm walking home from work after a particularly successful day; when I'm walking home from work. I think about the stuff, in particular, on Friday and Saturday nights. I think about it every time I go into the local grocer's to buy cigarettes, every time I pass an off-licence, and every time I watch my colleagues opening a bottle of wine, or leaving for the pub. I think about it over lunch – particularly lunch in a good restaurant – and I think about it over dinner. Then I dream about it. What do you mean, I think about it too much? I'm an alcoholic. Of course I bloody think about it, if only to remind myself of the choices that there are in recovery.

I found a new route to and from work. I make plans for Friday and Saturday nights that don't involve booze, parties, early-morning taxi-rides, failed attempts at intercourse, lipstick, or anything to do with Wales. I buy my cigarettes from a different Pakistani grocery, and last time I looked at the off-licence, a young homeless woman was sleeping in the doorway at 6.34am. If it comes to lunch and dinner, I try to avoid Indian restaurants, where my mouth forms the word 'lager' before it has time to form 'popadom', and pretend to prefer something unidentifiable and Chinese, that I can wash down with green tea. And usually, I avoid bars, particularly the bars in which I used to drink, where I know I'd be greeted with a smile of recognition, and something approaching a sigh of relief.

Sobriety can be uncomfortable to be around, if you're a local, an *habitué*, a regular, or just a passing drunk. I know this, since I was at different times all four, often simultaneously.

Drinking and the memories of drinking are like a track hacked out of, or burned into, my neural pathways. Every crisis, every happiness, every opportunity asks to be celebrated, mourned, or discovered over a drink. Yes, this is a learned response, but I don't buy the psychotherapeutic view that claims that alcoholism is *merely* that 'learned response'. If it's a response, it's also a life-threatening form of addictive illness – well, yes, I still prefer 'condition' – and if I learned to be ill within that condition, the sickness estranged me so much from myself that I couldn't recognize the learning or the sickness, and barely remembered what I was responding to. What? Who? Where? I drank, in the end, because I'm a drinker. I needed no excuses to drink, even while I constructed them.

I need to apply the same proliferation of inventiveness to remembering the reasons for staying in recovery. As one more realistic friend said: 'None for the road.' I still have a job I sometimes love, words I can mean and remember, a few people I can trust and laugh with. There's food in the house, and although the bank balance isn't altogether happy, it will improve itself, slowly. All I have to do to maintain this state of affairs is make the right choices – the choices that mean I won't end up tomorrow morning at 6.34am lying in a doorway, or hurtling towards the dark of Somewhere in a rogue taxi while clutching the knee of an anorexic transvestite called, and just for the sake of it, Ken. Make the wrong choices, and I'd end up alone in a ditch somewhere near Wrexham. No job, no house, no friends, and no bank balance would be waiting when I came back. If I came back.

The choices, at least, are simple. It's just living them that seems complicated.

8.   2 March 2000

Somebody asked me why I'm writing these pieces under the generic heading 'Goodbye, Mr. Wonderful'. Well, it's a snappier title than 'Diary of a Nobody', which I think has been used before. It's better than 'Confessions of an Alcoholic' – which would make me think of what journalistic colleagues would doubtless call '70s soft-porn romps'. It's classier than 'Sobriety Made Simple' – and in any case, I've spent a lifetime making things complicated. And 'Goodbye, Mr. Wonderful' just happens to contain a germ of truth. Actually, I think it encodes a whole virus.

The booze thought I was Mr. Wonderful. Since booze eventually thought through me, I imagined I was Mr. Wonderful, too. I needed no convincing, even when I was vomiting over the bin-bags outside a Chinese restaurant at 3am, turned up weeping at a city centre hotel at 4am, or ended up drunkenly at a rail station on the other side of the Pennines the morning after – or was it the morning after that? I was Mr. Wonderful all right. Mr. Generous, Mr. Witty-and-Charming, Mr. Champagne, the man who held the table at a roar, the man who knew, the man who held the floor (until he keeled over into its unmerciful embrace). The man who was never knowingly under-talked. Mine's a large one, although I don't like to brag...

It was all pretence, it was illusion, and it hurt. I guessed, dimly, that I was having fun while I was drinking in the days. Now, if you sense the fist of coercive sobriety clenching at this point, don't worry. There were, in truth, some good times, particularly early on in the alcohol career, and sometimes Mr. Wonderful almost lived up to his name. There was generosity, there was laughter, and there was a frail and desperate kind of trust, if only that the bars would open on time and that there'd be someone else there to hear you order the first stiffener of the morning. But increasingly, it was pretence. The jokes turned inward, into irony and self-defeat, or they turned outward only into sarcasm. The trust, frail to begin with, segued inaudibly into mutual disillusion. The generosity and warmth appeared to dry up as the wallet emptied. In the end, the only voices left were those of that perplexity, an overdrawn account, and a waitress from Bolton who kept asking about kir. No one was there to hear my long, elaborately constructed, effortlessly funny monologues. My, how I laughed. Look, people, there's Mr. Wonderful, mumbling to himself again. They weren't to know I'd stumble home, cry with appalling self-pity, and then crap myself.

In the trade, the cliché has it that alcoholism is the only disease that tells you that you haven't contracted it. I don't altogether agree with this. I think – it's merely what I remember from my own direct experience –

that part of you does know you're sick, out of control, hurting and hurtful. But of course, drinking, using, you're Mr. Wonderful. You're the charming piece of defeated illusion whom the world laughs with. You've invested months, years, your own and others' lifetimes in the construction of this imago of Self, and you need to sustain your investment. It's the only cover and protection you know. No wonder you love Mr. Wonderful: in the end, he's all you've got. He's the moderator between you and the world. He'll tell you you're right, and that every phrase of love and concern in your life is wrong. He'll tell you you're Bill Gates's salary, the National Gallery, you're Cellophane, and that tomorrow is roses and champagne. Somewhere, even in the hysteria of a good drunk, you know that his words can be translated as 'you're sick, you're selfish, and you're insecure', but what's left of you isn't listening. Mr. Wonderful wants a double, and he wants it now.

There may in the end be some of you reading these words who will imagine it was your fault. It wasn't, any more than it would have been your fault if I'd developed cancer or diabetes. And for the sake of emphatic clarity: *the fault was mine*, whose only and biggest problem was, always, himself. I took the choices, not you. And I, not you, made the mistakes. It wasn't you on the train to Nowhere. It wasn't you in the police cell and the genito-urinary clinic. It was Mr. Wonderful, who also happens to be a part of the accident of voices and illusions that is writing this. If I could murder the fractured fragment whose rictus of presence caused all of us so much grief, I would. But I can only try to see him clearly, and listen once again to his cracked, spoiled voice. Then, for my sake and for yours, I have to say goodbye to him. Recovery's just the art of finding a different kind of wonderful.

9.   8 March 2000

I was trying to find some sort of image for alcoholism, a way of easily and quickly picturing it to myself. I don't usually have time to haul the whole thing into my head accompanied by a freight of metaphysics – guilts and histories, shocks and disconsolations. I need to be able to check in with my own condition as efficiently, and as often, as I'd look at my watch.

There was a time when I thought that alcoholism was merely a single, surmountable problem. Fix that ('of course I can fix it'), stay sober, and life could go on more or less as normal. I was wrong. Alcoholism was so advanced that it had begun to take on other faces and other functions in the mess of personality that happens to be Chris McCully: it affected relationships, work, money, time. It affected everything, and consequently I wasn't, in the end, addicted merely to alcohol. I was addicted to anything…and everything.

It was as if, slowly and without my conscious knowledge, some kind of Addiction Program had begun to run in my psychological hardware. Whatever I did, and however sober I temporarily was, the Addiction Program was (and is) always running, interfacing with other programs – the sex program, the work program, the food program, the buying airline tickets program, the how-to-be-with-the-family program, the now-I'll-play-the-piano-again-(badly) program. It reminds me of the bits and pieces I can never actually delete from the computer. There is, for an example, a Microsoft icon that came pre-installed on this machine; it's apparently indestructible, even though that particular program apparently has nothing to do, and has been recently upgraded anyway. The Addiction Program's rather like that: it checks every waking function, it hums into life as soon as I open my eyes, and probably whirrs away while I'm asleep, too. I'm an addict. As long as I live, that particular program will always run. There's no way of deleting it, or co-opting its functions. There is no cure.

At the same time, as I learnt more recently, sobriety – or better, recovery – can also function as a program. The Recovery Program. It acts a bit like a virus checker on this laptop, screening every action, every process. I schedule it to perform specific tasks, like attending recovery meetings, but at the same time the program is always doing its stuff. It's beginning to govern my use of time, the kinds of restaurant I eat out in, the opportunities through which I enjoy my friendships, the way I approach my work.

The two programs – Addiction and Recovery – are today, and will be forever, working simultaneously. Together, they send mixed messages to the rest of the software, and the hard drive that happens to be me sometimes gets confused. Perhaps this is why early recovery is often so precarious: every action, from the greatest to the smallest, is being both driven and screened – first, by habits acquired over a lifetime, and deeply embedded in the Addiction Program, and second, by the newly installed Recovery Program.

Maybe it's the case that over months, years, the Recovery Program will slowly begin to interface with more and more programs in this psychological game of time and chance. It will have more and more to look at, gently and productively infiltrating other systems, so that they in turn run with more clarity and more truth. If this happens, then logically, the Addiction Program will find itself, like the program concealed under that undeletable Microsoft icon, with less and less to do. It will always be running, but its running will have nothing actually to play with, since those systems are already engaged with the Recovery Program.

I don't know whether this image works for you, but it makes a kind of sense to me. It also helps to explain why I get so bloody tired. I used to be able to work, as well as to fantasize, for hours at a stretch, while the Addiction Program was fizzing away unconstrained. Now a couple of hours' hard concentration leaves me ashen and wiped, which is frustrating. And yet I know that the tiredness is a product of the fact that the Recovery Program's functioning everywhere, at each moment of crisis or vision, defeat or happiness. As a friend pointed out to me at a recovery meeting this week, the brain, with all its hardware, weighs less than 2lbs, but its operation accounts for 25 per cent of the body's energy use. I think in this case, and at the moment, my brain and its warring programs are accounting for 50 per cent, so excuse me while I head towards the Jelly Babies and a darkened room.

10.   9 March 2000

The phone rang last Sunday night. I'd just come home from work, and was looking forward to an evening with the piano, the crossword, and a frozen pizza. It's not that I normally go in to work on weekends, but I'd left something undone, and it was eating me, so I went. Last Sunday night, I wasn't admiring my dedication so much as wondering where all the energy had gone. I didn't want to handle the phone, any kind of crisis, or another screed of words.

The voice on the other end said: 'You don't know me, but...' This always worries me. It's up there with the opener 'Is your name Chris McCully?' These kinds of discourse gambit make me think of overdrafts and hot flushes of shame. She sounded exasperated, too.

She had every right to be. It turned out she'd been round to see a friend who was deep into a relapse. It wasn't a casual 'slip'. He'd been drinking Scotch for four days, and there was no sign of him letting up. Feeling rather like some kind of implausible middle-aged vampireslayer, I picked up a Prayer Book and a crucifix (I'm not kidding), and poured myself into a taxi. I took the Prayer Book, incidentally, not because I'm a minor Christian homilist of the broken heart, but because I knew I was unlikely to get through to the drunk friend unless it was by using words he loved and recognized and had remembered from childhood. In the minutes pre-taxi, I also spoke to the man himself and asked him if he had any food in the house. Yes, he said, after a fractured pause, adding earnestly 'I need you'. Be there in twenty minutes, I said.

Twenty minutes later he'd forgotten I was going. His lady friend had left. He opened the door in a night-shirt soiled by God knows what, and proceeded to crawl around the floor, muttering the word 'whatever'. Even his dog looked mystified. The house stank of Scotch. At least he was still alive.

There isn't much to do on these occasions except to make sure the dog's been let out and fed, and to put the kettle on. We accomplished both actions, but not before spending another twenty minutes trying to find the procedure that would magically open the back door. He'd forgotten the way to do this, in a wilderness of Scotch and fumbled keys. 'I can't fucking...' he kept saying. God he repeatedly invoked. 'God-god-god... Oh shit.' Then he started crawling over the floor in his stained night-shirt. A man in a dirty house, among the wreckage of his dreams. 'I still fucking...' he said in a rare moment of lucidity, 'I still think [pause for a dry retch] I'm on-programme.' Then, much more distinctly, 'But I do need, and I mean need, more booze.'

It's possible, though it's risky and difficult, to come down from a bad relapse using alcohol as a detoxifier. I've rarely known this to work, and from my own experience I also know that the alcohol-detox. has often been a covert and insane opportunity simply to carry on drinking. It's the beckoning of obliteration, dressed up as the desire for control. I've heard most of the relevant excuses before, and don't trust them, even while I know I constructed some blinding and insincere apologies for my hurtling, alcoholic self.

He began to throw up weak tea all over the carpet, collapsing from hands and knees into a sodden adult foetus. He'd started to jibber. The eyes that looked back at me, dull and unseeing, weren't eyes I recognized, and the voice wasn't his. The pain came from knowing that somewhere in this person who'd become almost pure alcohol there was a friend who recognized the depth and extent of his own humiliation. And of course, in looking at him, I saw myself, the vanities, illusions, and deceits of alcohol poisoning, and the exasperating, hurt necessities of human care.

It was a hard thing to do, to walk away. Somehow he'd climbed into bed. I left the Prayer Book on his bedside table. He wrapped himself in the quilt, still muttering his endless string of 'whatever's, snorting occasionally, and making the kind of choking sounds that I couldn't distinguish as a cry, a laugh, or a retch. All I felt I could do was to phone him later.

People die of this…condition, as it turns into disease. They die because real life's so insupportable. They die because they choke on their own vomit. They die because of internal ruptures. They die because they drive their cars over seaside cliffs. They die because they hang themselves from bridges. They die of cold and exposure. They die when their last cigarette has set fire to the bed. They die chaotically, with a lukewarm cup of tea still by the bedside and a sheaf of unpaid bills scattered over the wet carpet. They die clutching inhalers and murmuring 'whatever'. For all the love that surrounds them, they die because they think they want to die.

When I got home, there was no piano, no crossword, and no frozen pizza. I sat on the edge of the sofa, living through some kind of mutilated afterlife until well beyond midnight. All I could think were older words ripped from a desperate sanity: *Lighten our darkness, we beseech thee, O Lord, and in thy great mercy defend us from all perils and dangers of this night…*

And then, at last, I cried.

2002 RETROSPECTIVE

The Simplification

D*espite the fact that I still had a job, despite the occasional grimaces of humour, they weren't easy, those first couple of months. Just coming back, to a place that didn't feel like home, was difficult. It was lacerating. I had images from an earlier life, of returning home from hospital (from some trivial medical operation of boyhood) to care, and calm, and solicitude. This was very different. I came back to a place that wasn't, and never could be, home, where there was only the relict of myself.*

I had at all costs to avoid the dramas of self-pity and resentment. This much I did know. I made myself a kind of pragmatic offer. 'You want to star continually in the drama of your own life, right? Well, today, how about just participating in what passes for the real world for a change? It may not be perfect, great, or even good, but you can at least turn up for it. Sober. And then see what happens.'

That first day back, I did nothing but delete the messages on the Answerphone, buy some bread, cheese, fruit, and milk, and decide to rearrange the furniture. Or perhaps not.

And so, feeling empty, shamed, and shocked, I rearranged the furniture, in this place that wasn't home.

It was one of the most important things I did.

There were others, with whom I'd been in treatment, who barely made it beyond the hospital gates. I could quite understand that. Programmed to drink, what does any alcoholic do with panic?

The rented house to which I came back looked and smelled more or less the same as I'd left it. I used to drink sitting on that sofa; I used to crawl up those same stairs towards the bathroom; I used to conduct the effortless early-morning monologues sitting, shaking, in that corner of the living-room; and there – the sweat from my back still stained the paintwork – there was the place where several months earlier, crouching to weep and racked with vodka-driven remorse, I had called the Samaritans.

I moved the furniture around, and then set about the layers of spiders and dust with a wet cloth and a bucket. I didn't want to sit in the same places, or allow the same gestures to trigger even one memory of one drink. It was the smallest but most practical of beginnings. It was just something I could do.

I was trying to become clean.

I moved the futon that functioned as my bed, because I needed to come round to a different perspective on the ceiling.

I moved the radio, because I wanted to listen to it from a different direction.

Some decisions I had taken in hospital. One of them centred on the woman with whom I was in the earliest stages of what might become, or might not have become, a life. What do you tell someone you're coming to love, in a circumstance like that? I told the truth, and as part of that truth, explained that if she wished to say goodbye there and then – as in her place, I would – then… And so on. Almost by return – by return, from Germany – came a reply crafted onto a tape, sent together with a personal cassette recorder on which to play the message. She wanted me to hear the loving reality that was her voice.

Others, too, had written to me. One of the most loving and significant letters came from my elder sister. 'I'm so glad,' she had written, 'that you've finally decided to throw in the towel…' It was exactly the right thing to say. I can feel my eyes stinging with tears even now.

Another decision centred on the people with whom I couldn't afford to remain in contact. I wrote to them, too, briefly explaining my position, and hoping they would eventually understand the reasons for my choice. With few exceptions, they respected my wishes, and I am still grateful for that.

If I was trying to become clean, I was also trying to simplify.

There were some things I couldn't clean or simplify. One was a troublesome and persistent case of genital warts. I mention this for two reasons. First, many alcoholics in early recovery have to deal with incidental pieces of physical damage caused directly or indirectly by their drinking. And I mention it because this particular

STD was persistent enough to demand weekly treatment at a hospital a longish bus-ride away, and getting to, then enduring, the shame of that treatment was... that is, it felt... hazardous, and for several months – no, a full year – before, I had only been able to endure the memories and the shame by fuelling myself liberally at a bar en route to the hospital. Now, in perilously early recovery, the continuing treatment also brought about a feeling of total dislocation, particularly with respect to my paid work. How do you explain to your employers that you weren't able to attend that committee meeting or this function not because you were drinking in a hole somewhere, but because you were having some fairly precise penile surgery?

I am very grateful to the doctor I will call Dr. Gurnard. In the end, having failed to respond to any kind of treatment because my immune system was barely operative (another by-product of alcoholism), I underwent a series of procedures during which Dr. Gurnard wielded an expert scalpel, and something disconcertingly like a blow-torch.

'Yes...' he said, squinting downwards, sucking in his cheeks in the effort of concentration, and tapping the edge of his scalpel – rather unnecessarily, I thought – on my flaccid, bleeding, and unprepossessing member. 'Yes... Your immune system is totally out. Not a vegetarian, are you? Lots of red meat. Enzymes, you see. Mmmm, well, that's come away beautifully. Be a bit uncomfortable for a day or two. You've got no plans for tonight, have you?'

I told him I had an appointment with a ten-mile bike ride, followed by another with the Swedish Ladies Volleyball Team. Then I asked him why he'd chosen to specialize in this branch of medicine.

He thought for a while about that one. As he dusted down the McCully Penis – it was dusted so that residual blood wouldn't stick the dressing to my shorts – he said this: 'I think it's because we can actually make people well.'

There was no judgement, no lecture, no blame. It was the democracy of the accidental and the broken heart, of final failure. Dr. Gurnard, and his lovely staff, simply administered to it. They, too, smiled at people properly.

I was being made well.

On each bus journey back, I would remind myself that the English words for 'heal' and 'whole' are closely related.

ANOTHER PROBLEM WAS money. Although my salary was notionally adequate, the payment of debts, the further monthly debt to the University (accruing from paying for treatment), and the interest on the debts, meant that I had only a tiny disposable income.

On the very few occasions I actually told people how much I was living on each week, they fell about laughing.

I made lists. Where necessary, I wrote to people, briefly, and as simply as possible, explaining what I was attempting to achieve in this new phase of life. I worked out how much I could repay, and when that would be. I tried to make sure that whatever happened, I would have an adequate, even a nourishing, diet. This didn't mean steak and restaurants. It meant bags of lentils; flour; it meant vegetables, and soup, with a chicken at weekends. Remembering Dr. Gurnard, I occasionally bought a cheap cut of red meat from the local market, where I also quite often talked to the stallholders, just passing the time of day. Apart from the phone, and recovery meetings, these were sometimes the only real-life, real-time conversations I would have for days.

I made more lists. The list-making habit of childhood and adolescence also had its driven, addictive side – I'll tell you later about the malevolent side of Lists – but it also functioned as the reminder of the framework I was trying to live. I was forced into a kind of ingenuity, with very limited funds. But I had survived that many times before – in the desert, in Morocco, in the travelling years – and the facts of ingenious survival now, in 2000, prompted me to ask an old question, but one with a new resonance: What do you actually need *in order to live?*

On any given day, I needed food in my belly, sufficiently sustained health, and a roof over my head. Given those things, if I lived that given day well, then tomorrow would look after itself.

After all the years of power, addiction, and acquisition, it was hard to try and live out of that perspective. And yet I had to live it, in order to simplify, in order to be well. And I began to live it precisely because *there were debts everywhere, because my means were so limited.*

I started to cook again, with cheap, basic ingredients, making each meal stretch. I started to read about food, and about the vitamins it contained. Even when someone came round to visit, there was always more than enough.

There was always, almost miraculously, more than enough.

I tried to be thorough, in the middle of a newly learnt simplicity. Or perhaps it was just that the attention to detail – the furniture-moving, the list-making – kept things simple, when they so easily could have become so poisonously complicated.

Meanwhile, people kept disappearing, or relapsing. And at work, one senior colleague told me that I was living on a sort of probation whereby 'Three strikes, and you're out'. I had clearly used up two – and a half, for good measure. I was also informed that I had not done 'any important work in the department for years'. It was all said in a kindly way, of course. Yes, it was meant very kindly.

And so, as kindly as possible, I repeated to myself the kind observation that I had apparently not done 'any important work in the department for years'.

Well, nice to get that learnt.

I could do little about the disappearing, the relapsing, the anger, or any of the other threats to recovery. But I knew also that there were still some final goodbyes to say.

March to April 2000

11.   9 March 2000

I went into a pub yesterday. It's the first time I've done this since I was in treatment. As I sipped at a double orange juice that would have been immeasurably improved, he lied, by three goes of vodka, I started thinking about pubs and alcohol, and somehow the inward conversation got mixed up with dentists, sex, and hospitals. This was probably because I'm in the middle of a week that has taken or will take me not only to the usual recovery meetings but also to my GP (to ask about procedures for regaining my driving licence); the dentist (to have six months' worth of black-coffee stains removed from my crooked lower teeth); and the genito-urinary clinic (where once again the fabulously skilled Dr. G. will, as it were, do my dick). In between the daily spans of 24 hours where I feel like an alcoholic fool, I'm also trying to finish a book, a couple of papers, a new essay, and to write the blurb for next year's collection of poems. ('Chris McCully's third full-length collection celebrates inconti-nence as a post-modern strategy, interrogating the present through the random deployment of fictive fragments of the past, etc. … McCully is a notorious teetotaller, and is currently uncertain about where he's living, etc.'). I'm also trying to plan a presentation of poems and techniques to a local high school (this for next week), set up a couple of international conferences, and bring a new Single Honours degree programme online. There are those who'll tell you that academics are people who harmlessly potter about on whiteboards, occasionally use a library, and have long summer holidays. Would that were true.

Anyway, the pub. I'd finished at the dentist's, and I was between trains. It was raining, I was in the Pennines, and I was thoroughly pissed off. There were no passing tea-shops in the vicinity, and the local station isn't known for the patronized chrome magnificence of its Costa Coffee and Sock Shops, although it does do a nice line in urinous, dilapidated rain-shelters and miscellaneous vandalism.

I ordered the orange juice in the warm fug at the bar counter. A couple of people were playing pool. Chalkboards announced guest bitters. A litter of prawn crisps behind the bar promised chemical salt for the thirsty. 'Ice?' You bet.

Something's happened to me, and I don't mean the hair that's started to grow on the palms of my hands. When I was 'merely' drying out, as opposed to trying to live in recovery, I used to go into pubs and order something non-malevolent just to see whether I could stifle the unbidden 'and could you put a couple of shots of...'. I used to feel like I was coming home, despite the fact that after half a day's worth of unbidden shots I wouldn't have recognized home if it came and bit me on the ear. But this time, I felt like a stranger, an outsider, scrunching the orange juice ice-cubes under a banner that promised live music (which there wasn't) and going through the rest of the week's schedule (which was real enough). I made my silent excuses to the dismal clack of the pool-balls, then left.

I go back six months, a year, and know that minor anxieties like doctor and dentist visits, let alone the terrifying and shaming trips to the genito-urinary nightmare, were excuses to drink. I simply didn't feel I could cope with life, and certainly not on life's terms, and needed to brace it before I could face it. Let's just have a livener, a stiffener, a loosener, I'd think to myself, riddled with anxiety and self-pity. I didn't want to hear, really, the fact that if I carried on drinking and working like this I had six months to live. I didn't want to know that my immune system had collapsed. I preferred to be the smiling, exhausted face whose breath stank like a wine-cellar rancidly on fire, whose teeth were stained with

Burgundy, coffee, and cigarettes, and whose over-elaborate manners failed to hide utter and complete desperation. And of course, I was Mr. Wonderful, hurling himself from the doctor to the violent disc at the bottom of the brandy glass, wincing every time he sat down because his dick was sore, having to wear boxer shorts so that Air Would Circulate...

One of the wise counsellors whose patience took me through treatment said that going into a pub was, for an alcoholic, rather like pouring petrol over yourself and then standing close to a bonfire. I think he's right. Perhaps I was just fortunate that when I came out of the pub, into an evening world full of schedules and responsibilities, it was still raining, endlessly, and there were no rogue sparks.

12.   15 March 2000

Alcoholism's been in the news. George Best is lying, bloated and yellow, on a hospital bed in the Cromwell Clinic in London. As the tabloids tell it, it's his liver, guv. ''Ere, I once 'ad that George Best's liver in the back of my cab...' And together with the rest of the world, I once had a drink not exactly *with* but, well, *near* George at Dublin Airport, in the days when he was looking like a raddled and watery-eyed old-timer and not a footballing god.

George Best's liver is only a quarter of the Bestie story. The other three quarters is taken up by George Best's immune system, his genito-urinary system, his central nervous system, and his brain. And that's just for starters. Alcohol affects everything. Imagine a million footballs, then multiply them by a million. The world's full of footballs. Now shrink them into billions of cells, each spinning with infection, bewilderment, and alcohol, and imagine that stuff coursing around in the body on the Cromwell Clinic bed. It could be you, dying for a drink.

George has apparently promised to Give Up For Good (this time). I wish him well, while noting that no one in the history of humankind has ever managed, once they're in the chronic phase of alcoholism, to give up by promising, through willpower, through the intervention of the Cottingley Fairies, and on their own. You can, true, be merely sober on your own, but for recovery to happen, and for it to be sustained, there has to be a carefully worked programme, involving family, friends, doctors, work, and, not least, group meetings. There is no cure. There's only management.

As usual, reporters and pundits fill their column inches by pretending, to a world looking delighted but askance at the story, that George Can Do It, good old George, simply by an effort of will. And I suspect there'll be many, many others who simply want the old George back – not the dribbling genius but the drooling, sick, glad-handing fall-guy who once screwed Miss World and is the scapegrace of everyone's folly. Ignorance loves its unreliable memories of the errant genius, the charming drunk. Ignorance in this case is wishing good old George a death sentence.

Down all the drinking years – a quarter of a century of them – I thought it would be my liver. A yellow, rheumy, messy death, and one that surely wouldn't happen to me. With a terrifying shock of recognition, I can still watch myself lifting another large vodka and tonic while thinking, 'My name's Chris, and I'm…bloody immortal.' In the event, it wasn't the liver that was primarily affected by twenty-five years of chronic toping. The liver was enlarged, true; but it was largely intact. So, by some miracle, were pancreas and spleen. As in a significant minority of alcoholic drinkers, it was the central nervous system where the clinical symptoms first took their immortal bow: numbness in the left foot, tingling and muscular weakness in the left hand. The doctors shook their heads and diagnosed peripheral neuropathy without hesitation. An exact quote: 'First, you won't be able to walk. Next, you won't be able to think.' Since my brain, or what's left of it, is my trade, this was a dubious form of immortality. Not knowing where, or remembering who; the fizz in the cocktail became an incontinent shuffle in a wheelchair; and all the fine words a slow shot of spit in the dark.

The liver's a fairly wonderful organ, and you only have one. Among many other things, it regulates the supply of blood sugars to the brain. If the liver's occupied with alcohol, this brain-supply function is interrupted. The individual brain is then deprived of its food: the person feels hungry, weak, nauseous, and has sweats. Welcome to the mildest form of hangover. Continue drinking, and welcome to hypoglycaemia. Many alcoholics also develop diabetes. In addition to regulating blood sugars, the liver also directly metabolises alcohol. Where the liver can't deal with continual doses of ethanol, it starts to manufacture its own fat. Enlarged, fatty liver is the result. This is a reversible condition, but if drinking continues, hepatitis may be imminent. Hepatitis means disturbance to the liver's normal process of metabolic operation, and inflammation of the tissues. Jaundice – hi, George – is a sign of the presence of hepatitis. Hepatitis may, or may not, be reversible. If drinking continues, there's more than an even chance that the individual will go on to develop cirrhosis – death of liver tissue, scarring, loss of metabolic function, disruption to the blood sugar supply to the brain… If you're diagnosed with cirrhosis, and continue to drink, you'll be dead within five years. Good old George.

It's not just George's liver. Elsewhere, what's been affected, more or less critically, is his whole gastrointestinal system; endocrine and central nervous systems; haematological, cardiovascular, genito-urinary systems; and respiratory system. And I'm afraid that no one is going to photograph these for the pages of *Hello!* magazine.

13.   19 March 2000

It's been a difficult week. Long periods of pedestrian dullness have been punctuated by surprise, and by what's almost happiness, though it's a happiness haunted by the bloated and sallow face of George Best. Welcome back, George, you're dying for a drink. Let the good times roll, until they're rolling on the floor and their tongue's turned black. Welcome back. Irish eyes are smiling, unseeing, at the end of their own bewilderment.

Welcome to Real Life. But for an alcoholic, as for any other addict, Real Life just isn't good enough. All that connectedness, all that responsibility, all that sheer bloody work. The word 'dull' is something that has to be bought off by the next fix, the next set of hired faces, the next round. Engaging with the day, and then not engaging with the day, becomes an expensive, and eventually life-threatening, aversion. Yet I'm reminded, and often, of a couple of lines a friend of mine once wrote. Life may be a lousy song, he thought – probably recalling, in a poisoned haze, the awful lyrics that plastered the back of psychedelic albums from 1968 – but there's a terrific repeated chorus… This past week, I've been aiming for the chorus. Most of it, I think I must have missed.

Of all the images that haunt and threaten my own recovery, the idea that life is first a kind of boredom, next a kind of fear is one of the most potent and the most hurtful. Recovery? It's like looking out of a kaleidoscope, a curious and known nightmare, into a tomorrow that seems like a railway track in Poland. There tomorrow is a set of iron rails and grey uncompromising gravel. Onwards the tracks stretch, a steel parallel setting their course into forever. However far you travel, there'll still be the same silent, damp birch forest on either side of the line. There'll still be the same mist hanging in the trees. And on you'll go, uncertain of any destination, uncertain about whether the rails, the mist, and the forest are in fact your destination. Even if by some miracle you do arrive at a Somewhere that could be Anywhere, you won't be able to speak the language, and won't be part of anyone's timetable. All you can do is grunt the same predictable and sober song through gritted teeth, hoping for the chorus while knowing that there's no one there but you to sing it through. The world's monochrome, it's always November, the pages are printed, the faces you remember aren't smiling, and all that's waiting is a final and endless winter.

Sometimes life is dull, Chris. It's about deadlines and bank accounts, and whatever may be in the freezer. It's about tax and washing machines, consultation documents, and loans. It's learning to gulp down a gulp of surprise at someone else's implausible shoes, or their views. It's tired politicians who are no better and no worse than you or me. It's the latest letter you don't want to read. It's everything your drinking self was crazily sceptical about. It may not be what you want, but it's exactly what you need.

And it's difficult. Taking life on life's terms may be second nature to whoever's reading this, but for any recovering addict it's not even third nature, and it has to be thought through without a fix. Not for nothing is a fix called a Habit. It may have lasted, in one form or another, most of our lives. We're reinventing the wheels of the Polish train, and embarking on a journey we don't altogether trust.

I think this may be why George Best – good old George – together with a few million recovering addicts has found it so difficult to stay clean. The bar's always there, the signals, the rituals of presence, the bought company and the paid-for voices. For a moment, for the length of the first brandy hit, perhaps, there's laughter, security, imaginary poise, and the city is promise, and primary colours. There are the random adventures of sex, the beckonings of the bottle. And the others, in this lit, uncomfortable illusion? They're virtually happy, as you pour in the mixer, that you're in the mixer like them. Nice one, George. Have another?

And so here I am, alive, in a birch forest in Poland. It's almost spring, and everywhere I look there are the same few hundred people, getting on with reinventing their own wheels, murmuring a similar chorus. One of these faces belongs to my bank manager. He's sober, always, and plays football. Last week, in the middle of a day that was greyness and worry, he called, unprompted. I nearly dropped the phone. It turned out that I was paying too much for the loan I'd taken out a couple of years ago. Er…a bank manager who tells you you're handing too much to his bank? It was a quotidian miracle, and the whole thing was fixed with a calculator, a file pad, and a few strokes of his immaculate pen. The result is that I'm nearly £1000 a year better off, cash in hand. I wanted to celebrate, of course, but the champagne and the faces were lost at the bar of a station I've already passed through.

14.   23 March 2000

A friend of mine wrote to say that a friend of his – it's always a friend, or a friend of a friend – has been in a bad way, that she's been suffering from black-outs, and is this a sign of alcoholism? The truth is that it could be. Since the woman involved has a history of heavy alcohol use, it probably is.

Black-outs are one of the clinical symptoms. For many people, black-outs imply unconsciousness, a warmly spinning darkness, sleeping it off next to a body you recall only dimly. Among the more addled, this is sometimes cited with a kind of shamefaced pride. Got the old leg over last night, couldn't remember who she was in the morning, feel great now… Want another? Well, no, thanks. But to chronic drinkers, black-outs aren't about unconsciousness. They're about consciousness you forget, about tracts of time torn out of your head. They're being alive without remembering how, who, or where. You can hold down a conversation in this kind of black-out; you can teach; you can drive, illegally; you can buy airline tickets and do the grocery shopping. To others, you'll possibly seem strange, disconnected, and you'll stink of vodka and defeat, but you'll appear to be more or less all there. Truth is, the powers of rational choice and of recent memory will be utterly gone, and you won't be anywhere apart from at the lost crossroads that is your poisoned self.

I've had many such black-outs, particularly during the chronic phase, the past five or six years. Let me emphasize that I don't mean simply collapsing into a drunken stupor, though I did have that. I don't mean merely waking up hungover next to someone you don't recognize, though I did have that. I mean making a chicken roast for twelve Irish fishermen in the middle of the night, and not remembering how the next morning. I mean coming round to the terror and bewilderment of a railway shelter a hundred miles away, not knowing when or how I got there. I mean having long non-conversations that have gone into nothingness and guilt.

When one of my most long-standing friends rang five months ago, I asked her, with apparently deep concern, about why her pregnancy seemed to have lasted forever. By my reckoning, after a difficult nine months, she was over a fortnight late. 'You don't remember?' she asked. 'I phoned you from the hospital, the day after Kit was born. We talked for over an hour. You must have been pissed, darling.' I'd missed the birth of my last and lovely godson. I'd missed the labour and the joy. I'd missed the fact that he'd been named after me. It had all gone into some pouring dark, where I was wide-eyed, and voluble, uncaring, and unconscious.

The great researcher into alcoholism, E.M. Jellinek, published in 1952 an account of alcoholism's aetiology. The disease, he claimed, developed through four phases: the pre-alcoholic; the prodromal; the crucial; and the chronic. In the pre-alcoholic phase, drinking is largely social, but it's become the individual's characteristic response to handling stress. In the prodromal phase – 'prodromal' = 'signalling disease' – you're not drinking socially, but critically, sneaking extra drinks at parties, looking for excuses to drink, buying company with drink, and feeling guilty about drinking. It's in this phase, claimed Jellinek, that black-outs – 'alcoholic palimpsests' – start to occur, 'amnesia-like periods during drinking… The person seems to be functioning normally but later has no memory of what happened.' The prodromal phase may last for months or years. In my case, I think it lasted almost forever, and co-existed with other, and increasingly serious, symptoms.

The neural mechanisms of this kind of black-out are only partially understood. It seems as if alcohol interferes with the production of proteins by certain brain cells, and so strategically damages memory function. This makes a kind of sense: long-term memory isn't radically affected, and you can use immediate memory (events occurring during the period of black-out), but short-term memory is shot, since the brain can't process events from short- into longer-term memory. It's a selective impairment. Individuals seem to differ in their susceptibility to this dys-function. Some younger 'social' drinkers have unpleasant, but non-critical, black-outs after particularly heavy consumption; but in general, if your alcohol use is already heavy, if you've had a history of pro-blematic drinking, if you've had more than one black-out, if black-outs are associated with another sign of this disease (early drinking, sweating, shaking, all the rest), then black-outs are probably diagnostic of incipient, or current, alcoholism.

Black-outs seem to indicate that you're no longer taking ethanol for social purposes, but that it's become a chemical risk that may well have already turned to a chemical dependency. You may not remember whose the face is at the bar or in the bed next to you, you may not know how you got there, but you do know, deep beyond memory or desire, that it isn't fun any longer. There are all those skeletons in the cupboard, including yours – and you don't even know whose they are.

15.   13 April 2000

And so the licensing laws are to be changed. There have been the usual unlovely glozings and glibberings from the Moral Right: 24-hour drinking will, it seems, license unbridled licence, and things will never be quite the same in the quiet cathedral closes of Mutterby-on-the-Marsh. Gangs of lager louts will despoil the dahlia beds. Violent and pouch-eyed academics will hurl imprecations at the postman. Drunks will wriggle vomiting on Saturday morning driveways, just when you thought it was safe to wash the car. Grandmothers will pump their bookmakers' accounts with gin. Slingshots will hurl at street-lamps at 3am, and the world will be a battery of unstoppable house alarms, of publicans, and of sinners. *O tempora! O mores!*

Alcoholics in active addiction don't care about the licensing laws. It doesn't matter whether the pubs are open for two hours or for twenty-four: there will still be, on an educated estimate, 20 per cent of the population who are directly or indirectly affected by alcoholism, and that's 12 million people to you. The damage will still go on, ramifying through families, through schools, through the courts, and through the workplace. It has gone on this way since the year dot, whenever that was. It went on in pre-Christian Palestine and it went on – it even intensified – during America's stupid, righteous, and doomed experiment with Prohibition. My name is Legion, and it doesn't keep hours.

Alcoholics will always find alcohol. If they can't find it, they'll make it. They're as twitchy and alert to its presence as diviners or dowsers. They'll stack it, stash it, hoard it. If almost everyone has at some time had an imaginary friend, so every alcoholic has, or has had, a secret supply. These poisonous dumps can sometimes be found at the back of an unused cupboard; in the cellar; in the toilet cistern; in the hot press; in the rafters of the garage; in the grass-cuttings on the compost heap; even – you'll like this one, and it happens to be true – even in bottles of miniatures cached by night in the eighteen holes of the eighteen greens of the neighbourhood golf club.

At present, in the benighted wasteland that is Cool Britannia, if you do want to drink in company, and after the pubs have shut, there are clubs, there are safe houses, there are backstreet shebeens entered via slurred and secret passwords. And just so all the addictions can line up nicely, there are licensed casinos, too. Make mine a double, and put it on something red. Membership is free, ties are optional, and the taxi's waiting to take you into the bewilderment and dry mouth of another shaking November morning.

It's useful to contrast this state of affairs with that which pertains in more civilized societies, where alcohol is more freely available. Yes, I'm talking of what British xenophobia labels Abroad – Italy, Greece, Spain. I'm not saying that alcoholism is less prevalent in these countries than under the shadow of the Greenwich Dome – it's still a 20 per cent thing in my own estimate, no more, no less – but I do claim that drinking is more companionable, more familial, and more dignified under a Mediterranean moon. For one thing, alcohol is there invariably consumed with food, and I don't mean a bag of pork scratchings. For another, there's no nonsensical rictus about Last Orders – a British ritual that's guaranteed to send gangs of loud and reeling teenagers out into a loud and reeling night. For another, drinking isn't appropriated by the cult of the individual achiever, the lonely and shattered success who treads out the street-lights one by one on the way home. It's altogether a more supported activity, surrounded by colleagues, by friends, by family – and by laughter, by songs everyone's learnt from childhood, by smiling that lasts beyond goodbye. It's precisely the kind of slow, wry, clever, friendly drinking I'd like to do if I could. Which, of course, I can't – at least, not today.

Greece is an instructive example. Take Corfu. True, Corfiots may sit in the shade over a late Greek lunch and take an ouzo and a small plate of *mezedhes* before tucking into *pastichada* so thick and rich it has to be followed by a siesta. True, Corfiots may sit late over a meal, laughter, conversation, and a bottle or three of wine (always accompanied by water). But you won't see idiocy and you won't see drunkenness. For idiocy and drunkenness you have to go to Kavos, to Kassiopi and Rhodopi, to the resorts – they're more like ghettos – where the Annabels and Kevins go red, get sick, go brown, and then go home, after their fortnight of disabled sex and hangovers. Drunkenness flexes its Essex muscles, and gets sand kicked in its peeling face. It's a complete mystery to local people, and Corfiots typically avoid all the ghettos in high season, unless they want to make money out of decibels and imported bottled beers. Civilization quietly gets on with itself elsewhere, and looks back at the antics of Club 15–Bus Pass with a mystified, and not quite indulgent, smile.

It may be too much to expect that civilization might one day come to Tony Blair's emotionally bankrupt and unintelligent Britain, but a relaxed and sensible approach to how we consume societally legitimate poison might be no bad place to begin to hope.

16.   14 April 2000

George Best has been discharged from hospital, vowing never again to touch even a wisheen of the hard, or for that matter the soft, stuff. I've been thinking about pubs, and how difficult it must be to be George Best, good old George, surrounded by booze everywhere, nor any drop to drink.

If booze is institutionalized in this non-culture, it's also fictionalized, and hierarchized. That the pub is a national institution one can hardly doubt: all those turgid images of the Rovers and the Vic, the second, and troubled, homes of the neighbourhood villains and 'eigh-oop, gor-blimey' Characters; the major investments of the breweries into 'theme pubs' with pointless themes and rows of books chained to the walls of the not-so-Snuggery; the advertising campaigns, the fat and perspiring darts teams, the awful Quiz-Nites, the even more awful karaoke machines; and the truly and utterly unspeakable existence of bloody pork scratchings… Welcome to Cool Britannia, Tony, and since they're calling Last Orders, make mine a treble.

If you want to meet a stranger, where do you agree to go? The pub. If you want to see a group of friends after work, where do you gather? The pub. If you want to take out a colleague to celebrate his or her retirement, her pregnancy, his stag night, or her promotion, where d'you go? The pub. Working lunch? The pub. And if you need to give directions, how d'you do it? 'Turn right by the White Horse, then go straight on till you get to the Flea and Firkin, then turn right, and go on for, um, half a mile until you get to the Old Cock Inn…' It's ingrained. I mean, you're not going to say 'Fine, Wendy, let's meet at the Olde Cote Tea Rooms', are you? 'Turn left by that café…er, can't remember its name, something like Cappa-something…then go straight on till you get to that market stall run by the farmer's ex-wife with the halitosis…' No, it's the pub every time, the girls out trapping off on a Friday night in Oldham, the whole non-pulsating, pitiful power of the pitcher and the pussy-magnet. 'The lights must never go out, the music must always play…' The liquid fortress; the zero resort; the local. The pub.

And even the pub is factionalized: the lunchtime trade, in suits and skirts, business lapels still nestling coolly over a cold and inedible Ploughman's, onion breath in the gin and tonic; the early evening trade, tired out in corduroys, lager rings from the bottom of the first pint fresh on the tables just wiped from the end of lunch, a couple of harassed husbands, a couple of drunks unable or unwilling to go home in Happy Hour; and then the night-time trade of rag-and-bone, false finery, chicken in a basket, cheap perfume, and the glitter of tights in a taxi afterwards. Haven't you got homes to go to? Yes, maybe, but this is the local, and its heartbreaks are better than real life. Frictions and factions, the darts team on Tuesdays, that black DJ on Thursdays (always a quiet night, boss), the Guest Beers on Monday, and every day a Happy Hour, guaranteed from 5pm until 7, Special Offer on the Breezers.

Institutionalized, factionalized – and hierarchized. Regulars at the bar, each with their own place, their allotted raised eyebrow bringing another refill, the preferential treatment; passing trade in the Snuggery, the Shrubbery, the Orangery, or the Buttery; the Ladies Darts Team and the Girl-Organists' Convention in the back room; and Old Joe in his one chair, always his chair, he'll be in at tea-time, regular as clockwork...

Old Joe interests me. He's there in every pub and in every life, just as every addicted life has an eighty-year-old grandfather who took two litres of Scotch before breakfast and smoked forty a day, never did him any harm. Old Joe's a mythical creature, a raddled survivor, mute king of the Happy Hour heap, gets going each morning with a nip of the golden magic in his extra-sweet tea, and for God's sake don't sit in his chair or else the music will stop and every eye be turned on you in accusation. Old Joe beat the rap.

Now let's take a look at Old Joe, who used to be called George, good old George, in his younger days. Look at him, wrapped up in his incontinence and his doctors' appointments, his hospital visits, and his catheter. There he is in his chair, the furniture of home, the crowned head of addiction and his aspirant, ape-shit courtiers. Not shaking too badly today, is he? Not slurring and spitting as much as... Buy him another? Maybe he'll tell us the one about the European Cup. How old is he? Well, now there's a strange thing. You wouldn't think... I mean, he's looking a bit untidy, and he hasn't cleaned his nails, but... What d'you think? Early seventies? Fact is, I had to sign his insurance forms after the fire, and he's only in his forties. Forty-seven next birthday, would you believe it?

I knew Old Joe when he was forty-seven. I knew the institutions that fed him and kept him barely alive, and they weren't called hospitals, they were called pubs. I knew the factions that didn't listen to his stories, and they paid for the pub. I knew the hierarchies and the order he craved and missed, the illusions of himself he drank down in the pub in his one chair. I didn't know Joe when he was forty-eight. He didn't make it, and it wasn't, ever, Happy Hour.

17.   16 April 2000

People sometimes ask – well, no, they don't ask, they *enquire*, silently, with a raised eyebrow or a telling hesitation – people ask what I think about booze, now. Am I about to be censorious? Do I disapprove of it, all of it? Am I on some sort of failing, one-man campaign to get the stuff banned? Am I a caped crusader, with a big S for Sobriety stitched unreliably onto his Sloggis?

In the absence of a passing telephone booth, and dressed in normal clothes, I say, as calmly as possible, that I have nothing against booze. I mean that quite literally: I'm absolutely powerless over alcohol. I can't beat it, ever, even if I were to wear crusaders' tights. I've fought it, surely – through the years of embarrassment, through failure, through all the tensions and destructions of denial – but I'll never beat it, and, like you, I never could. I've fought it in petty lies, and I've fought it in forgetting; in mock-honesty, in health. I've fought it in excuses and celebration, in apparent happiness, and in books. I've fought it throwing up and impotent. I've fought it in bedrooms and on the floor of Accident and Emergency departments of stray hospitals whose kind and concerned faces I couldn't remember. I've fought it through gritted teeth and the rictus of a smile. I fought it until I had not that much longer left to live. And I have nothing against it.

Let me put it this way. If alcohol isn't hurting you, if it isn't hurting your work, your family, your bank account, or the people you love then it's the greatest legal drug on the face of the planet. It's a breeze, a walk in the park, a shot in the arm. But life's not roses and champagne, and as you pop the Bolly and read the Interflora message, you could choose to remember that there are two Class A drugs. One's heroin, the other's alcohol. One happens to be legal, the other isn't. They're the only two drugs in the world where addiction means clinical intervention, and detox. But if the one, alcohol, isn't hurting you, if your addictive patterns aren't lining up around it, if no one you know or love has a problem with the raised glass in your hand, I wish you well, and hope you'll have a refill, however rueful, for those of us who can't. And I hope you enjoy it.

This said, I don't keep alcohol in the house. I used to, in the almost-dry days, the two years I spent stumbling after the wagon. I'm still too close to those lunchtimes, those evenings, when I uncorked the terrible supermarket plonk I'd bought – ha! – just for cooking, and ended up 48 hours later vinegary, dirty, abusive, and lost to myself. Let's hear it for the days of wine and bruises, and of the one word, Sorry, etching itself like age into my forehead. So I'm still too near the corkscrew and the cocktail shaker to want to go near the neck of an opened bottle. Then again, I know several recovering alcoholics who do keep bottles, and even cellars. After all, they argue, the world is full of this stuff, and why deny anyone else's pleasure? I agree, and maybe some time I'll get to this easy generosity. I hope so, but the hour's not yet.

I also think I'd find it difficult, at the moment, to serve anyone alcohol. Let me repeat: I have nothing against the electric soup, but I just don't want to be switched on in the kitchen, the bathroom, the bedroom, or anywhere else I used to drink. Maybe... But despite all the maybes, I remember an eminent academic, who – many years ago, with his first year of enforced sobriety still fresh on him – bought me a bottle of whisky, proceeded to pour it for me, and who was dead two years later. I can see him shaking yet, with the defeat, and the desire, and the anxiety of compassion in his eyes. 'I still dream about it, dear boy,' he said. 'Still wake up shaking, and sweating, and all the rest.'

I thought it couldn't, and therefore wouldn't, happen to me.

Aftershave I still use, and after flirting manfully with some awful alcohol-free stuff that smeared on like soapy semen, and tasted worse, I stuck to the poisoned brand. I know I can't drink it, because I tried this once, with consequences for my tongue I haven't forgotten, and choose not to repeat. I also spray on some cheap deodorant, whose ingredients, the label tells me, include 'Butane, Isobutane, Propane, Aluminum Chlorohydrate, Dioctyle Adipate, Talc, Silica, Parfum...' and 'Alcohol

Denat', whatever that is. Given the other contents, it's a good job I don't smoke when I'm towelling myself down, or I'd die of auto-immolation.

Please read my lips: *If it isn't hurting you, or the people you love, alcohol's the greatest drug on earth.* It always has been. But as you retreat into all your yesterdays, as they become all your tomorrows, I can only raise a smile and two cheers as you lift the tumbler, knowing that my smile, at least, is very much steadier and more real on none for the road.

18.   21 April 2000

I was in court yesterday. Two years ago, there was an argument between a passing policeman, a bottle of vodka, and a BMW weaving the wrong way down the tram-tracks in the centre of this ostensibly fair and rain-swept city. I was banned for three years, sentenced to 200 hours' community service, and fined. Earlier on the same day, I'd had a terrible and conclusive row – the word's too light – with my oldest friend and his wife. The friendship, to my sorrow, is no more. Neither is the BMW, though I'm still paying off the loan. It was one of the most turbulent and awful days of my life, and its consequences, notwithstanding the near bankruptcy, were the deepest shame and loneliness I've ever felt.

My alcohol breath reading was 131/35. That's over three times the legal limit. In that sort of state, you're heading rapidly towards coma. I wonder now whom it was that I wanted to kill. This was the year of drawn curtains lasting all daylight, of sleeping with the means of auto-destruction under the pillow or close at hand in the bathroom. Whom did I want to kill? The answer is, of course, the shame that was myself. But on BMW night in Manchester, it could have been you. It could have been your partner, or your parent. It could have been your child.

Two years into the three-year ban, and you're entitled to apply, via the Magistrates' Court, for the reinstatement of your licence. I applied, enlisting a firm of good solicitors who've come to know me a little too well over the years. Briefing them was one of the most uncomfortable parts of the process, since it meant revisiting reasons, alcoholism, motives, shame, and loneliness. It meant looking again at the chaos, acknowledging it, and feeling its reality. There's nowhere to hide – no polite or impolite evasion, no unreliable self-image, no alcoholic massage with a large brandy and a group of unwilling hangers-on. What you're looking at are the actions of a drunk, whose every failure is himself. And in looking at the actions of this particular drunk, I briefly, but badly, wanted a drink.

We went to court. It was an unusual business, in that we weren't applying for reinstatement because I needed a licence for my job. We were applying because life's limited, isolated and isolating, without a car. We were applying because running a car will enable me to inject some good, orderly direction into the planning of evenings and weekends. We were applying because I might be able to go fishing again, to places I love and with faces I love. But above all, we were applying because regaining the licence might prove to be a symbolic, and therefore important, part of the whole process of rehabilitation.

The solicitor ran through the details of personal and professional life, emphasizing the court's powers of discretion. I only blushed once, when it came out that I was, it seemed, a 'nationally respected angling journalist'. Yes, with a readership of three, two of them, my sisters. He ran through the history of attempted sobriety, and more recently, the history of treatment and recovery. He ran through the minimal achievements and the plans.

'Chris said something to me, privately,' said the solicitor, 'and I don't think he'd mind me sharing it with the court. What Chris said was "I'm trying to get my life back…"'

Feeling deeply self-conscious and awkward, I confirmed the lot under oath. At least we'd made a straight case. The magistrates retired, and my small world held its breath.

'The court will rise.' We rose. Outside the traffic was a muted stain on the air, and a squeal of bus brakes. An April wind shook the slatted blinds of the courtroom. Somewhere, a police sergeant unobtrusively picked at a surprising stain on his fly. 'We have no hesitation whatsoever, Dr. McCully, in removing the disqualification, and confirm that your licence will be reinstated subject to independent assessment by the DVLA's medical advisers. We'd also like to wish you well in all your various enterprises.'

I tried to look modestly nonchalant and entirely grateful, while filling up like an idiot and swallowing the tears that were almost certainly in the back of my throat. The magistrates were smiling. My solicitor was smiling. Even the Chief Constable's solicitor was smiling.

I walked out into the April wind and the unreliable sunshine. What d'you do, when you've won a court case like this? My deepest and longest-standing instinct was to head for the nearest bar, buy something with some fizz in it, and borrow someone's mobile phone in order to muster enough mouths to sup at five champagne flutes. Yes, working lunch, tiny celebration, life back in order... But life wasn't back in order, or at least, not quite and not quite altogether. I don't know how I'm going to pay the solicitors, or the kind and expert consultant whose letter of support spoke so strongly in my favour. I don't know how or whether I'll ever be able to afford to drive. But the whole point of the process was that as of yesterday I have more choices than I had the day before, and that means more freedom. Recovery, beyond anything else, does mean freedom, and that is worth celebrating, as is the expertise of all the people on whose help I'd so crucially relied. I imagined that the champagne would have tasted like acrimony, like years-old vinegar, and chose, out of loneliness and gratitude, to get a cup of coffee and a haircut instead.

19.   26 April 2000

It's the Tuesday after Easter. This is sometimes how it is – the Tuesday after Easter, rain falling in stair-rods, the Bank Holiday over, and five consecutive days of loneliness. I don't think I've spoken face to face with anyone since last Thursday, though of course there's been the mercy of the phone, the Internet, and the perennial company of books. But I can't settle to the books; to anything. Along with the appalling shadow of self-pity, I also have to confront myself – a saddened, middle-aged man who's a chronic alcoholic, who doesn't know how to pay his bills, whose house is freezing cold, and who'll try to make a 99p supermarket chicken last until Thursday.

I think this all began when I started to worry about other people's worries. In particular, I was worrying about an accountant called...let's call him Cartwright, whom I barely know, but who called to say he was struggling. His problems in sobriety – house problems, relationship problems, the usual problems – were very close to my own. I don't think I could have helped him much, since he apparently misheard – or perhaps, chose not to hear – anything I was saying. I put the phone down. No one, I thought, with all the arrogance of ignorance, should have an accountant called Cartwright in their life. And it was Easter Monday, sport on the television, the world in blown cherry-blossom, heading towards the pub. At that moment, and for the rest of the day, I wanted to be like other people, and to pour myself into a bottle of champagne I couldn't afford. I tried to read, to work, to sleep. Then I began to brood, about money, about my dissolved marriage, about lost friendships, about the whole broken and backwards world, with its addictions and its sham, its drudgery, its predictabilities, its hatreds, and its losses. Eventually, some-where in the deeps of my head, I arrived at the sentence 'I am a man more sinned against than sinning'. The deals I'd been dealt were so raw they were bleeding. I still had the scars on my dick from treatment of a persis-tent and uncomfortable case of genital warts. I had paid for one divorce, paid for very large parts of a critical disaster with someone else, including the engagement notice, and was still paying for a car I'd bought in 1998, and would never again drive. I had £8 and some coppers to last the next three days, including cigarettes. There seemed to be only the remainder of an unreliable overdraft between me and the gutter. Elsewhere, the day tucked into its Easter eggs, and milled around in Garden Centres. I, too, had enjoyed the postage-stamp garden, when I'd had one, before the crash. The crash, that had come unbidden, and was helped on its way by other people's insults…and several supermarkets' worth of vodka.

'I am a man more sinned against than sinning.' Oh, please. Welcome to self-pity, tossing about in my head like the topmost bough of poison-ous cherry-blossom in a high April wind. Why me? Why do I have to be a chronic alcoholic? Is this what the training was for? Is this what the laughter and all the love were about?

I paced about, then tried to read. I sat on the corner of the borrowed sofa and shook, until hours had passed. I still wore the T-shirt I'd slept in, and hadn't shaved. Nor had I eaten. All the small rituals, the small disci-plines of safety, were forgotten. I tried to think of the future, and it still looked like a grey and empty railway track somewhere in Poland. I picked up the phone. Even when Jonathan, kind Jonathan, had invited me round to eat a leg of lamb, I wouldn't go. I have to work, I said. You work too hard, he said. Okay then, I work too hard, what do you know? All I knew was that I had to feel whatever it was I was feeling, without anaesthetic. And then I had to let it pass through me, somehow, and then somehow, I had to let it go.

Five and a half months into recovery, and I've had a couple of these awful days, the days of shaking and loneliness, when my head's haunted by accusation and a woman's face, by bank accounts and losses, by shames and hopelessness. They are precisely, exactly the times I would have been the first into the bottle, any bottle, anywhere. The oldest truth in the book is that alcoholics drink on such poisonous feelings, on resentments and self-pities, on hunger and loneliness. There's also the thought that if recovery can feel this bad, why be sober?

I shook stylishly for a few more hours. I dragged myself towards a bit of pasta, couldn't be bothered to wash up three pots. Then I climbed into bed, and just to cheer myself up, read something about Samuel Beckett, in a world of mouths and grey cries.

Today's better. It's not great, I'm not singing, but I'm not shaking with worry either. Bad days have a merciful habit of coming to an end, and all the fragile and shattered hopes remind me this morning of the remaining cherry-blossoms I can see from the window: they come, they're obliterated in these stair-rods of rain, but they're part of a structure of a tree, a life, that not even Bank Holiday weather can uproot. No more am I uprooted, even if it's to live into another day to confront the remains of a 99p chicken and an accountant called Cartwright.

20.   29 April 2000

I received this e-mail letter from a friend. I quote it, very slightly edited, with his permission.

Dear Chris,

Found the latest columns terribly moving, particularly the one about the court case. One small step for Chris, one giant step for freedom. Yeah, brought a load of stuff back for me – re. court cases. Stuff I'd long since blanked out. Second time I was in court, after going completely AWOL on Tequila Slammers, the paper's court reporter was there. I spent ten minutes trying to talk her out of covering the case. But to no avail. The shock and the shame were wind-tunnel strength. Icy. And total sense of unreality: that this was happening to me. Must have been someone else, guv. And the thing is: it was, in a sense.

Think the columns are important work. This stuff needs saying. Like the nitty-gritty bits about bad days, good days. The reality check stuff. That's what it's like. That's what alko's can't stand. Even now I can't stand it, sometimes. Letting yourself experience and work through the emotions is key as well, as you point out. Again, alko's would rather do anything than face those. They wanna by-pass 'em, sell 'em a dummy, give 'em the slip, duck, dive, weave and bob. Or wallow in what they imagine them to be. But, ultimately, you can't live, or love, your life like that.

Did you see interview with George – after coming out of hospital? He looked suitably chastened. Asked what made him think he really could give up this time, given he'd tried so often before, he said: *Well, I've never really given up before. This time I've got to.* Then he was asked how he was going to do it? He obviously didn't have a clue, had no strategy. Hadn't really thought through the extent to which he was going to have to overhaul his lifestyle. Then it emerges lovely young wife Alex likes a drink – and certainly wasn't going to stop drinking wine in the house. His manager cum agent, nice, but clueless, liked a drink and was going to carry on drinking round him. Just wine, though. In other words, every fucker he was going to be around was going to be drinking. And the first pix of him days later was of him leaving a pub! But it was interesting seeing the friends etc. being interviewed. They clearly found the question of how to help him stop as difficult and embarrassing as he did. They clearly needed counselling in how to help him (just as much as he did). Yeah, I really think there's mileage in friends and family angle. [...]

Then there's the whole question of how family and friends react to you once you've changed. Turns out they fucking hate the 'new' you. They preferred the drunken waster – for all sorts of reasons. You had an important role to play – as incorrigible family black sheep, didn't you realise? You've upset the systemic apple cart. Suddenly, girlfriends don't find you as attractive. The dangerous party animal they fell in love with has disappeared – replaced by a sober bore whingeing about his health. This last is exactly that happened to me in my marriage. I 'sold' myself [...] during courtship as this Wild Thing – 'cos that's what I sensed she wanted me to be. Then, when she starts living with me, she's horrified to discover this rather serious intellectual, who spends days locked away with books, writing poetry. Talk about boring! Also: she discovers that the wonderful confidence I exuded in the pub masked real insecurity and vulnerabilities. (Now there's a surprise!) And was she interested in supporting me not drinking? No way, dah-ling. Was she interested in castigating me and taking the piss out of me for being a wimp? You betcha. (But even there it wasn't as simple as that. I was and can be the party animal – AND I can be more serious. I'm both. But that was too complex for the wife to get her head round.) The unwritten contract we'd drawn up together had been broken – she certainly didn't want to change – and the consequences were fatal. So change full stop can be deeply threatening, if not destructive.

Another thought: even now, I've got friends I just can't not drink with. Our friendship is based to such an extent on having a good time drunk that to stay sober when I see them seems like a betrayal. But it literally kills me keeping up these friendships. 'Cos I come back from weekends with these people in pieces. They don't see that. Witness last weekend. It's a complicated thing. I don't have the bottle (how apt!) to say, I'm not going to drink (although I've done it now and then). And, the reality is: I really do have a great time when I'm pissed with these people. Plus, they seem really hurt and shocked (and bored) if I say I'm not going to drink. All of them are people made uncomfortable by the idea of people not drinking around them 'cos they themselves drink far too much (and are alko's, truth be told). But they're not at the stage where it's hurting so much they can't drink. And so it goes on. (So, I go on these weekends – and have to psych myself up in advance – and plan in at least a week's recovery time.) It's easier with 'new' friends 'cos you can present yourself as a non-drinker from the off. With old friends, there's all that shared history – and the shared history is shaped and constituted by drinking. It's a non-stop problem.

Given a choice, though, I'd prefer to see them and not drink. All of them. And the reality is, more than not, now, I don't have a great time being drunk with these people 'cos I feel so ill. Another thing I notice, more and more, is that there are important illusions being sustained when me and me friends drink. One is: we're still young and not, as we palpably are, well on the way to being over the hill. Two is: nothing's changed. We're still those young gunslingers heading out on the highway about to take the world in a love embrace. Forget the intervening bouts of alcoholism, the broken marriages, the bastard children. So the drinking is a form of nostalgia.

Sorry, didn't mean to go on like this. But there are very few people you can really talk honestly to about alcoholism. And stuff only occurs to me when I write. Do you find that: your best thinking occurs as you write? Auto-genesis, or something. Feel free to use any or all of this.

And so I have.

The Loneliness of Gratitude

And so it was underway, the recovery and the fret. It hurt, and it went on hurting. Once again, you can hear the hurt in the attempts at humour. The irony was a weapon, made by thirty years of fear. With some things I was preoccupied – with genital warts, with regaining the driving licence, even with George Best's recovery as an instructive analogue of my own. You can hear the preoccupation in the repetitions. I was repeating myself in order to instruct the days. It was rather like learning a new language, but far more frustrating, because the raw material was the syntax and morphology of myself, and these didn't fit together at all coherently.

Still there was freedom, and there was increasing decision and clarity, in small matters as in larger ones. There were many days when I had to remind myself that to achieve clarity, or just to make one decision, was a hell of an improvement over the nullified days of nausea and drawn curtains.

Some things I couldn't fix. As my friend's letter had so truly put it, there were old friendships that were founded on very little but alcohol, and both the friends and I felt somehow embarrassed. To some, I guess, my recovery felt like an affront, or a challenge. Some didn't care – but why should they have done? Some friendships didn't last, despite my attempts to apologize, or to start afresh, and that was, and is, a matter of very deep and lasting regret.

People move on, they have their own lives, they go away, they do forget. At this period, it began to strike me how very little I actually knew of the people whose *friendships I claimed, with such vehemence, so much to value. And because I knew or understood little, I had tried to fix the friendships in endurance, something permanent, something utterly reliable, something always there, something that would always do, immediately, what it promised on the label... That is, I had treated many 'friendships' as if they were bottles. I knew what bottles did, after all, and these were part of my emotional landscape because their effects were predictable. I could buy a bottle, I could pretend to manipulate a bottle, I could pick it up when I chose. This was something I knew how to do.*

I was like a dependent child. The bottles were taken away, the friendships were withdrawn...and I could have cried. And reaching that point of understanding, I felt violently pathetic. Self, self, self.

You are avoided, as if you are an unlucky place. You are the wrong railing.

And after all, and despite the decision of the magistrates, it turned out that I wasn't entitled to regain my driving licence. The independent medical reports – 'independent' reports made by DVLA-appointed doctors – showed that I was barely a year in recovery, and therefore a poor risk ('Dr. McCully is a high-risk offender...'). I was told first of all that I was entitled to drive, and then, by letter, that I was not so entitled. I had paid for the privilege of medical examination, and also arranged my own independent tests and reports. And besides, I had given all the relevant information to the court that had determined that I was eligible to drive again...

I kept reminding myself that the whole damn thing was my own fault. I kept thinking about the people I could have killed. And apart from obsessing about the frustrations of dealing with the Medical Branch of the DVLA, what this episode had taught me was that I had further freedoms in recovery.

Time, I kept telling myself. Take time. And then another recovery cliché, 'Time Takes Time'.

'SORRY' DOESN'T BEGIN to cover all this.

I had to live the sorrow, and make it creative, smiling, grounded. In the business, this is called 'living life on life's terms'. Many people apparently know how to do it. I didn't.

Some days, it had to be good enough just to feel conscious. On other days, abandoned days, I sometimes wondered whether I had truly died, and whether this apparent life was some sort of after-life, poisoned by regret, exiled from friendships, despised or mistrusted in one's place of work.

Feeling the continual pull of self-pity, I tried to be merciless, to question or examine everything. I was always tired, working what seemed like a mess of time and truth. And there were also times when recovery meetings seemed to be full of bleating and gibberish, though dumbly I stuck with them, and was lucky to have had them.

Slowly, very slowly, life was improving. I don't mean that it felt normal, whatever that may be, only that it felt just a little more comfortable. One friend had lent me some furniture, so I had an easy place to sit, and a television to watch. I made some chocolate cake, and taped Alien. *I dealt with the household bills. I walked to work, came back from work, went to at least one recovery meeting a week, sometimes two. I tried hard to feel grateful, while feeling terribly lonely.*

There's no way out of it. However many the faces and voices around you, however encouraging the recognition of recovering fellow addicts, the loneliness has to be reckoned with, and with that reckoning, the shame, the blame, and all the uncertainty.

YOU WILL BE abandoned by some of the ones you thought you loved. Even to the family, even to close friends, you will seem like a reproach. They can't follow you to wherever it is you seem to have gone. Why should they? You have hurt them too badly, and besides, for them to follow you would mean that they questioned themselves so far as to reveal the depths of their own fear, their own ignorance, and their own prejudice. And who is willingly prepared to do that?

IT'S THE NOVELTY of abandonment – abandonment in real time, not drinking time – that translates so easily into loneliness. But being alone *is not quite the same thing as being* lonely. *In early recovery, you may well be both, though it helped me to remember that the unchosen loneliness would pass, sooner or – more probably – later. This is why some form of support is so critical. I don't care if it's an AA meeting, or some other form of meeting, even some meeting to do with a hobby or a club. There just has to be some form of human contact, in a form that allows your own meta-language – the language of your recovered self – to be spoken, and authenticated. You can't do recovery in loneliness. No one can. On the other hand, you can do recovery alone, so long as you're alone with others who are equally alone with you.*

THE UK GOVERNMENT did not, after all, change the licensing laws. It appears that this gesture was merely a pre-election, re-election bribe. Meanwhile, the personal use of cannabis has been effectively de-criminalized, and further resources will be used to tackle the social evils of 'hard drugs'.

AFTER HIS LAST detox., George Best was equipped with Antabuse implants. He has recently (2002) been discharged from the Cromwell Clinic after a liver transplant. These events can't have been on the CV of the promising young footballer whose talents made him a god. We're embarrassed, so close to hubris and mortality, and therefore we say 'Good old George'. It's as if we were to say 'Good old Icarus'. And then after what we do say, we don't know what to say.

IT'S IN THAT gap, that speaking silence, that your recovery begins. You're caught between the gestures of one world, and the uncertainty and fear of the next. You could almost be glad, except your hunted, hurtling self has forgotten how to be glad.
  You can learn to speak your own gratitude primarily by listening to others.

THE PLOUGHMAN WATCHED Icarus crash into the sea, and because the failure made him angry, he left the body and its eyes for the gulls.
  The same night he made an unusually long libation to the gods.
  His wife didn't understand that at all.
  The next morning there were other things to get on with.

IN EARLY RECOVERY, there's no such person as the prodigal son or daughter. They will return to find their parents' house vandalized, and their parents dead.
  They'll just have to deal with it.

April to July 2000

21.   30 April 2000

People further into recovery than this bare few months keep telling me that continued sobriety has a Hump. The Hump tends to occur when the early enthusiasm wears off, when life reveals itself as the complicated, broke, broken, and pitiless mess that it is, and when the illusions of oneself as slightly more than a travelling sum of accidents can't be sustained. What the hell, you think: if recovery feels this fucking bad, why not have a drink? Meanwhile, the whole world drifts to the pub on Bank Holiday Monday, while you eye the telephone as if it's just gone into the red – which, in a way, it has. I guess I've got the Hump. Life suddenly seems pear-shaped. Quasimodo looks back from the bathroom mirror.

There were symptoms, and I ignored them. First, there was the use of spare time. I'd been working so hard that I barely noticed Easter creeping up, with its riot of ice-cream vans, rain, and Bank Holidays. This year, Easter's been rapidly followed by a pointless Mayday Monday. Two successive long weekends – and I hadn't planned for them. Nor do I have the spare cash to take a train, go fishing, get into the country. Even finding a tram fare to Altrincham – a princely £3 return – is difficult, and I need to find that twice a week just to get back for treatment. So the alternative is to do the washing, the ironing, the cleaning. To catch up with writing projects. To do research. But I spend my entire life doing these things, going cross-eyed with fatigue, reaching for the Optrex at midnight. Two thousand words a day for four months is no fun, believe me (no one else will). The upshot is that I look at everyone else having the wits and the cash to do something with their free time, and then I feel excluded, and restricted. Bad.

Second, there's irritability. Also bad. Irritability's driven by not feeling I'm using my spare time to relax; by other people's apparent lack of any kind of understanding [sob]; by the constant hassles of work; by the lack of freedom there is in this 'recovery'. I feel as if I've paid, and paid again and again, for other people's irresponsibilities and wrong choices. I've certainly paid for my own.

Third, there's the sick, hollow feeling of being dull. All work and no play. I don't even feel I want to talk to anyone on the phone, since unless they're critically interested in verseform, adverbials, meme theory, or sea-trout I don't think I have a great deal to say that's either interesting or acute. I'm tongue-tied and lost, self-absorbed and thoughtful. When recovering alcoholics reach this point, helpful partners have been known to say 'I preferred Chris McCully [or substitute your own name here] the drunk…' Well, thanks.

Which brings me rather too neatly to the fourth thing that's under-wiring the Hump: painful memories. Memories of sex, of financial freedom, of irresponsibility. These memories are poisonous, since they bring me too close to what's called, in the recovery trade, euphoric recall. In euphoric recall, drinking was great. There were the allures of sex, of the erotic chase. There was the laughter, the craziness, the lack of consequence. It was all Easy Rider and a pair of long, suntanned legs. It was California and Venice. I know: the hell it was. It was dry-retching, it was a hurt and twisted face, it was pissing yourself in fear somewhere in Salford. But in euphoric recall, you remember promises and sunshine, and the contrast, then and now, when Now is hurt and tired and a wrecked chin submits to the razor… The contrast is like a perennial disaster, a misery-hill, a human hump in which someone, probably you, has planted a flag that blazons the skull and crossbones, and the one word, vodka.

It's just past five on a Sunday afternoon, and I'm bored, fractious. I know I need to use the phone, get to a meeting, plan the coming week. I just keep thinking 'Fuck it'. I don't want to talk to anyone. It's taking all my energy just to get to the end of the day, a bath, and an early night without getting to a drink first. A drink. Several drinks. No one would know. And a whole bottle would still the fractured pouring of memory and disaster through my head, just for a moment. Oblivion.

Then again, if everyone knows that denial's a river in Africa, then oblivion to an alcoholic is a person from South America. Well...I think I'll have to carry this Hump until bedtime. Fuck it.

22.   1 May 2000

The Hump has dwindled to the size of a persistent and ugly wart – and I know about warts. I woke up this morning sober, again, and a ridiculous little tune was sounding off in the dim bells at the back of my head: *Riddle-me-roh, and riddle-me-ree / Life's a rictus of vitamin B...* The thought that I can do alliteration at this time in the morning meant that I hit the toast and Marmite, then reached for a bottle, a pill bottle, that comes from Bollocks & Hairnet, or Hairoil & Barnet, whatever they're called. It's some kind of expensive shop that specializes in designer health. They sound like a firm of Wilmslow solicitors, and charge as much. 'Conveyancers to the broken heart, the addict, and the drunk.' Somehow, I don't think that will catch on.

However, to vitamin B. When I was Mr. Wonderful, I thought that boozing would eventually wreck my liver. I didn't know quite *how* it would destroy this vital, and singular organ. The word *cirrhosis* swirled about somewhere in my ignorance, as did the colour jaundice-yellow. A messy death, I thought – and can hear myself adding, 'Yes, but it'll take a while, and in any case, I'm immortal.' Truth was that I had no idea what ethanol would do to my insides. I didn't know how my insides worked. And I had no idea that one of the things vast quantities of ethanol do is wipe out the body's supplies of vitamins – in particular, vitamin B.

You've been looking at vitamin B on the back of cereal packets for years. The B vitamins are a complex that include thiamine, riboflavin, niacin, pyridoxine, and vitamin B12 (which doesn't seem to have a name ending in –in(e)). As any pill bottle from Balding & Worried will tell you, this complex of vitamins is essential 'in order to maintain a healthy nervous system'. Vitamin B is actually rather more important than that: acute vitamin B deficiency is heavily implicated in the development of organic brain disease, notably Wernicke's syndrome (named after the researcher who discovered this area of the brain). Korsakoff's psychosis, often linked with Wernicke's syndrome, is also closely tied to alcoholism.

Some definitions (from Kinney and Leaton 1995, pp.138–139):

> Both are caused by nutritional deficiencies, especially thiamine, a B vitamin... Wernicke's syndrome involves injury to the midbrain, cerebellum, and areas near the third and fourth ventricles of the brain, whereas Korsakoff's psychosis results from damage to areas of the brain important to memory function...and is often associated with damage to peripheral nerve tissue as well. Prognostically, Wernicke's syndrome has a brighter picture. When recognized and treated early, it often responds very rapidly to thiamine therapy. Korsakoff's psychosis is much slower and unlikely to improve. Someone with Korsakoff's psychosis will probably require nursing home or custodial care.

Other symptoms of vitamin deficiency include malnutrition and anaemia. Happy days. This diagnosis, these definitions, come to you free, courtesy of Dr. Vodka.

The problem with taking alcohol is that the body's fooled into thinking ethanol-calories are real calories. They're not. It's also possible (as in my case) that the liver, pancreas, spleen are all intact and functioning, but that the central nervous system is more or less damaged. I still remember the face of the consultant, critically worried: 'First you won't be able to walk, then you won't be able to think.' He was hooking up peripheral neuropathy with the possibility of my developing what's sometimes, picturesquely, referred to as 'wet brain'.

In early recovery, therefore, alcoholics take, or are given, massive doses of B-complex vitamins. These may take the form of injections, or high-strength vitamin supplements, accompanied by a regularized diet. For months, I took a non-prescription pill that I shadily obtained from Boots, asking *sotto voce* for 'B-co'. We're not talking 'Recommended

Daily Allowances' here, either. You need something like nine times the RDA of vitamin B1, for example. The pharmacist at Boots looked at me as much as to say, 'Oh, another piss-artist.' She might as well have printed 'For alcoholics' on the label of the bottle she reluctantly passed over the counter. Several months on, and I still take vitamin B supplements, though these aren't as strong as the B-co Boots-pills, and come with a vitamin C included. And of course, there's no use taking these things *instead of* a proper diet: you take them *as part of* an adequate food intake, one that includes minerals, anti- oxidants, and what-have-you. So I try to construct what I eat fairly carefully. This has a consequence in that I can sometimes spend an idle hour working out menus for the coming week, when the alternative would be to head for another consultation with Dr. Vodka, and some more empty calories.

23.   10 May 2000

Another friend is deep into a relapse, and there's nothing I can do for him. Mutual coherence over the phone is impossible. He's either whimpering with self-pity, or cuts across anything I attempt to say. I told him I didn't feel I could have a rational conversation with his condition. 'So, you're abandoning me too, are you?' Only it didn't quite come out like that. It plunged through ten miles of cable as 'Shureabninnytoo, yuh?' He was talking echt-Drunk. Or possibly hoch-Drunk. Linguists should study echt-hoch-Drunk for their research projects. Come to think of it, someone probably has. As it was, and at my friend's request, the best I felt I could do was to call my friend's mother, who's in her unreassured eighties.

'Why is he like this?' she kept saying, silently accusing herself of his descent into the third relapse in as many months. 'His father was a clergy-man…' And then, heart-breakingly, a small, lost eighty-year-old voice: 'I'm too old for this, Chris.'

Alcohol doesn't respect professions or parentage. It doesn't respect age, income, competence, friendships. It doesn't respect care, reading, intelligence, or whatever lies on a birth certificate. I would add another thing: alcohol, as it turns into alcoholism, doesn't respect love. Alcohol has only one function: it wants to be consumed. That's something that no one ever tells alcoholics, or their worried, eighty-year-old mothers. A drinking alcoholic's deepest relationship is with the bottle. He, she, is giving, using, creating, listening, with the bottle. Only the bottle isn't listening, or giving. It doesn't want to have a conversation. It only wants to be consumed. Eventually, as an alcoholic (by which I mean a drinking alcoholic) lines up all his or her addictions around that deepest of relationships, all other relationships become just like the one the alcoholic has with the bottle. Those around the alcoholic start positioning themselves in order to manage an addiction they often don't recognize. Alcoholism starts to leak, towards sex, wives, husbands, children, mothers, sisters. But once these configurations begin, the drinking alcoholic no longer wants flawed, funny, responsible human relationships. He wants relationships just like the one he craves and listens for, just like the one with the bottle. Welcome to the lies, to drunken monologues, to insults, and manipulations. Welcome to the broken faces of bruised friendships. Welcome to *I don't know what to do*, to mothers blaming themselves, to husbands tearful in divorce courts. Welcome to 'I'm too old for this, Chris'.

'I'm too old for this, Chris, and nobody here' (she referred to the home in which she was staying), 'nobody here would understand. They're all clergymen's widows, and...' Her voice tailed off into hopelessness, behind which was the singing silence of absolute despair.

I don't know now, and I didn't know then, that I could give her the certainties, the healing, and the forgiveness that she wanted. I could only be practical, and tell what little truth I understand. Alcoholism's a disease or, if you prefer, a condition. It's progressive, it's fatal, and it affects not just the drinking alcoholic but the people closest to him, all of whom, without exception, are caught in a relationship that's difficult if not impossible to understand. *Why is he like this? Why is he abandoning all responsibility, all dignity, all laughter? What makes her do it?*

The answer, as always, is 'It must be me'. Failure, self-blame, begin their dance around the bottle, singing lines like 'If you loved me you wouldn't...' and 'Unless you stop I'll...' It's the 'If-or-Unless' two-step, and by now, everyone's dancing, while the tune is Anger, modulating into Resentment, and coming to a stop only at the crematorium curtains. *Dance, dance, dance till you drop.*

It is worth repeating that in my view, for whatever it's worth, alcoholism doesn't respect the love that often lies so desperately around it. It cannot be loved away, however great a mother's love, or a wife's, a friend's, a husband's.

No one's to blame. Does anyone blame themselves for causing cancer, or diabetes, or heart-failure in the people they love? No. These illnesses are the result of time and conspiracy, of misfortune, genetic predisposition, and, it may be, wrong choices. Is alcoholism any different? Does anyone really think that the drinking alcoholic is having a good time? That the bewildered, snivelling body that soils and disfigures itself and hugs itself into a vomiting unconsciousness is really having the best days of its life?

All the relationships around the alcoholic, the user, the anorexic, the bulimic – in short, around the Addict – arrange themselves around the simple fact of an illness. Decisions are taken, lives lived and partly lived, around the estrangement and duplicity that leak from the someone who isn't listening, and has never listened. That someone is the bottle, the tackle, the fix. Alcoholism, as a disease, can't be cured. The minor piece of good news is that recovery is possible, but it's only possible with understanding, and acceptance. In fact, even the understanding isn't effective unless it's underpinned by acceptance: there is no cure, and everyone is powerless, but everyone, including the alcoholic, still has choices.

The choices begin in powerlessness, and in chaos, in surrender. From that defeated and paradoxical affirmation, everything becomes possible, even miracles – and they're something clergymen's widows might recognize.

24.   19 May 2000

Several people, both alcoholics and non-addicts, have asked me what happens in a detox. I can only speak for detoxification from alcohol. There are other, and different, forms of serial withdrawal from multiple addictions – addictions to, say, alcohol and barbiturates.

Alcohol suppresses the normal working of the central nervous system (CNS). Alcohol's a depressant: the relaxation you feel after one or two hits is the beginning of a depressant state; the slowness of reaction after a skinful is another indication, as is slurred speech. Repeat the depressant dose over fifteen, or twenty years, and you're in trouble. (I was in fact treated for clinical depression for ten of the drinking years. In retrospect, this was a misdiagnosis. My patient, exasperated doctors and I should have been looking at alcoholism instead.) At the same time, over one, five, fifteen or twenty years, you've developed a tolerance for the drug that's screwing your neurophysiology. Further, increased amounts of the same drug are necessary for you to achieve the same effects – of illusory relaxation, of chilling out – that you once enjoyed. In the end, you're drinking just to feel 'normal'. If you then discontinue use of the drug that's allowing you to feel 'normal', you get withdrawal symptoms.

Anyone who's ever had a hangover has experienced a mini-withdrawal, with its nausea, shaking, sweating, its irritability and edginess. Similarly, anyone who's ever had the fabled hair of the dog has been drinking in order to treat their own withdrawal. Bloody Mary, drunk in this way, is a form of medication, since the sure way to handle the symptoms of withdrawal is to administer a touch more of the drug that caused it in the first place.

It follows that there are two basic but different types of managed withdrawal.

1.   There's withdrawal without clinical intervention. Effectively, this means carrying on drinking, but self-administering carefully monitored smaller doses until the body's free of alcohol. I've tried this dozens of times. It doesn't work for me – but then I'm a professional alcoholic, it wouldn't.

2.   Then there's the commonest form of detox., where clinical intervention, and the administration of further drugs, is required, plus nursing care at home or in hospital. I've undertaken this form of treatment three times (1997, 1998, 1999).

Once tolerance to alcohol has been established, stopping the ethanol means that the body and brain are released from the accustomed depressant effect. The mildest results are shaking, sweating, palpitations, irritability, and anxiety. The CNS, having escaped from its depressant, goes haywire. Disturbed sleep patterns are very common, both through with-drawal and into early recovery.

More serious effects of withdrawal are auditory and visual hallucina-tions. My hallucinations were visual. They involved humanoid birds with iron-green wings, and they were alarming, both to me and to the people around that desperate week. The hallucinations began with the onset of withdrawal, and lasted, in spells, for two to three days. Other common hallucinations involve insects, rodents, or hearing accusing voices. These images or voices are 'real' to the victim, so real that self-harm can some-times result, which is one reason for nursing supervision.

Delirium tremens – the DTs – are the sustained outcome of severe withdrawal, having the components of *delirium* (hallucinations, disorien-tation) and *tremens* (shaking, raised blood pressure, flushing, and fever). Like other symptoms of withdrawal, they're critical in the first 24–28 hours, but subside over the course of a week.

Detox., then, involves supervision of the victim during withdrawal from the effects of ethanol. It's now commonplace, in this form of detox., to administer a benzodiazepine such as Librium, which has a sedative effect, so that the physical symptoms of shaking and sweating are eased. ('Shaking?' you'll think. 'Huh. So what?' Now imagine your whole body, down to its every cell, vibrating like a nail continually struck by a hammer.) Dosage of Librium is calculated so that the biggest dose kicks in at the start of withdrawal. The dosage is then decreased over a week to ten days, by which time the neurophysiology of the victim has begun to return to a functional state. Here again, nursing supervision is required, since several alcoholics I know have tried to drink through detox., and combining any quantity of ethanol with large doses of Librium is poten-tially lethal. This is why the nurse or doctor who begins to administer the Librium will normally measure blood alcohol concentration (by taking a breath test) before continuing treatment.

There's a further reason for detox. Alcoholics are lost and estranged people. Buried in their illness, in their grandiosity, self-pity, delusions, their shame and grief, you might not have been able to find them or talk to them for years. Detox. means that at least some of the masks have been removed, and that you can begin to speak through the isolation and the shock into the lasting individual beneath. Who knows? They might even begin to hear you – if they're listening.

Detox. is unpleasant, humiliating, and urgent. But withdrawal in its severest forms can be physically dangerous, and the safe administration of benzodiazepines is surely preferable to choking on vomit, or dying in convulsive seizures. Even then, survival isn't guaranteed.

25.   24 May 2000

Alcoholism's a form of addiction. But what does 'addiction' actually mean? I don't mean, what is its dictionary definition ('The, or a, state of being addicted to a drug…; a compulsion and need to continue taking a drug as a result of taking it in the past…'), but rather, what are the signs of (a) the state of addiction, and (b) the immediate consequences of addiction?

I'm addicted to alcohol. I always will be, until someone turns off the hard drive that's me and all the lights go out. Characteristics of this addiction were the following: manipulation of self and others; excessive vanity; arrogance; failure to listen or connect; grandiosity; self-pity. And that's just for starters. I've called this composite 'Mr. Wonderful'. Mr. Wonderful was full of spectacular gifts and equally spectacular vulnerabilities. (This is another feature of Mr. Wonderful, the Addict. He or she may be among the highest of achievers, and yet the Addict inside is lonely enough to create imaginary friends.) Unfortunately, stopping the intake of alcohol won't 'cure' the Addict. There is no cure. There's only management, and management means handling not only the alcohol, but the whole complex, addictive patterning. By the time alcohol's recognized and accepted as the chief suspect of increasingly inappropriate, damaging, and bizarre behaviour, all the other potential forms of addiction, with their residues of manipulation, grandiosity, self-pity, and fantasy, will have lined up around the bottle. When the grip on the bottle's loosened, these addictive propensities are still very much in place. This is why there's a difference between 'mere' sobriety – though I still think a day's sobriety is a small miracle – and recovery. Sobriety is a 24-hour decision. Recovery's a lifetime's commitment to understanding and renewal, completed one day at a time, stranded by choice on the island of today.

I read of these distinctions first in books. I was taught about them. But of course, I'm an addict, and thought I was above the definitions and the principles. They didn't apply – to others maybe, but not to Mr. Wonderful, who was intent on Going It Alone, even if the going was only into the gutter.

Then I lived through, and still live through, the other symptoms of addiction. Take the alcohol away, and that tired circus-animal, the mind, still insists on playing its usual tricks, since these it has learnt more fundamentally than anything (or anyone) else: vanity, illusion, the blind of the next hit, the unthinkingness, the lack of connection, the isolation and withdrawal from the world, the fantasy. Call these crazy, or call them 'acting out', call them what you will, what they mean is that the old, sick, addicted self (or should that be a capitalized Self?) still lurches through the day with all its manipulations and deceits intact. And other addictions line up to take the place of the primary addiction that's now on hold.

What are these other addictions? Technically, physiologically, they may be less harmful than the primary addiction, since addiction to coffee, or Jelly Babies, digestive biscuits, gambling, cigarettes, or Internet porn won't result in withdrawal so severe it needs clinical intervention. But psychologically, and if they replace a primary addiction to, say, alcohol or heroin, they're damaging, since they provide the mind, dressed fundamentally in its addictions, with a place for acting out.

I realize this again because I've just spent an hour looking at pages of Internet porn. Porn is worth something like $15 billion a year to the US economy, so someone must be looking at (and paying for) this stuff. As it is, porn both intrigues and repels me. The allure isn't women's (or men's) naked bodies. Nor is it the fantasy of masturbation, contrary (I guess) to popular belief. Porn offers an illusion of becoming, and even of power. In front of these turgid images of second-hand desire, one can choose to be what one needs, at the moment, to be. While the illusion lasts, you're in the deepest of relationships with something that can't answer back. Responsible only to the structure of one's own illusions, you're in the most dangerous kind of control. For me, sitting looking at these images was almost exactly equivalent to living the customary self-justifying, barely controlled relationship whose conversation was the bottle. But crucially, neither the bottle nor the porn image wants to have a relationship. They only want to be, they only exist to be, consumed. Cue pity, and cue also self-disgust.

Wiser voices said that other addictive possibilities would step in to alcohol's breach. An hour after I closed the browser, I feel as if I've just come back from a consultation with Dr. Vodka – not shamed by my own imagination, but haunted by its self-reflexive powers of illusion. It's rather as if I'd sat in a bar for an hour with the metallic after-taste of orange juice, craving not just the fact of vodka, but the whole evening of power, of acting out.

And I know now that alcoholism's just one facet of an addictive condition, and that those wiser voices were right.

26.   25 May 2000

On the back of last night's piece I've been thinking again about the complex of structures that is addictive illness. Addictive illness isn't just the sick man or woman in the gutter, on the park bench, the needles in one pocket and the half-bottle of vodka in the other. Addictive illness is, it seems to me, a propensity to behave in ways that will cause physical and psychological damage not only to the Addict, but to those around him or her. The end result may not be the fact of the gutter, but the fact of the unmanageable life. Addiction is the illusion of control, playing against a fundamental powerlessness.

I'll tell you how crazy this stuff can get. In the last, lost, terminal throes of active alcoholism, I was sharing a house with a delightful man who managed his alcohol intake so that, barring one or two nights a month, he rationed himself to two or three glasses of wine each evening. Meanwhile, and even as I envied his apparent self- control, I was failing to manage the vodka: dry for weeks, or months, eventually the wheels fell off and for the following few days I'd suffer through black-outs, nausea, the whole clammy gamut of withdrawal. One night, though, I was struck by an inspired idea. 'Roger,' I said, concealing his true identity in order to protect the entirely innocent, 'Roger, I have an idea. What about the casino? It's a place to go out at night without drinking [the casino has no licence]. I mean, we could drink coffee, play blackjack…' A few days later, we went. I still remember, and remember with acute shame, the dreadful passport photograph someone took for the purpose of the membership card: a sick, leery, drunk, and bloated face failing to smile back at the lens. Then I was inside, in the terrible calm of the turned cards, the smell of perfume, and the click of the roulette wheel.

It's true that I broke even. It's also true that I remember very little about the time I played blackjack until 4am and drank endless coffee. The turn of the cards, the notes, the faces, the motionless hands of the dealers…they meant nothing. I was living in a blind, existing through a hit. Real life, with its responsibilities, its back gardens, its deadlines, and its bird-tables, was suspended, and while it was, I reeled between Pole and Tropic, in the never-never land where I could apparently choose to be anything I wanted, even Mr. Wonderful. And of course, though I was drinking coffee, I was still drunk from the vodka of the evening before. Fantastical, bizarre, I was acting out. What was living in me was a rebel mind whose self-constructed victim was a slave.

I can hear my own rationalizations. It was convenient, it was free entry, it was open until early in the morning, it was a place to go without drinking, it would mean you could go out for a night without feeling like a solitary toss-pot (a term which, incidentally, has its lexical roots in alcohol)… And so on. Rationalizations, excuses. I hear the same thing, have used almost the same words, about booze: *It's good for my heart, I use it only in moderation, it's a digestive, it's the hair of the dog, it's cheaper than ever, we bought it on holiday, one for the road, one for no reason at all…* Rationalizations, excuses, and that key word, denial.

An old, repeated joke: *To an alcoholic, denial's a river in Africa.* To those non-addicted, denial is exasperating to the point of fury. If you saw, for example, a diabetic who refused to treat himself, if you saw a cancer sufferer ashen, wasted, and refusing treatment, what would you think? What could you do? You'd urge, argue, even beg. And unconsciously, you'd begin to position yourself and your whole life around the fact of the addict's denial. You might also join in with the denial: *She hasn't got a real problem, she just drinks too much sometimes.* Meanwhile, in the deepest and most secret places of the interior landscape, the human scenery is configuring itself slowly around the addiction. Otherwise harmless pieces of acting out, of fantasy, of illusion, form like crystals in a copper sulphate solution, clinging to, and growing from, the one, undeniable crystal suspended within them. The harm spreads, the chemical process hurtles into the future, and there's no let up, no arrest, no remission, and every promise is broken. Welcome to dependency.

My own potentials for addiction – to gambling, to sex, to sugar, to coffee – slowly configured in this way around the central addiction to alcohol. Somewhere beyond denial, you know that this is happening, and you're powerless to arrest the chemical process. Abandoned to oneself, lost to the world of promises and mortgages, marriages and laughter and mess, you're unable to choose human freedom and dignity. Instead, you choose the deepest of relationships, with the bottle, the image, the turn of the card, the needle in a darkened car-park. It's what you know how to do, caught in the process of a search that's gone badly and blindly wrong. And swirling about in the disk of brandy, haloed in the car-park lights, there's a word that exists behind all the rationalization and denials in the world.

The one word is Fear.

27.   26 June 2000

I seem to have been living on airplanes the past two weeks. First, there was a deadline, and a trip to a conference in the States. The jet-lag only just shaken off, and there was a subsequent trip to Düsseldorf and Amsterdam. Some people tell me they envy this, er, lifestyle. This, er, life-style involves continual wary looks at the drinks trolley, and at airport bars.

I once wrote somewhere that airplanes are venues for erotic ambition. I also remember dear, delightful David Niven writing that he had only to step onto a plane for his incipient erection to become the size of Belgium. I couple these apparently stray remembrances with the increase in air-rage incidents, and the institution, in LA (where else?), of Mile High Flights, where you and your partner, if you have a partner, can hire a Lear, and for an allotted and expensive span, make sex in the clouds. And I link these imaginative presences with the report of a long-ago acquaintance who worked as a flight attendant. On transatlantic flights in particular, she said, otherwise Respectable People were known to behave in ways so abandoned that they'd be lost to polite reportage. One immaculately suited businessman, for instance, routinely used to stroll down the walkways of his intercontinental 767 and casually urinate on his fellow passengers. 'Aisle seat, sir?' 'Um, no thanks…'

When you travel, you don't necessarily travel as yourself. The bundle of weary accidents that's you travels as the person it needs, at that moment, to be. Uniformed in invisible luggage, this guessed-at persona has time, a captive audience, a local habitation, and a name, Legion. In sum, airports, airplanes, are places where addiction can act itself out.

I used to travel as Mr. Wonderful. For some reason, the drinking would begin days before I was actually scheduled to fly, with the result that when I did in fact hit the check-in desk I'd be nursing a hangover. In Mr. Wonderful's drinking lexicon, hangover meant Bloody Mary. Three of these in an airport lounge, together with a packet of Camels, and I'd feel no pain at all. Just to make sure the painlessness stayed painless, I'd load an extra couple on board before unsteadily hitting the gangplank. Their effects would last until the merciful appearance of the drinks trolley at 30,000 feet, when I'd seamlessly, and with no style at all, switch to cheap champagne.

The results were embarrassingly predictable. I'll spare you the drunken litany of the faces, the voices, and the places that I aimed at, and sometimes missed. I'll spare you the mystification and the busy grief. They are parts of a past I have to own, and which I can't change.

What interests me is that I'd usually reserve the really heavy stuff for coming home. On the outward run, I could work through a hangover, pretend to be cogent, academic, and world-class on a mere bottle, or a few beers. On the way home, though – home from a conference, from a research visit, a fact-finding tour, a poetry reading, from a love affair – I'd dehydrate myself on vodka so badly that it would be a week, and more alcohol, before I'd grow back into my own name.

The effects of ethanol are exacerbated by height, speed, pressure. You get drunk more rapidly. You get sicker, quicker. For a drinking alcoholic, the only remedy for sickness is more alcohol, and the second, and subsequent, passes of the drinks trolley. And since many alcoholics are deprived of their usual nicotine fix on aircraft, they drink more in order to allay the discomfort of nicotine withdrawal. They drink more to allay the discomfort that is their lying, travelling self. They drink more to allay the discomfort. They just drink more.

It's a relief, to check in to airports sober. It gives me a better shot at talking my way into an upgrade. It's a relief, to know where it is I'm going, and not to lose anything, including myself, in the process. It's a relief to look at the clouds and see them as clouds. It's a relief to be able to handle accidents, minor turbulence, and the hurtling schedule – and to have time to do so. It's a relief not to feel sick, and not to feel estranged. Yes, true, as the drinks trolley comes down the aisle I also find the phrase 'Just coffee – and water, please' wanting to form itself into 'Large vodka and tonic', but to date it hasn't managed to get that far.

Above all, it was good to fly back from the States, after a long and exhausting struggle with the airline at Philadelphia airport, and to feel fresh enough to walk straight into the department and pick up some work and deadlines as if I'd just come in from down the road, and Chateau Recovery. There was some kind of freedom in this, and some sense of responsibility. The payoff was that the same night, having put in a normal working day, I slept the kind of peaceful and deep sleep reserved for those I'd often envied as virtuous. I was just Chris – travelling, worried, working, and sober – and I preferred his company to all the Mr. Wonderfuls in the world.

28.   26 June 2000

I've never to date used these pieces as 'Dear Diary' entries. *The Intimate Confessions of Mr. Wonderful*, aka Chris McCully, would be another piece of work entirely. But in the past two weeks I've hit two problems which have been difficult to discuss, and about which it's impossible to complain. The problems essentially involve the attitude of the so-called Caring Professions to alcoholism, recovery, and treatment.

I have to be watched at work. The university does the watching in a discreet, even a caring, way, and I've been more than lucky to have this care and concern. It's been repeatedly pointed out to me that anyone else would have been sacked, but somehow this doesn't reassure me. The watching itself is a form of humiliation, but it's also a consequence. Part of this consequence is a meeting every month or two with the head of Occupational Health.

She's an admirably professional and formally correct woman whom in other circumstances I'm sure I would like and respect. She has an almost impossibly difficult job, whose remit extends to travel inoculations, drunken senior lecturers, and the adventures of Medical School porters. Translated into the university context from health care somewhere in Cheshire, she has apparently some experience of alcohol-related problems, and has put it on record that alcoholism is an illness. Now there's a surprise. In an almost unprecedented move, she's also putting together a university policy on alcoholism. Entering her office is entering a world of cool, almost polished, mannered enlightenment. I wish I could have met her without the hyper-sensitivity and defensiveness that so much characterize my recovering life, and which so much fault me.

It was more than unusually unnerving when she began to refer to alcoholics in the third person plural, the generic *They*, the objectified *Them*. 'They're so difficult to treat. It's so difficult to know what to do with Them.' To all intents and purposes, we could have been two complicit non-alcoholics having a strategic professional chat. I looked over my shoulder to see if anyone else was in the room. There wasn't. By 'they', she meant me. By 'them', she meant me, too. I pointed out, as gently as I could, that I was in all truth One of Them, which after all was why I was there. To give her credit, she apologized, generously and profusely, for what she called her 'use of English', but it wasn't the grammar that was remarkable. It was the underlying assumptions. I doubted she'd use the same meta-language in order to talk through treatment for a diabetic, a cancer sufferer. It's also true that she was right, and I am grateful to her: alcoholics *are* difficult to treat, relapse *is* common, and less than 10 per cent of alcoholics make a sustained recovery.

I was still thinking through Attitudes to Alcoholism when by a technical accident I was obliged to consult the chief psychiatrist of the hospital that treated me back in December. During our two previous consultations, several months before, he'd taken notes, asked apparently interested questions, and had written a crucial letter of support as I put in the application to have my driving licence reinstated. I was also – I still am – very grateful to the man, who has an international reputation for his work on alcoholism. But perhaps on this occasion I expected too much. I didn't expect the fact that he hadn't remembered my name, that he hadn't consulted any previous notes, that the consultation lasted ten minutes, and that he wasn't prepared to listen to anything whatsoever that I had to say. I didn't want, and felt I shouldn't have needed, to rehearse the details of my former marriage or present employment. Nor did I want to be the object of the comment that I had 'good insight'. Nor did I want to list – I didn't have time to list – the reading I'd been doing on alcoholism and addiction. Form answers seemed to be all that the Great Man required, the only spur he needed to resume his effortless and well-used monologue on the facts of alcoholism. I felt invisible, unnamed, un-name-able. Or was it just defensiveness and hyper-sensitivity, yet again?

It's not that I need to feel important, or different, or full of 'insight'. I think the problem is this: I'm an individual, I'm an alcoholic, and alcoholics have individual rights and freedoms, particularly those rights and freedoms they earn through recovery. We aren't a generic *They*, we're not invisible, and we have opportunities for human growth, for truth, and for laughter and dignity. It's reassuring if the people who are overseeing our cases know our names, and have some little idea of the local clarities and textures that make us up as we live recovery. In the case of the Great Man, I'm afraid I wasn't about to roll over and play the awed dead because of the fact that he has actually – gasp! – Written A Book about alcoholism and employment. I mean, I've written a few books myself, and still hope I can remember my students' names, and write accurate references and reports for them. My standards might be those of an alcoholic, but that doesn't mean they're wrong, disreputable, slipshod, or double.

I guess what I'm saying here is that everyone in recovery will have difficulty handling other people's ostensible standards, and other people's apparent attitudes. My own difficulties with these things are sharpened by personal faults I must work even harder to manage: hyper-sensitivity; defensiveness. As it was, I think what galled me most was being faced with a large bill for a 15-minute consultation with a European Eminence who should, really, have known better.

29.   27 June 2000

The *Big Book* of Alcoholics Anonymous (AA) is shot through with references to the medical profession, possibly because one of the founders of
AA was himself a doctor. It's unfortunate that no one in the UK can these
days rely in any way on receiving understanding, practical help, or treatment from a GP if they suffer from alcoholism. We have more chance of
treatment if we're addicted to heroin, cocaine, or heroin and cocaine
derivatives. Largely because alcoholics are held to be unreliable and
untreatable, there has been a massive diversion of resources from alcoholism and into the treatment of 'Drugs'. 'Drugs' are newsworthy, 'Drugs'
are high-profile, 'Drugs' are sound-bites for politicians. Meanwhile,
during the last twenty years, alcohol treatment centres have closed, detox.
programmes are underfunded (and subject to long waiting-lists), and the
public perception of alcoholism is the sick, yellow, bloated face of George
Best. Good old George. But George's case, and mine, points up the fact
that it's difficult to get effective treatment for alcoholism unless you pay
for it. Hopelessness meets the rehab. clinic over the thud of the
cheque-book.

   I can only write from experience. When these alcoholic problems first
became critical, when I was drying out, shaking and hallucinating in
Salford, I'd just moved house, and hadn't registered with a new GP. I was
incapable of phoning to register. I was incapable of talking. Or walking.
There was no money in the bank, so checking in to a treatment centre or
private hospital was beyond my means. The only recourse was to seek
treatment through the NHS, which of course meant prior registration
with a GP.

   Have you tried to register with a GP in the UK recently? In the event,
my sister, and my ex-wife, had to call on my behalf. In the mists of shame,
I seem to remember that they called half a dozen surgeries. Several lists
were already full. The lists that weren't full rapidly became so when the
word 'alcohol' was whispered into the phone. No GP wanted to take on
an alcoholic, and to use public, and accountable, funds for a programme
of treatment. We'd have had more success if I'd been a heroin user. Eventually, I was asked to go along to an elderly Irishman, whose surgery was a
mess of concrete, glass, and splinters somewhere on a bomb-site. Under
normal circumstances, 'going along' would have been fine, but without a

car, and in the throes of alcoholic hallucinations, diarrhoea, and disorientation, 'going along' was virtually impossible. Without my sister's and my ex-wife's help I wouldn't have been able to go along anywhere. But we went along, together.

The elderly Irishman opened up with a reminiscence of Dublin, continued by remarking casually that most writers were alcoholics anyway (he himself, to be sure, had had a drink with Brendan Behan, once) and ended by asking had I taken the pledge? 'What fucking pledge?' I thought, incapable of thought. Was my father an alcoholic? I didn't know. My father was long-ago dead. Was anyone else in the family etc. etc.? This took time. It took diarrhoea time and hallucinating time. Eventually, the doctor, who'd drunk with Brendan Behan (once), wrote 'This man is a CHRONIC ALCOHOLIC' on his notes (*my* notes, *my* record), and gave me some pills – Heminevrin? Librium? – with a casual instruction to start taking them at once. He also made an appointment for a consultation, an 'assessment', at an NHS hospital four days later, with a view to referral for treatment, which was to take place anything up to three months later.

I was grateful, but I'm glad I didn't start on the tablets at once. Since I was still drinking, merely in order to stop the hallucinations, the pills could have killed – as the detox. team subsequently confirmed. And yet it was clear to everyone, even to me, that something immediate was required. Something immediate is required in the case of every alcoholic who actively seeks treatment. But public funds don't stretch, within the NHS, to something immediate, and alcoholics may get turned away at the surgery door. It seems to me that instead of immediate intervention, many alcoholics seeking treatment in the public sector may well receive something ignorant, slow, unwilling, and possibly fatal. And even when (or if) you finally reach the tawdry nirvana of a detox. programme, 'controlled drinking' is still offered as an option. 'Controlled drinking', for an alcoholic, is controlled death. It simply keeps you mute, lost, and vaguely manageable as you die, a statistic unknown to the politicians who have ordained your taxes and NI contributions for this purpose.

30.   6 July 2000

Out of the abundance of well-meaning advice given to alcoholics in recovery, one truth seems inalienable, and self-evident. In the first year of recovery, you shouldn't make major changes. You shouldn't change your job, your house, your car. You shouldn't apply to become part of an astronaut training programme, or take a PhD in Chaos Theory. You should simply live each day as it comes, as gently and easily as possible, planning for the future but not expecting any particular outcome. Marooned on the benevolent island of today, you should aim to live that as well as you can, without excessive aspiration, without hurt or remorse. Above all, continues the advice, you shouldn't develop a relationship with a new partner. The sex, the laughter, the intimacy will come later, but they're not for these endless moments of Now, as Now is lived in early recovery.

I'm afraid I got everything wrong. In the first seven months of recovery, I set up two new international projects, and a couple of international conferences; I developed contracts for a series of new books; I have travelled very extensively, in different continents; I'm writing a new series of freelance articles (including these occasional pieces); I'm planning to share my time between England and Amsterdam; and above all, I have developed a new relationship, though perhaps it's more true to say it's developed me.

I'm still an alcoholic, which means that I'm still underpinned by all the unrealistic fantasies and ambitions that support, or fail to support, alcoholic thinking. It's true that everything I do on the island of today is checked out against the fact of alcoholism – do I shop here, where I used to buy vodka, or there, which is a dry environment? Do I walk to work past the pub where I used to drink, or do I go the long way round? Do I choose to carry a local resentment, or do I just let it go? But in larger and less quotidian senses I'm still ambitious, idealistic, fantastic, and often bizarre with unrealities.

This bizarrerie shows itself in that I try to do things too quickly. Like every alcoholic, I can't wait. Whatever I want – a woman, a job, a book, a bus ticket – I want it now, and preferably, yesterday. I get impatient with myself, and with other people. Impatience with other people in turn leads to resentment, and alcoholics can't afford resentment, since they'll use it to drink. I also do everything to excess. It doesn't matter whether it's time spent writing and working, or having a bath, playing the piano, or eating a quarter (make that a half pound) of Jelly Babies. Everything's excessive: I play an easy arrangement of 'As Time Goes By' on the piano, and fantasize that I'm playing the Carnegie Hall. I write 2000 words of a new fishing article and dream I'm James Joyce. Instead of being content with what modest achievements I can muster – and they're real enough – I want more, and I want more, now. What am I trying to prove?

I'm trying to prove, to the world and its drunken grandmother, that I'm not an alcoholic. This shows itself in devious and subtle ways, and I can hear myself thinking, 'Well, I may be an alcoholic, but alcoholics can still be world-class, responsible, useful, and productive human beings.' This is true, they can, but the formulation is ghosted by the haunting thought that I may not be an alcoholic – I mean, not *really* an alcoholic. Perhaps I'm just a man who once had *a hard time*. Enter self-pity, snivelling, and carrying a tumbler spilling full of vodka and tonic.

Or perhaps I'm trying to prove to myself that underneath the implausible, smiling public face of the forty-two-year-old man there's a boy who was of use to other people because he was Mr. Responsible. This younger self – he worked for the team, the House, the School. He played up, he played the game. He won his colours, and some (though not all) of the glittering prizes. What was he trying to prove? Ultimately, he was trying to prove he could be loved, and that he would be loved the more, the more responsibility he took on.

Responsibility. Unrealistic expectations. Ambition. Travel. Work. The tiered rows of faces in the lecture hall. They hurtle together into a glass called grief. And I stare into the glass called grief, and what looks back is any woman's face, a set of victims – victims of ambition and need – swirling around with the ice cubes. It could have been, it sometimes is, the tear-streaked face of my ex-wife. It could be the self-professed 'intimacy junkie'. *I can love any, so she be not true*, as someone once said. How viciously unfair I was. Then I think of the relationship, the love, that I'm currently living through, with all its futures and ambitions, its shuttling between two European cities, and I wonder if that's any different, or whether I'm just acting out again the old fantasies of chase, and desire, and need, despite the self-analysis and care I try to bring to it. 'Everything's changed', true, but change has dangers as well as delights for alcoholics, and sometimes, the cultivation of patience, or detachment, seems impossible, and you're left merely with dry-mouthed heartache, and once again with the perplexity of an empty wallet.

31.   7 July 2000

I'm having to work hard on this. It's not been a good or easy week, and anger and resentment are to blame. Not for nothing does AA stand, among other things, for 'Altered Attitudes'. I don't think my attitudes have altered fast enough. Perhaps they haven't altered at all. If not, I'm heading for relapse.

There have been too many changes recently – in working pattern, in location, in bank accounts. One week of unsettled peace has planned the following week's foreign trip. The foreign trip has been followed by a week of fractured recovery, during which the following week's foreign trip has been planned. In truth, I've not been in the country much, and miss the reality and the idea of home. Faces; people; parties; dinners; papers. Words, words, words. It doesn't actually matter that each event, almost each face, has been a delight: it has involved change, and since all change, even good change, involves loss, the continual small adjustments have been wearing. I begin to resent the schedule. On top of this, having been landed with some menial and tedious jobs at work, I begin to resent the once-more-expressed opinion that I have not, apparently, done 'any serious work in the department for the past few years'. Since my sloth over those last few years has run to bringing one-sixth of the entire undergraduate syllabus online, since it's involved the creation of an entirely new degree, since it's involved a couple of books and a brace of international conferences, together with a programme of readings and lectures and a great deal of international recruitment, I think that opinion is wrong. The words – and they were, I'm sure, meant kindly, very kindly – felt like a large slap in the face. Justifiable resentment, then? Whether justifiable or not, any kind of resentment, any species of anger, is fatal to an alcoholic. We can't afford them.

And on top of this, I'm beginning to mistrust myself in terms of the relationship I'm trying to develop. Am I simply pouring myself heart and soul into another broken dream, and losing myself in the process? Will the flying, the travel, the unsettlings hurt research time? Will they eventually hurt both self-esteem and recovery? I try to reconstruct myself into the future, when my real focus should be on today, and feel lost and bewildered.

Anger, resentment, mistrust. They add up to a cocktail of problems. And what does any alcoholic do with a cocktail?

There are things I'm not doing. The fault in this is mine. Foreign travel means it's difficult to stay connected with the recovery programme, and with AA or other meetings. It's not impossible, and many resources are available to the alcoholic over the Internet, when all else fails (or even when all else doesn't). At the same time, though I've kept up with readings on alcoholism, I could have done more. Instead of doing more, I've spent too much time in finger-pointing, in useless worry, and in silent recrimination aimed at self and others. And instead of productive peace, I've hurled myself into work, and then more work. As I've asked here before, what am I trying to prove? Behind all of this, there's been a smear of resentment, of anger spread thinly. Work, exhaustion, worry – and time fractured by a difficult schedule. Part of me, and it's still a large part, thinks, 'Sod it. I know what'll fix this.' And Mr. Wonderful wants immediately to march to the nearest bottle with bubbles in it. The beads on the outside of the glass, the smell of crisp apples… Welcome back, Chris, what'll you have? Good to see you looking so well… I'll have a glassful of grief, please.

Alcoholics and addicts have a special kind of disastrous magic thinking. Non-addicts want some peace, security, self-esteem, and laughter, and they quietly and patiently work towards these small, real, and important goals. Addicts want exactly the same things, and want them passionately (particularly in recovery, when there seems to be everything to prove). But the passionate wanting doesn't translate into quiet patience. It translates into three nights in the gutter, trouble with the law, broken promises. Our actions blow away the things we most need – stability, genuine friendship, a sustainable life. We're programmed for chaos. I'm programmed for chaos, and angrily head towards it, fuelled by resentment, wagging a couple of fingers to the world, its wife, the cook, the thief and his lover as I go.

I have to remind myself that today, I can choose. I can let the anger go, since it's non-productive anyway, and really, who gives a toss whether I'm angry about work? At the same time, I can analyse the resentments, since they're ultimately my fault: I *allow them* to happen. I can quietly become aware of my own chaos, and its magic thinking, supported as that is by acute touchiness. That is, I am discovering again that my biggest problem isn't other people. It's me. And I can choose to live a quiet and settled routine, even among the continual demands of travel and writing. I can choose to look after myself, and I can choose to connect again with a programme of recovery that will take me, if I let it, as far away from chaos as a Long Island Iced Tea is from a bowl of raspberries.

32.   7 July 2000

Drinkers have friends, and they usually have family. Alcoholics have few real friends, and their family relationships are always and everywhere more or less damaged. The problem, for both drinkers and alcoholics, is that long-standing relationships fall into patterns, and they're often patterns of dependency. The friends and the drinking partners come to rely on Mr. Wonderful buying the rounds on a Friday afternoon. The family is used to the mood swings, the unpredictability, the unrealistic aspirations, the magic thinking. In these patterns, everyone has a huge investment in lack of change. The tacit rubric is 'We're going to keep things like this'. The choice is the devil you know.

In many, if not in all, families and friendships shot through with alcoholism, it's possible that in the early stages, and at gut-level, no one wants anything to change. The long-suffering husband gets used to the wife relapsing every five weeks, gets used to finding bottles at the back of the closet. Suffering this, and handling it, paradoxically makes him think he's needed: the pattern boosts his self-esteem.

The wife who endures Saturday nights full of vomiting and beer-fuelled farting from a drunken pig of a husband thinks, 'It must be my fault, and in any case he's not so bad when he's sober... And I have to put up with this because it's all my fault, and there aren't really any alternatives.' Such fatal endurance again translates into self-esteem. If I can put up with this, I'll feel better than perhaps I deserve.

The guys at the bar on a Friday afternoon know that Mr. Wonderful will buy the next round, talk about horse racing or women, tell the same jokes, and give the assembled non-company the illusion that everything in this dubious world is in fact delightful and amusing. Good old George. Vicarious pleasures become, by slow bleaching, vicarious self-esteem.

None of this stuff is real. We're dealing with illusions here, a painted gallery of faces and glasses, a museum of minds. The psychological investment in lack of change, in patterns of dependency, eventually becomes the false and meaningless smile, the indulgence that masks a brittle anger, the unwillingness to tackle the problem. Within families, where emotional bonds and sensitivities are presumably greatest, the patterns are perpetuated because change brings loss, and loss brings hurt, and no one wants to hurt the people whom they love. Shuffling about in this imaginary museum, we function as the victims of ourselves and each other. The drinking goes on.

It's a paradox that the people closest to the alcoholic, whose patience, from the alcoholic's perspective, translates into condescension and mis-understanding, often enable the alcoholic to keep drinking. Caught in a web of illusions, the drinker takes a drink to fuel his self-importance. The alcoholic carries on drinking, and will fight to the death to keep things the way she knows. Often enough, the promises to reform, the treat-ments, the attempted changes simply don't work, or don't work for long. Everybody's programmed for chaos, and prefers the known heartbreak.

In my case, as in many, it took a crisis, or more accurately, a set of crises. I was surrounded by acquaintances who, wittingly or unwittingly, were enablers, and I used them to carry on the deepest relationship of my life, that with Dr. Vodka. Nothing, but nothing, was allowed to touch, to come near, or to threaten that relationship. If those around me configured so that McCully and vodka could continue, well and good. If those around me didn't configure in a way that would sustain my drinking, I tried to manipulate them until they did. If I couldn't manipulate them, I wrote them off, and used the anger to generate itself into the next drink. 'The next drink' was not, therefore, anyone's fault but mine. Some people were very used to the anger, the manipulation, the slow configurations around the stream of beers and bottles. Some people even liked it, because when McCully was 'on form' – pissed as a toad, and barely able to stand up – he was Mr. Wonderful, and a perilous guarantee of a squalid adventure. These emotional investments, coupled with the fact that drinking estranged me from myself, meant that the alcoholic drinking continued unchanged for years. And how I seized on any hint that I wasn't an alcoholic. Perhaps I was a workaholic (this seemed good); perhaps I was a sex addict (not so good, but vaguely interesting); perhaps I was a gambler, a stricken poet, a Bohemian (whatever that is). I was anything but an alcoholic, and I knew this because my drinking buddies said so. Meanwhile, back at home, the dinner burnt in the oven, and my ex-wife was in tears of worry and anger.

The only way out of this is truth, and truth is usually driven by crisis. The crises are hospitals, the divorce courts, the solicitor's office, the prison cell, the shamed sacking, the headline in the local newspaper. Disastrous, perhaps, in themselves, these events are simply signals that truth has to be told, and told at gut level, until freedom emerges from chaos, until the facts of change bring about a better configuration of faces and voices, and until liberty is earnt, and re-learnt. Dependency in the imaginary museum, the static patterns of alcohol and grief, will kill, sooner or later. It's as serious, and it's as good, as that.

'The Slush-Fund'

O ne of the things that was difficult was money. The financial damage of the drinking years had gone very deep. It wasn't just paying for the booze. It was paying for all the stuff that happened as a result of the booze. There were moving costs, lawyers; holidays that I told myself I deserved, but couldn't afford; there was a new second-hand car which I couldn't use, and hadn't needed anyway; there was company, or the illusion of company; there were the credit-cards. On top of it all there was the matter of travelling between the UK and Düsseldorf, and later, the UK and Amsterdam. I scrounged for bargain airline seats.

I planned, scrimped, saved what I could. To those who took an interest, I explained what I was trying to do, and why. That wasn't always easy. Then again, I say here that those to whom I did explain what I was trying to do were always – always, as in invariably – helpful and supportive. This goes for the representatives of my bank, too. In that context, I tried to forget the account manager who had told me, in the final throes of my drinking career, that he was the only person that stood 'between [me] and the gutter'. But in recovery, and with some visible, though precarious, financial stability beginning to obtain, it was different.

Through it all, I also minded some good advice I was given at the outset of this phase of recovery. The advice came from a counsellor, and a fellow-addict.

'I kept a kind of slush-fund,' he said, 'a sort of secret account. Every month, I'd tuck a bit away. It didn't matter how much it was. Could be the odd £50, or even just a fiver. Come to that, it could even be a pound or two. Or less. The important thing *was that at the end of each month I'd made some sort of contribution to my own slush-fund.*

'The other important thing was that this slush-fund was just for me. Nobody else knew about it, nobody else could use it, and I told no one I was keeping it. It was just for me. In the beginning, I didn't spend it, either. Just kept adding to it.

'Of course your instincts are to spend any loose change on booze. But I kept going with this...stash. And I determined that I would never spend it on booze. It was for presents, and the presents were pretty much for me. If I wanted a new coat, say, or a holiday – something useful, a present in recovery – I could always use this secret fund. It was always there.'

I made my own slush-fund. It was great advice. For the first time in years – decades – I had at least one bank account that was always in credit. (That reassured the people who audited my accounts, too.) And any spare cash I had went into this secret reserve. The amounts were, to begin with, laughable – but I wasn't laughing. Some months it was a pound or two. On another occasion I deposited 50p. But then, as I began to write and work properly again, there were occasional fees, from essays or poems. There were sometimes cash gifts at Christmas, too. I was lucky to have these.

Over a year, two years, this secret fund came to resemble a respectable amount of sterling. At need, and when all other possibilities were null, I used the Chris Fund to buy airline tickets, trying to keep straight a sense of priorities. ('Recovery first. Then home and family. Then work.') But increasingly, I used the fund to buy fishing tackle. New plugs for the pike fishing I was becoming ever more interested in; a good set of waterproofs; a new rod or reel. And I bought the very best stuff I could afford. The result was that I began to assemble a functional, durable, and useful set of angling kit, stuff I could use in the hobby I was beginning seriously to resume. The resumption, the hobby, the time, and the absorption – these were all benefits of recovery.

As we moved, later, to Amsterdam I kept the slush-fund going. A year on, and I thought it would be useful and interesting if I bought my own boat and outboard. Even a basic aluminium boat and a second-hand outboard don't come particularly cheap, but I looked around, compared prices, haunted boatyards, and eventually bought the best I could afford. I bought the boat and outboard largely out of the slush-fund, too. And a fish-finder, anchors, a comfortable boat-seat, all the accessories.

'A boat?' You are thinking 'the bloody man bought a floating gin-palace'. I did not. I bought a 13-foot boat for pike fishing. Because it's painted olive-green, my more unkind friends call my boat 'the wheelie bin'. I call my boat 'Boot', because it is precisely that, in Dutch, and after all, it is a Dutch boat and lives on Dutch pike waters. It has been a joy. And in truth, more than a joy. It has helped me to understand the construction of my adopted country, its polders, fens, weedbeds – and all the life in and around the water. That understanding came only indirectly through the slush-fund. More accurately, it was another, and direct, gift of recovery.

17 July 2000
(with 2003 Retrospective)

33.   17 July 2000 (and November 2003)

Addicts are hit on by other addicts. To an addict, another addict is a focus of fantasy, of power, and of the kind of hopeless (non-)relationship that the addict most deeply recognizes. Add to that the inalienable truth that misery loves company, and you've lined up sex, abuse, despair along with the row of vodka bottles or the discarded gear.

It's not so much the idea of drinking partners – the gang of terrible youths all of whose faces are yours. It's not so much the idea of having a few beers and then having the Dutch courage to go to a strip-joint (together). It's some deep down compulsion and recognition we're looking at. Perhaps this includes the gang and the strip-joint, but it's more than that. To a drinking or using addict, another addict is homecoming, and the illusion of arrival.

I say this because there have been two things on my mind this past few days. One is the newspaper report which states that the present government is asking for red meat, chips, and beans to be served at school lunches at least three times a week, in order to combat the alarming rise in eating-related 'disorders' among girls and young women. The other is the fact that I was for a brief while, and at the height of the drinking, involved in a relationship that was also addictive. No other word will do. And the fault in this is mine. I am not proud of the fault. Into it are coded some of my deepest realities, and deepest shames.

I sometimes look out at the world and think it's the world that's addicted. The visible world seems to slide by on compulsion, servility, power, the evanescent changes of the fantastic body, the 101 Ways To A Better Orgasm, the fatal necessity of perfection. I may be wrong, but surely it's this horrifying image of perfection that stalks the dreams of the anorexic, the bulimic. 'I am powerless, but I can show my power, and be perfect.' The bathroom scales, the locked door, the pathetically minimal vomit, the bedroom mirror: anxiety, power, and addiction checks in with perfection and puts two fingers down her throat. Conceptually, it seems to my imperfect understanding that there's no distinction between this condition and that exemplified by the leery blue raincoat with a half-bottle of ethanol in its pocket. They're junkies, working out their illusions while big money pays governments to sustain a culture of hopelessness, ignorance, and betrayal. And this is Cool Britannia, whose teenage sons are drunk alone in Leicester Square, and whose girls look back at emaciated Little Miss Wonderfuls through haunted and malnourished eyes.

OF THE RELATIONSHIP that developed – no, not in the heights but in the depths of my alcoholic behaviour and bewilderment – I will not write. I can say, though, that the hard words, the insults, and the shames endured for a long time into this phase of recovery. I found it difficult to forget some of what was said; what I knew and could remember of what was done; and what I could remember of what I did. Memory hurt; some kinds of reading hurt, because they brought memory with them; travelling hurt, because memory travelled with it; even the smell of sunlight on tarmac hurt.

And of course, the days that were Then were an appalling landscape of perpetual drama, endless crisis in which there was also the continual pull of Sorry; and then another pull, from all the nauseating arguments of self-justification; and then another pull, from the beauty and terror of memory; and another pull, from justified or entirely unjustified anger...

Walking out of this landscape, and putting by the known claustrophobia, the self-obsessions of the mutually destructive, were among the hardest things I did, and, I hope, will ever have to do. Hard, too, was the thought that no apology, however gentle, would fix the past. I couldn't even begin to set things right without causing further pain.

I lost myself. But I can write here, and with justice, that the most difficult realizations came in the present phase of recovery, when I recognized that this relationship felt very much like, and had much in common with, the deepest of all the relationships I have ever made — the relationship with alcohol. Fantasy; pride; self-pity; anger and bewilderment — these were the dubious hallmarks of that authentic thing, addiction. And addiction, I was learning, didn't stop with the needle or the vodka. It extended into the past, and into the future, into friends, family, lovers. And though it extended into lovers, family, and friends, it couldn't and can't be loved away.

It felt like power, but recovery showed that it was chaos.

It felt like intimacy, but recovery showed it was insanity.

IT FEELS LIKE being consumed, and the faults in all of this are mine.

I look out of this suburban window and feel sorry for today's sunny July day, and for the addictive and shaming misery that lives in a million and more homes, now, in Cool Britannia. But today is to be lived, and lived well, and there can be an end to addiction, starting merely on this unlikely and forgiving page whose point is the next 24 hours.

July 2000 to April 2001

34.   23 July 2000

A friend sends me a clipping from *The Observer*, a report detailing the
tragedy of Audrey Kishline, the 'outspoken founder of Moderation Management' (MM) in the US, whose book *Moderate Drinking: The New Option
for Problem Drinkers* functioned as MM's central text. Kishline has recently
been convicted of driving while three times over the legal limit. In the
midst of her moderation, Kishline drove into 38-year-old Danny Davis,
and his 12-year-old daughter, LaSchell. Both were killed. Kishline has
been jailed for 'vehicular homicide'.

MM

The report claims that in the US, vivid and heated debate is ongoing
as to whether total abstinence, or 'moderation', or some unlikely combination of both, is the key to the treatment of alcoholism. The same debate
– the Alcoholics Anonymous (AA) route of total abstinence and 12-Step
recovery, versus 'controlled drinking' – is apparently held, sometimes,
regarding treatment strategies in the UK.

I've never believed in moderation, and I've never, until early this year,
tried to live it. Well, I wouldn't. I'm an addict, and the addiction doesn't
stop at alcohol. I can be addicted around people, addicted to sex, the
Internet, nicotine, work, sweeties. It's slightly appalling to realize that
taking the drink out of my hand is only one small step in a long and diffi-

cult process of recovery – a process which is also one of re-discovery, of loss, of occasional joy, and of breaking not just the habits of my own lifetime, but my attitudes to the habits of others' lifetimes as they've impinged on mine.

In this context, it would be impossible for me to have even one drink. I have tried controlled drinking, and for me – I repeat this because I need to remember it – it didn't and couldn't work. The addictive patterns run too deep, and though I may forget the fever and the fret of vodka, my body will never forget. At this point, I guess it might be possible for me to have one drink, perhaps two, and perhaps I'd leave it at that...for a day, a week, maybe a month. But this illusion of a 'successful drink' would be fatal. In another week, another month, I'd be consulting with Dr. Vodka as if there was no tomorrow – which, in a way, there wouldn't be. In any case, even if I were tempted to drink, even if I actually swallowed the stuff again, would I be happy with it? The bloody awful truth is that I can never drink well, successfully, or comfortably again. I would be too uncertain about what would happen. And therefore I prefer today's freedom of total abstinence, aligned with recovery. It's easier.

I have known addicts who seem to be able to handle two or three glasses of stuff each day. They form an addictive pattern around their own moderation – never having a drop before 8pm; only drinking on the weekend; always drinking out of the same glass, or in the same place. Meanwhile, in other areas of these lives, it's often been the case that addictive patterns riddle themselves out – in money, sex, gambling, work. For all that the drinking is 'moderate', the rest of the life isn't sober. At least, it doesn't seem like it to me.

One problem here is the presence of Alcoholics Anonymous, whose uncompromising insistence on abstinence, and the reality of the 12-Step programme, can seem counter-productive. Let me be blunt: although I'm not by any means a regular attender at AA, I thoroughly like the 12-Step programme as a framework for recovery; I thoroughly like many, many active members of AA; and I'm glad the programme works so effectively for so many millions of people. The trouble is, AA membership can also become addictive, and for the sceptics and rationalists among us, the 12-Step programme has no basis in logic or science. In the *Observer's* Kishline report, for instance, Professor Nick Heather (University of Newcastle) is cited as saying that the 12-Step programme is 'akin to a cult': 'I'm a rationalist in favour of scientific evidence, but it's mumbo jumbo.' To which I would counter that alcoholism isn't a rational disease. It's a dislocation of the emotions, a chaos in the psyche. I also think – and I think it because I live it – that this chaos isn't confined to alcoholism: alcoholism is only one symptom of an addictive patterning that can viciously underlie an individual's behaviour and thought patterns. This dislocation can't be treated by logic. Christ, there are those of us who have even done good science, and who tried to tackle the problem with all the intelligence, the reading, the structure and insight we could muster. All those things are great – but they can't, singly or in concert, beat alcoholism.

As far as I can see it, 'moderation' doesn't work for addicts. In fact, 'Moderation Management' is a rather telling title. If you have to 'manage' your moderation, you're not really being moderate. The fact that moderation has to be 'managed' suggests that there's some chaos that underlies the management process. Unless the chaos is looked at, named, recognized, it will remain as chaos, however it is 'managed'. What remains true, however, is that 'controlled drinking' is cheaper for any society to offer to its addicts. The alternatives – of mass education, of re-training, of recovery-in-sobriety – would be prohibitively expensive and therefore difficult to contemplate. In an addicted world, 'controlled drinking' keeps us relatively fixed, and relatively unhappy. It keeps us off the streets and out of too much trouble – until we drive into a man and his daughter one fatal evening.

35.   24 July 2000

On the back of yesterday's piece, on the debate between those who advocate total abstinence, and those who advocate 'moderation', I was thinking again about treatment strategies, and damage, and self-recognition. Maybe if you're a 'moderate' or a 'social' drinker – you only get pissed once or twice a week, and your body isn't yet shattered – you could get away with 'managing' your moderation, if not the rest of your life. If you're an alcoholic and an addict, I don't think there's any other route but total abstinence, and the freedom of total recovery. But how do you know? Are you merely a drinker, or an addict?

There are several widely used tests for alcoholism. I don't really believe in any of them, since individuals vary in their patterns of consumption, and I also believe that alcoholics will – deep down, and too deeply down for the words of their denial – well, they'll just know. For what it's worth, I have included one famous diagnostic set, *The Johns Hopkins Test for Alcoholism*, on the next page.

This solipsistic self-assessment, though, doesn't seem inclusive enough to me, even though I scored an imperfect 19. Those affected by others' alcoholism, by others' problem behaviour, may themselves be clean and/or sober, and yet show all the traits of addiction. Another diagnostic set, *Did You Grow Up With a Problem Drinker?*, follows on page 116.

Although I didn't 'grow up with a problem drinker' I scored rather highly on this diagnostic, too, possibly because I grew up with myself.

I draw no conclusions – at least, not for you – from these questions. All I'm doing here is thinking aloud. In doing so I remind myself (a) that alcoholism isn't treatable by logic; (b) that it's fatal unless its progress is arrested; (c) that it's usually aligned with other forms of addictive patterning, in self or family; and (d) there is no cure.

36.   21 August 2000

Ten days ago I was on holiday in Greece, two weeks in to a three-week holiday, when the mobile rang. The remains of a frugal lunch – cheese, biscuits, peaches – were on the table. The heat, filled alternately with cicadas and with Greece's love affair with the internal combustion engine, was heavy, almost inflammable. The voice on the mobile was the voice of a friend from England. 'Chris, there's some bad news.' I thought instantly of family. 'Jonathan...died two days ago. He was in withdrawal. He had a heart attack...'

Back in December and early January, I was in treatment with the man I shall here call Jonathan. Jonathan the gifted musician, the organist, the choir-master. Jonathan who had lent me Hanon's *Exercises for the Left Hand*. Jonathan who had testified so vibrantly and with so much hurt to the wastage of his marriage, and to his own solitary relationship with

The Johns Hopkins Test for Alcoholism

1. Yes/No Do you lose time from work due to drinking?

2. Yes/No Is drinking making your home life unhappy?

3. Yes/No Do you drink because you are shy with other people?

4. Yes/No Is drinking affecting your reputation?

5. Yes/No Have you ever felt remorse after drinking?

6. Yes/No Have you had financial difficulties as a result of drinking?

7. Yes/No Do you turn to inferior companions and environments when drinking?

8. Yes/No Does your drinking make you careless of your family's welfare?

9. Yes/No Has your ambition decreased since drinking?

10. Yes/No Do you crave a drink at a definite time daily?

11. Yes/No Do you want a drink the next morning?

12. Yes/No Does drinking cause you to have difficulty in sleeping?

13. Yes/No Has your efficiency decreased since drinking?

14. Yes/No Is drinking jeopardizing your job or business?

15. Yes/No Do you drink to escape from worries or trouble?

16. Yes/No Do you drink alone?

17. Yes/No Have you ever had a loss of memory as a result of drinking?

18. Yes/No Has your physician ever treated you for drinking?

19. Yes/No Do you drink to build up your self-confidence?

20. Yes/No Have you ever been to a hospital or institution on account of drinking?

- If you have answered YES to any one of these questions, there is a DEFINITE WARNING that you may be an alcoholic.

- If you have answered YES to any two, the CHANCES ARE that you are an alcoholic.

- If you have answered YES to three or more, you are DEFINITELY AN ALCOHOLIC.

(Reproduced from www.recovery.org, with permission.)

Did You Grow Up with a Problem Drinker?

1. Do you constantly seek approval and affirmation?
2. Do you fail to recognize your accomplishments?
3. Do you fear criticism?
4. Do you overextend yourself?
5. Have you had problems with your own compulsive behavior?
6. Do you have a need for perfection?
7. Are you uneasy when your life is going smoothly, continually anticipating problems?
8. Do feel more alive in the midst of a crisis?
9. Do you still feel responsible for others, as you did for the problem drinker in your life?
10. Do you care for others easily, yet find it difficult to care for yourself?
11. Do you isolate yourself from other people?
12. Do you respond with anxiety to authority figures and angry people?
13. Do you feel that individuals and society in general are taking advantage of you?
14. Do you have trouble with intimate relationships?
15. Do you confuse pity with love, as you did with the problem drinker?
16. Do you attract and seek people who tend to be compulsive?
17. Do you cling to relationships because you are afraid of being alone?
18. Do you often mistrust your own feelings and the feelings expressed by others?
19. Do you find it difficult to express your emotions?
20. Do you think parental drinking may have affected you?

Alcoholism is a family disease...

Scotch. Jonathan who had often phoned. Jonathan who'd kept drinking, and was drinking himself further into isolation and chaos. Jonathan who seemed never to be able to stop, who never quite got the message. Jonathan I'd not phoned for weeks. Jonathan I hardly recognized, or perhaps, recognized too well under the crazy, broken voice on the other end of the wire. He was in his early fifties. He had an estranged wife, an elderly mother, both locked into their different distances and their broken hearts. He had two small children.

Ten days on, and I'm still bewildered. I remember the voice on the phone, the moment the news struck; the peach stones on the tablecloth; the vibrancy of the heat that was suddenly nowhere. And the feeling of anger, of utter futility; of English remorse somewhere on a Greek balcony; and the hot tears pricking with rage, uselessness, absence, and yet more anger.

Jonathan's death – his addictions, his alcoholism – is in the crudest sense a reminder that addictive patterning is a disease – a condition, a set of conditions – that can and does kill. It wasn't the heart-attack that killed Jonathan, although 'coronary' rather than 'alcoholism' will have been properly, mercifully, recorded as the cause of death. No. What killed Jonathan was booze. If there had been no periodic bingeing with Scotch, there would have been no withdrawal. And the way Jonathan was using the stuff, the withdrawals themselves were getting worse: insane shakings, fever, sweat, nausea, dry retchings. And the heart, abused, overworked, pumping in laceration, in fear. And then not pumping at all.

Jonathan wanted to stop drinking. Through treatment, after treatment, Jonathan said he wanted recovery. But he didn't want recovery enough. I can still hear my own arrogance of two years ago: if this is an illness, it's the world's most unique illness, because you can simply choose to be well. This was and is untrue. It's only a lying heartbeat away from 'I can choosh to shtop any time I wanna'. But once alcoholism – once any addiction – is active, you can't choose to stop. You have to retrain everything in order to help you stop, and crucially, you have to make these choices in the company of other people. That's part of the wanting, when you want recovery enough. And in the end, what was left of Jonathan wasn't doing that wanting. Whatever was left of this human being was having another kind of non-relationship, with the fatal, stricken fantasies of Scotch and withdrawal.

There's a Japanese saying that does the rounds in recovery: *A man takes a drink. A drink takes a drink. Then the drink takes the man.* Alcohol took this man. It has taken, it continues to take, millions, irrespective of their gifts, their status, their intelligence, their warmth, and their laughter. And intelligence, warmth, laughter were some of Jonathan's many properties.

Alcoholism does not respect any of these gifts or properties. It doesn't respect love itself.

'All deaths have meaning,' I think to myself now just as I thought when Jud relayed the news of Jonathan's coronary. But the meanings often take months, years, decades to unravel, and maybe we can never, in our own imperfect mortality, see the end of whatever unravelling it is that is taking place. I can't see the meaning or the unravelling of this. Not yet.

As I write, I can see Jonathan playing the opening bars of Chopin's *Fantasie Impromptu* on a beaten-up upright piano somewhere in a cold village hall in Cheshire, before an AA meeting was scheduled to begin. Today, on the piano downstairs, Hanon's *Exercises for the Left Hand* lies open, as do easy sonatinas by Kuhlau, another Jonathan loan. I can see myself, on a Greek terrace, with a mobile phone in my hand and disbelief creeping into an afternoon of unreal and unremitting heat. If alcohol exiles forever, mine was just a different kind of exile, with its forcing to bear witness, its shock, the peach stones lying on the tablecloth, the sea fractured by the rings of mullet, the sliced tomatoes, the not knowing what to say. And Jonathan…dead.

37.   24 August 2000

Holidays are difficult times for addicts. I think they're probably especially difficult times for drunks. What does a drunk do, when the pressure's off and he wants to celebrate a well-earned sense of rest? What does she do in the departure lounge, the ferry terminal? What does he do on the plane getting there, on the plane coming back? What does she do when all the preparations for the holiday are so much last-minute that the clocks of all the deadlines are running? What does he do when he comes home, and feels strangely let down, almost post-coital, and needs a pick-you-up?

Right.

I could count on the fingers of two hands – okay, I'm an addict, make that three – the number of holidays I've screwed up because of booze. The places visited but unseen; the airplanes full of queasy unconsciousness; the celebrated arrival that turned into a nightmare of loss and betrayal; the bad feeling; the sour faces; the pub; the fridge; the loss. Come to that, I could probably navigate my way up some old, abandoned, favourite haunts, such as the west coast of Scotland, by licensing hours and bars. I'd get lost on the way, surely, but I'm on holiday, what the hell? You take the high road…and I'll stay where I am, because it isn't Throwing Out Time. Yet. And make sure there's some stuff for later, will you?

I was – that is, we were – in Greece. I think I've written about Corfu and alcohol somewhere else, and about the possibility, the bare possibility, of drinking like a gentleman on that simple, messy island. Ouzo and *mezedhes* for lunch, followed by a siesta and a swim, followed by an aperitif, and a late dinner with a bottle of Makedonikos or, better, Theotoki. *Khialo bukali krasi, parakalo.* Actually, in bad Greek, bring one for each leg.

As it was, many parts of Greece are fairly sober, and it's perfectly acceptable, outside the terrible resorts (such as Ipsos, which has a bar amusingly called 'Alcoholics Anonymous'), to drink several kinds of coffee, to drink soda, tea, or even ginger beer – *Tsin-tsin birra*, a legacy from the nineteenth century, and the days of the British Protectorate. Look round on the Spianada at midday, any day. The working habit of ouzo and *mezedhes* – the Greek equivalent of a pie and a pint – is outclassed and outnumbered by the sodas, the juices, the coffees, and work continues over the mobile phone.

I was sober. If anyone had told me, eight months ago, that I could have gone through three weeks of holiday anywhere, let alone Corfu, while staying on the wagon I wouldn't have believed them. It helped, it more than helped, that Monika brings such close understanding into the days we share. It helped that the walking, the swimming, the plans were of such a realistic, gentle, peaceful nature. The result was the most wonderful, and restful, and changing vacation I can remember. And a further benefit of this was that I saw more parts of the island than would ever have been possible in the old, crazy, drunken days under the arcades. We drove north, and walked. We walked into the hinterlands, into valleys where the nothing that was there was murmurous with heat and cicadas. We climbed. We swam. And one unforgettable morning, there we were at the top of Mount Pandokrator at sunrise, looking into Albania, and down across the limestone scarps of the mountain, where at that unearthly hour there were only distant goat-bells and the sounds of our own breathing.

I felt uncomfortable only twice. My Corfiot friend, Mary, had known me in the arcade days, the days of ouzo and forgetting. She seemed to find those spectres – of my own shames – somehow remarkable. 'You had crazy summers in Corfu,' she said, laughing indulgently. Yes, they were crazy summers. But they were also disease-ridden, loss-ridden summers. And then again, there was Nikos, turning up late at night for dinner with a gallon cask of retsina so resinous that the aroma from the opened neck filled the room. Well, *yammas*.

The past is the past, and however amusing my friends and drinking partners might or might not find it, or me, today is today. I just kept choosing all the todays, vibrant with heat and light, and full of a relationship so deep and growing that it seemed of a piece with my own deepening sense of peace and well-being. It seemed of Us, and for a week, for three weeks, ours was the day, the Corfiot earth, the sky, the laughter, and the whole bloody ocean.

Yes, it's anti-climactic, coming home, adjusting again to loneliness and work. Yes, I woke up last night at the old, bad time of 5.10am, and for a bare and disorientated moment considered pouring myself into a taxi and towards a 24-hour market. But I had woken up to another day, and today, I choose not to drink. In the yesterdays of marred promise, I celebrated my non-freedom with a bottle of something that threatened to cheer, but brought only heartache. Today, holiday or no holiday, I simply choose to celebrate this freedom with freedom.

38.   13 September 2000

People say – recovery people, people who know better than I – that in the first year of sobriety an addict should never make big decisions, never make sweeping changes. Don't sell your house, your car; don't trade your job, or your partner…assuming you still have a job, house, car, or partner. Don't travel, don't put yourself into high-pressure, and therefore high-risk, situations. Shopping is fine. Exotic foreign holidays are distinctly suspect.

It's grand advice. I would have taken it, were it not for the fact that during the past three months I've travelled to the States, to mainland Europe, to conferences. I have learnt to live with strangers who are, however temporarily, sharing this house. I've had to work under fairly severe pressure, meet unexpected deadlines, and make plans to construct a life in Amsterdam, far from this known city which, for all its unloved inconveniences, is still a kind of home. And three days ago I decided – we decided – to get married.

The result of the high-risk, high-pressure life is that I feel happier than ever, and in a strange way, more grounded. Nevertheless, I have to work hard, and then harder, to stay with the Reality Factor. An addict can't afford to be swept off his feet; he'll only end up in the gutter.

What does the Reality Factor mean? It means living with the days, living with events, being equable about the good and the bad. An example: one week ago, I learnt that despite repeated assurances from doctors, and from the DVLA itself, my application to have the driving licence reinstated had been turned down. This, despite the court's decision of three months ago to grant the licence (subject to medical approval). The problem is in the parentheses. Yet I can only think that the bored hand at the Swansea desk hadn't read through the file of the case, since it doesn't appear to be legal to overturn a court's decision when that decision's been made, and when the medical approval, the money, the paperwork are all in place. When I opened the letter of NO, foolishly expecting a licence to be inside, I was devastated, and turned the whole matter over to the lawyers. Even as I did this, it felt like being kicked in the stomach, and tasting the bile of resentment. A day later, and I was flying out to Spain to do a piece of work. A day after the flight, and I was engaged. Life, when it moves this fast, doesn't seem like life. It seems like some kind of technicolour frieze: vivid, exciting, and alarming. And what does an alcoholic do when he's vividly excited and alarmed? What's the first thing you reach for over the conference decompression, or after the business in the jeweller's? What do you do with the bad memories, the residual guilts, the uncertainties?

Of course, I thought about drinking. I thought about sex. I thought about celebrating over a cup of coffee and a blackjack table somewhere in Barcelona, until I realized again that the turn of the card could just as easily stand for the push at the optic. Feelings aren't to be fixed. They're to be appreciated, inspected if necessary, and then let go.

I'm still unsettled. Tonight, exhausted after flying home from Santiago, I heard via e-mail that I have unknown cousins in Canada, and that Monika's mother has had a dangerous car smash somewhere near Krefeld. She's currently lying in Intensive Care, and was lying there even as I was telephoning around with the news of marriage, next May, and Amsterdam. I feel not only concerned, but guilty, somehow, at being so unstoppably happy. To cap everything, I have blood relations I never knew I had.

There's nothing more I can do tonight, nothing more that Monika can do. It's time for some tea, some biscuits, maybe some television news. Time for a bath, and perhaps a look at some fishing tackle catalogues before turning in to sleep. And tomorrow morning, as always, there's the small discipline of early meditation, of focus, of reminding myself to keep everything in the day. If drinking was a habit in the end, so I think that these easy disciplines may also become habits, and productive ones. These small observances always remind me of the blacksmith's nail. Do you know that rhyme? 'For want of a nail, the horse was lost. For want of a horse, the rider was lost. For want of a rider, the battle was lost. For want of a battle, the kingdom was lost...' Lives go on, in their infinite varieties and their infinite processes of entailment. The smaller decision impacts on the greater. The art of analysis lies only in proper connection.

Yes, it is like looking at some kind of medieval frieze, a Bayeux Tapestry choked with events, with deaths, surprises, local details, local clarities. Things happen, and you watch them pass. But these things also are happening to you, and while you're looking at a tapestry, you're living it, creating it. One morning you'll wake up and find thread in your hands, and the day will surely be full of events, but also of making, connection, choice. As I wearily sign off this piece, I ask you as I ask myself: Did you have that making, the connection, and the choice, when you were drinking?

39.   15 September 2000

One of the things to go, when you're fixing or drinking, is your hobby. It doesn't matter if it's needlepoint or netball, stock-car racing, gardening, or playing the trumpet. The hobby will be sucked into the self-obsessions of the addict. It will be displaced by anxieties and time spent on the addictive process. Fishing was one of my own casualties. I think I spent more time drinking, finding drink, and worrying about where the next drink would be, than I ever did on the river or the lake. Gradually, I lost my capacity for that kind of happiness. And then I lost the happiness altogether.

To talk of 'hobbies' invites an indulgent smile. A man with a hobby conjures an image of someone middle-aged and uxorious, a garden-shed-potterer in a string vest. 'Hobbies' are to real life (thinks Mr. Wonderful) what a cup of tea is to a vodka martini. A man with a hobby is a man who wears a string vest in the summer; he wears open-toed sandals with unfortunate socks. He's a nerd, an anorak, a geek.

Put aside the loaded lexical weapon of the word 'hobby', and think of the word 'recreation'. Think of it truly in terms of its morphology: re+creation. Something is re-created, begun anew, made afresh. It's not merely the passive consumption of time, it's a radical construction. And what's constructed? Only that most precious of commodities, one's Self.

It's not accidental that through 1996 until now, the entries in my fishing diaries dwindle into paragraphs and wistfulness. Where I used to go fishing once, perhaps twice a week, and where each summer was filled with at least one seven-day trip somewhere, in the critical years I didn't go fishing at all. In the throes of hangovers and nightmares, I was too sick to go out even with kind friends who'd offered me lifts. Then I was banned from driving, the relationship with my closest fishing friend ended in black disaster, and it was impossible to think of fishing at all. To think of fishing was to think of the past, and of happiness, and of all that had been lost. It was as if memory was being cut apart. Meanwhile, the days filled with accident and anger, guilt and shame. Even on the few occasions I managed to get out, I found it hard to fish alone, my mind was too fractured and too full. The day was there, but I couldn't, somehow, seem to reach it.

In the course of the last year, the fishing has come back to me. It isn't that I set out to find it, it's not as if I forced myself to spend time tinkering about with flies, catalogues, bits of tackle. It's rather as if, like the friends I let down, like the time I wasted on time, it was simply waiting for me to come back to myself. Instead of staring obsessively into an evening filled with vodka and illusion, I wanted to tie a few flies, write an article, engage again with the structured mess of pike gear under the stairs. It happened slowly, at first. A handful of flies; putting some new line on a reel; looking through a catalogue; reading a book at bed-time. Such simple, sustaining things allowed me to re-create myself. They still do. The past is still full of trouble; but the future has the gentlest kind of hope. Ordering a few pike spoons sets me dreaming of a Bassenthwaite shoreline, and the pike hitting perch-fry down a heat-stricken day in midsummer. Messing around with a shooting-head helps me dream of sea-trout, and Danish tides. And three weeks ago, as I bought my first permit in the Netherlands – something complicated, in efficient Dutch triplicate – I began to think positively about pike, perch, and polders, autumn days in the boat, frozen days on the bank, with a wan sun and the volcano kettle. Next week, after giving a paper at the university in Leiden, I'll be out there, learning to think about new fishing in a new language. And I'll be alive, connected with the day, and connected, I hope, with all that process of entailment that is life underwater.

If addicts are obsessed with themselves, it's because we're obsessively creating a false Self, rather than allowing that Self that is us simply to be. I don't know how to put this in properly psychological terms, but it seems that each of us lives through a process of radical illusion, a kind of mythical and terrible journey. Even to put it like this dignifies the hurts and the human misery that tangle in the wreckage of the process. But the process itself, the search, the blind illness, isn't wrong. It's energy looking to re-create itself in all the wrong places, acting itself out in fantasy and anger. It's the expense of spirit in a waste of shame.

I know about shame, have even courted it. It's as familiar to me as the motion of these hands on the computer keyboard. It became a habit. Still, in place of that fruitless habit there's also the habit of re+creation. For me, this happens to be fishing. It could be a garden shed and a pair of secateurs; it could be dancing or knitting. Whatever the form of the reconstruction, I understand now, and not merely with what's left of my intellect, why the unknown author of the first fishing book in the English language wrote that angling 'was principally for your solace, and to cause the health of your body, and specially, of your soul'.

40.   18 September 2000

I never thought I'd end up writing the best part of a thousand words in praise of chocolate, but there you are. Addictions take you down some strange roads.

It's a sugar thing. Take a drink, take several, take many drinks over the course of a couple of decades and your body thinks it's being fed. The result is that you're high in pure sugar – don't believe that junk about all the sugar turning to alcohol – and low in carbohydrates and vitamins. When the blood-sugar level drops, what's a drunk's instant reaction? Right. Another hit, and yet another, and though the body might be bloated, the system's malnourished. I saw it in my own flabby, wasted face: no complex carbohydrates; no vitamin B; and damn all else.

Take the drink away, and the body, habituated by abuse, still craves sugar. Therefore it seems like a good idea, if only as a temporary measure, to drink something sweet when a craving hits. It's also a good idea to keep a chocolate bar somewhere in the briefcase. Chocolate, or Jelly Babies. I have bitten the heads off so many Jelly Babies recently that they could be DVLA officials. And at the same time, you may find, as I do, that desserts suddenly become an attractive proposition. Sticky toffee pudding; ice cream; weird fudgy stuff. You wouldn't have been seen dead eating these concoctions three years ago, as you unsteadily stirred the vodka martini with the cocktail olive that was your only solid food for the day. And yet now... Now you live under a different dispensation. Part of that dispensation is eating properly. Eating well.

I thought I'd put on weight, eating sweet things. At my lightest, and worst, I was an emaciated eleven and a half stone, around 160lbs. For someone 6'3", that's too light. Nevertheless, I looked at myself in the mirror and saw Michelin man, the pneumatic self-pity of a moon- faced boy. I wanted to slash my cheeks with any convenient sharp edge, and quite deliberately used to starve, living on vodka and nerves. As the weight fell off, it didn't fall off neck or face. I would never look like Albert Camus, nor was I Meursault, high cheekbones over a half-smoked Gauloises. Instead, the weight fell off my legs. These were turning numb from the big toes upwards, and at the same time my left hand was begin-ning to feel muscularly weak. In the alcohol trade, I'm told this is called the 'gloves and stockings' effect. It's otherwise called by its Sunday-best name of peripheral neuropathy, and it sure as hell isn't cured by more vodka. Its effects are only partially reversible, and then with a good diet, which means a proper balance of sugars, carbohydrates, and vitamins.

In the event, I have put on weight, and now the scales show a fairly comfortable twelve and a half stone. Somehow, this is a healthier weight. There's none of that saggy bloatedness that comes, however thin you are, from vodka-and-Lucozade cocktails. Occasionally, I look down in the shower and see incipient middle age, in the form of a small (but perfectly formed) belly, and think that this is merely an insurance policy, rather than a ticket to the Endlessly Unlovable Ball.

Sweet tea. Chocolate. Jelly Babies. Desserts. I'm not urging anyone to go out and ingest these things forever, without discrimination, and to the exclusion of everything else. But I do think that comfort food is useful to an addict in early recovery. Just monitor your consumption. You may find, as I did, that instead of having one digestive biscuit with the mid-morning coffee, you have a sudden urge to eat half a dozen. Come to that, you may drink half a dozen cups of coffee, too. And the chocolate bar you thought would break into halves, one for midmorning, one for mid-afternoon, you scoff at one standing. Well, fine, you're an addict, and you can be addictive around anything, even biscuits, for heaven's sake. But in early recovery, I use anything just to stay away from today's drink or today's fix. I can work on the other addictive patterns later. For now, I try to handle the primary addiction. As that's processed, as life slowly becomes easier, as you feel both stronger and more comfortable in your own skin, you'll have the ability to see the other addictions for what they are, and deal with them in their turn.

This isn't merely theory. This is how it has been, and this is how it's worked for one addict, aka Mr. Wonderful and Michelin man. I happen to carry, almost always, one or two chocolate bars in the executive briefcase, and you wouldn't believe how pleased I was when a friend of mine, whom I hadn't seen for months, said 'Chris, Jesus…' ('Yes,' I said) '…you're looking so lean… And mean…' She might have added '…and magnificent', but as it was, I was walking testimony to the power of chocolate, and bugger vanity and the bathroom scales.

41.   18 September 2000

I was re-reading some of the 'official' diagnostic tests for alcoholism. Nine months into recovery, I thought I'd write my own self-diagnostic. I was trying to identify the difficult situations into which this…condition…sometimes takes me, and I have suggested to myself some remedial actions at the end of the diagnostic list.

Self-diagnostic for Active Addiction

Answer YES/NO

1.   Are you beginning to isolate?
2.   Are you talking to yourself?
3.   Are you constructing imaginary situations?
4.   Are you leaving things undone?
5.   Are you always running late?
6.   Have you let up on the disciplines of reading, phoning?
7.   Is everything too much trouble?
8.   Are you carrying resentments?
9.   Are you leaving dishes unwashed, the ironing undone?
10.   Are you spending too much time in 'displacement activity'?
11.   Do you feel uneasy or unsettled for no apparent reason?

12. Do you feel you aren't listening to other people?

13. Are you lacking connection with the small things of each day?

14. Do you feel that you're always being judged?

15. Are you making unreasonable demands on yourself?

16. Are you fantasizing?

17. Are you grieving the might-have-been?

18. Are you neglecting to wash, shower, shave carefully?

19. Are you putting things off?

20. Are you wearing one or more masks?

If you've scored ONE or more with YES

(a) bring things back into the day – this particular day

(b) take several deep breaths

(c) remind yourself of the small realities, the small courtesies

(d) phone someone

(e) don't leave things undone

If these remedies fail

(i) take a long, hot bath

(ii) do some light reading

(iii) do some 'recovery' reading

(iv) write a letter, but don't post it yet

(v) eat a chocolate bar, then go for a walk

(vi) play the piano or listen to some music

(vii) make a casserole

(viii) do a crossword

(ix) plan a fishing trip

(x) go to bed

I don't know whether this is useful to you. It seems like a fairly safe and middle-aged list, but it's worked so far. In particular, it's the facts of connection that seem to make sense – not isolating, not fantasizing, not worrying and dreaming simultaneously. Bad feelings do pass, I remind myself. One trick seems to be simply to allow oneself sufficient time to let the shames, the resentments, the self-pity and anxieties the space to pass through, to evaporate. I reach for convenient clichés: *This too shall pass.* Let it go.

In all truth I've probably made this list seem too strategic. What I do find is that I spend huge amounts of time merely listening. It doesn't matter whether this is listening to words, or to advice, or listening simply to silence as it passes. Strangely, it's the silence, properly construed, that seems to have so much to say, and what the silence says is very different from the hectic self-absorptions of active alcoholism. To listen to time as it passes suddenly seems like a uniquely valuable connection with all the merciful instants of Now.

It's one of AA's oldest pieces of advice, I realize: 'Give time time.' I give this advice to myself today, in the hope that it's useful to someone as they overhear it.

42.   5 October 2000

Last week I found myself at two in the afternoon in the teeming and seedy midriff of Amsterdam's red-light district. Officer, I wasn't there by design. I was passing through on my way from Waterlooplein, home of Europe's best open-air market, to the Centraal Station, where I was scheduled to take the tram home. If you don't believe the geography, look at a map of this fair city: from Waterlooplein to the Centraal Station takes you through the streets east of the Damrak, until you emerge among the hamburger joints and neon of the Damrak itself. It's a bit like Oxford Street on speed. Then you turn right and cross a glutch of canals before heading underground to the Metro.

On this journey, I reflected merely that I was a middle-aged drunk in the middle of territory where there were multiple opportunities to score. The bars were open. Couples sat outside in the early autumn sunshine, sipping designer beers. Men of Caribbean extraction shifted around in doorways, waiting for trade or the next hit. Someone walked their poodle, carefully stepping around dog-turds as she did so. Yellow signs proclaimed the dubious virtues of Oriental Massage. Red signs lured the unwary, the reckless, and the drunk into tattoo parlours. Shop-fronts concealed stained plush interiors where bored women lounged in almost nothing at all, listening to Tina Turner's cover of 'Only The Strong Survive'. Meanwhile, only next door, sensible architects sensibly designed the rest of Holland, throwing in parts of Belgium for good measure, and Tina Turner's voice haunted the slide-rule and the anglepoise. In the canal-side streets, hungover builders on cheap three-day holidays from Sunderland and Swansea wondered why they felt cold and homesick, and goose-pimpled bravado shrank into their underpants and their too-tight T-shirts. It was Amsterdam, the burgher-like, suburban face of addiction, raddled with a polite despair. It was needy, disreputable, human. The nearest I can come to describing it is to ask you to imagine a middle-aged businessman, from his trim hair-cut to his steel-framed glasses to his expensive mohair overcoat. Then imagine he takes off the mohair overcoat, and throws it on a chair. Underneath his veneer of civilization, he's naked, his arms are track-marked, and in a razor-scar down his lower abdomen there are very small, very beautiful, and very deeply burrowing larvae.

If I know this man, I also know his territory. I knew I could slip into it like slipping into a well-worn conversation. I know the look of addiction. I know the faces, the voices, the deceits, and the uncontrollable, silent angers. Above all, I know the smell of drunks – the nicotine and tar stitched into the clothes, the stale fume of too much night, the sweet, sour petrol on the breath, the dried sweat of effort clogged to the skin. Failure smells like that. The apparent freedom of nothing-left-to-lose translates only into pock-marks, cigarettes, and chains. And at this point, I rather badly wanted a beer. Sit in the shade of a tree by a canal, sipping something effortless that came from somewhere unknown in Belgium, something that tasted like liquid coal, warm with burnt sugars. Sit for a while, and be, er, cosmopolitan. Let them find me in the shady side of a square at mid-day, with a notebook open on the table and what's left of the mind oozing poison and poems...

I told Jud this when I revisited England last weekend. 'I kept my head down, Jud,' I said. 'I looked neither to right nor left, and headed through the place as quickly as if my life depended on it.' He raised an eyebrow. 'Kept my head down, didn't look, didn't stop, didn't wonder, didn't worry...' He raised his other eyebrow. There was a heavy pause.

'Okay, well, yes, it's true. I did come face to face with a giant dildo in a shop window. But then I was going to call you…' Jud's eyebrows were raised so far that his face was vertical, and laughing. 'I just wanted to say, I mean, "Here I am in Amsterdam, looking at a giant dildo in a shop window"…'

There was one of those silences that are so meaningful that they re-write the meaning of meaning. 'You jerk,' Jud said, lovingly. 'And you didn't make that call. But you know what I would have said to your "I'm looking at a giant dildo in a shop window"?'

I didn't know.

'Just comb your fucking hair and get out of there.'

43.   5 October 2000

Sleep is one of the most basic human requirements. To sleep, add shelter, an adequate diet, and some peace of mind. I realize that these necessities may sound deeply boring. To a drunk in recovery, though, sleep – profound, untroubled, normal sleep – is difficult, to the point of being impossible. And even when you achieve sleep, there are drinking dreams, or waking up feeling as if you're in the worst of a hangover. For two years, my sleep patterns were so disturbed that I couldn't get off, as it were, without listening to the radio (Radio 4 merges seamlessly into the World Service at 1am, after the Shipping Forecast and the National bloody Anthem), and I still adopt this minor tactic of the bedroom if and when I sleep alone. (I no longer sleep with the knife and the paracetamol under the pillow, though.) And for those two years, chronic sleeplessness made me feel so lousy that I wondered whether sobriety was worth it. And wondering whether sobriety is worth it inevitably means that you'll drink again. I did. Sleep, therefore, means survival. It's as boring as that.

I took heed about sleep. One piece of good advice was never to asso-ciate the bed with a place where you feel restless. After half an hour of tossing and turning, get up. Wander about. Watch some television. Make some tea. Then go back to bed, and try again. You might have to do this a dozen times a night (I did), but it's better than terminal anxiety, queasi-ness, and night sweats; eventually your body, whose memories are so intangible yet so powerful, will learn to associate bed with rest. You might also want to try the Radio Trick, though I don't really recommend it: tune the radio so that it's easily audible (straining to hear never rested anyone's nerves), and use it as connection and company until you feel settled enough to drop off. And also, be warm. Hot water bottles on a cold night may sound like the acme of worried middle age, but if they help you sleep, let middle age take care of itself. And speaking of middle age, there are also the Old Wives' remedies, of which the chief is a milky drink at bedtime. I think I should have taken out shares in low-fat Horlicks.

Drinking dreams, from this direct experience and that of many others, are relatively common in early sobriety. Three times during the past ten months I've woken up panic-stricken, disorientated, and almost in tears, until daylight has brought the merciful realization that the brandies were an illusion. At one point, I think I even woke up sobbing, 'I'll have to go into the Relapse Group...' But of course, since dreams are, among other things, a kind of clearing-house for the junk of conscious-ness, naturally you're going to dream about booze. It's your deepest rela-tionship. Accept it, think about it, move on. Maybe these dreams are trying to tell you that something in your recovery's not quite right. If so, I think it's possible to learn from the errors and promptings of the night before. It's a hell of a lot better than waking up not knowing where you are, or whose is the body in the bed next to you.

Waking up feeling hungover is also common, even many months into recovery. One theory – actually, it's only my theory, so take it for what it's worth – is that the body never forgets. Bad, battered, uneasy nights. The wreckage of memories and guilts. The vicious pangs of remorse, of shame. In recovery, these things are still parts of you; you just handle them differently. But you still carry them with you into however-much-broken sleep, and you can wake up feeling wretched. It's the feeling wretched that your body remembers. 'I feel bad, cramped, wrecked, sleepless. I must have had a skinful...'

Muscles have memory. Tendons, sinews, circulation. They all have memories. If you doubt this, ask any pianist how they memorize the rep-ertoire, and they'll tell you about muscular memory. So no wonder, in your repertoire of glasses and failures, that your body remembers practising, on so many faces and bottles, all those difficult pieces for solo despair.

Another theory about the 'recovery hangover' is more mundane, but equally plausible. 'Normal people' sometimes wake up feeling wretched. Normal people have headaches, worries, anxieties. Normal people have stuffy noses and sleepless nights. Normal people catch cold, have backache, listen for burglars. Maybe, just maybe, your recovery is re-joining you with the rest of the human race, and in some sense, you may be becoming normal as the latest germ at work. Yes, it's strange to feel this normality as a privilege, but the alternative, remember, was Mr. Wonderful waking up in a field somewhere with a transvestite called, just for the sake of it, Ken.

44.   11 October 2000

One of the prime factors that keep this recovery going is the idea of freedom. When you're drinking, using, you're a prey to all the ungovernable craziness of the addict. Your wants – all the miseries of Want – are so close to the surface that they always and incessantly demand time and attention: you have to act out, trapped in illusions and fantasies. In doing so, you become other than yourself. In the terminal throes of drinking, perhaps the truest thing I said, to a close colleague, was 'I don't know who I am'. And what imaginative landscape was I inhabiting, when I said this? It was Yeats's Byzantium. What Yeats perhaps forgot to say is that this Byzantium is only for the ill, the captive, and the exile. In the end, living as a slave to your own need isn't altogether romantic.

It's difficult to admit to even some of my own fantasies. One thing I'd do, often late at night over the lees of something made in France, was imagine I was being interviewed as The Great Writer. If this sounds pathetic, it was. I'm blushing as I write. Yet there's an analogue of this in the reality of today's recovery: I imagine I'm being interviewed, five years down the track, as The Great Survivor, someone who endured not only the whips and scorns of loss, but also the hallucinations, the illness, the rebel mind. The Great Survivor? Come off it, Chris, just look at yourself in the mirror. What stares back is an uncertainly smiling, middle-aged man who worries about his chins. Why, in any case, do I have to be 'The

Great' anything? It was Mr. Wonderful who wanted to be The Great. Chris McCully's deepest need is to be plain Chris McCully. Chris has choices, and therefore, has freedom. Mr. Wonderful, The Great Nothing At All, had none.

This said, imagination has surprising, and real-time, power, and that power can often coerce reality into the desired shape. Imagine yourself leaping gracefully backwards over a two-metre-high bar, and you're slightly more likely to achieve the improbable vault. Imagine yourself attractive, and you will be – a cliché that has spawned a hundred glossy magazines. Think of yourself as the most successful pike angler who ever walked the planet, and it's just possible that you'll take more pains to catch pike, and therefore, really connect with that elusive 30-pounder. The trick, if it is a trick, is to align these coercions with real life, the life of mortgages and back gardens, of bank accounts and bird tables, of the endlessly pouring moments of Now. It's no good fantasizing about what might happen five years into the future, since you might be dead by then. You might be dead tomorrow, or next minute. There's only the surprising instant, which, as it happens, is just about long enough for you to inject with hope, and with whatever dream of realism comes to hand. That is your gift; it's also my freedom.

When I was actively using, I preferred fantasy. Fantasy seemed much more amenable than the ferocity of the life I was actually living, with its vomiting, its unreliability, its handful of purple shit, and all its fear – fear of being found out, fear that no one would come, fear that someone would come, fear of light moving, fear of shadows, including my own. Projecting Mr. Wonderful into an alcoholic dream way-off yonder kept some part of Chris McCully safe, and kept Mr. Wonderful invulnerable. Mr. Wonderful needed those illusions in order to survive, unmarked by the messiness of today. Chris McCully needed them like a hole in the head.

And yet he lived them; he allowed them to happen. The result was a kind of imaginative slavery. There were no real choices to be made, and therefore, no freedom. I suppose I must have gone on somehow with the sheer business of living, with food and schedules and petrol and travel, but I also remember that I relied very heavily on other people. Ex-girl-friends turned up with food, my sister turned up with lunch; someone lent me a cab-fare, or the rent. Sometimes, when other people ran out, I simply hid the bills, left the food, and poured myself into another fantasy and another bottle. What kind of man can't even make choices to eat, work, or sleep, and is shamefully unable to look after himself?

An addict can't make these choices. And so today, as I stare at the computer in Amsterdam, and look at the garden I'm digging this October, or inspect the closet I've just cleared out and painted, or think of the zander and pike I'm going to fish for next weekend, it doesn't seem like anything other than a quiet, relatively peaceful, constructive and happy life. And now you must excuse me. Tonight I'm expecting Monika back from Spain, where she's been doing something starry at a conference, and I have to make a salad. It might not be the greatest salad in the world, but it will be edible, there'll be plenty of it, and I'll be smiling as I make it up. It's reality, groundedness, the detailed construction of Now, and there's freedom in it.

45.   23 October 2000

Returning to the UK to do some mundane work with bills and banks last week, I also attended an after-care meeting at the hospital where I was in treatment last Christmas. I was reminded again that it's only a minority that makes it into, and through, recovery. Depending on whose statistics you access, between 70 and 80 per cent of diagnosed addicts relapse sooner or later, and usually sooner. My guess is that addicts undertaking private treatment, with all the benefits of after-care and support, fare rather better than those undertaking treatment through the NHS, and then through AA or an equivalent 12-Step group. For addicts suffering through this last route, my educated guess is that fewer than 5 per cent actually make it.

It's easy, put like this. It's a matter of finding the % key on the computer. Behind the graphic, the reality is that relapse probably means death. 'Not making it' means dropping dead with DTs, while the taps are still running and the dog's not been fed. It means not being found for days. It means dying with no meaning, dying alone, dying under the arc-lamps of a car-park somewhere in Bolton, dying of hepatitis and bad needles, dying of shock and hypothermia.

I've seen them, the families crazed with hopelessness and grief who literally beg for their husbands, fathers, wives, sisters, and mothers to be admitted to treatment. I often wonder why it is that many of these same families, who had once been on their knees with anxiety, end up saying, maybe a year later, 'I preferred you when you were drinking.' In that environment, what chance does anyone have?

The truth is, I think, that families, wives, husbands, and partners all, often, desperately want the addict to stop. They'd part with the family heirlooms, sell their pets into slavery, flog the Volvo, hock the mobile, anything just to get him to Stop. But very few realize that 'stopping' means fundamental change. To stay stopped is to stay in recovery, and that needs change, and work, too. Any fool can give up the booze for a week or a month, but that's not recovery, it's often desperation, blackmail, and fear. Recovery isn't about those things. It's about freedom, and freedom means choice, and choice means change. While they want the drunk to stop drinking, families and partners often don't want to acknowledge the need for subsequent change in recovery, and then comes the plaintive 'I preferred you when you were...'

The drinking, the using, is a known emotional landscape. Everyone positions themselves around that landscape in familiar patterns. The compass needle trembles to the terrible Pole, and another bottle. Meanwhile, disposed around magnetic North, are mothers, wives, husbands, aunts, uncles, and Uncle Tom Cobleigh. The positions are familiar, and therefore, safe. The same dispositions involve colleagues and friends. There are cover-ups, vital and meaningless promises, the urgency of desperation... And there's love, too, abundant as the compass, generous as geography.

For recovery to last, it has all got to change.

Meanwhile, what's the addict in early recovery actually thinking? I'll tell you what I still think. I'm absolutely terrified of being boring, of not being drunk and charming, of not living with excitement and danger, of not taking ultimate risks. The drinking life was chaos and it was disappointment, but I had the illusion of becoming, and I could choose to Be Interesting, even as I smelt like shit. The hit, the laughter, the illusion of being witty and in control, of being who I wanted to be and felt others wanted me to be... These were parts of the buzz, the becoming, the search, the pattern, the need. And so when people turn round and say 'I preferred [insert your own name here] the drunk' they're speaking to one absolute fear, and speaking out of ignorance, or cruelty, or both.

The truth is that the kind of love and stability I'm living is about as far from boring as the Antarctic is from Spitzbergen. It's interesting, it's constructive, it's funny, and I can write and live and have sex again in more radical and creative ways than I ever felt would be possible when I was Mr. Wonderful. The friendships, the fishing, the sustained joy are all real, too, and frankly I don't care too much if you think that putting in a few hours on this garden is Boring. I like it that way.

Other people's attitudes are killers. Whoever's reading this might, for a start, look to theirs – before they hide the gear or knock the drink out of someone's hand. Before any family, friend, or colleague asks or requires an addict to stop, let each one ask himself whether he's prepared to undertake all the changes another person's recovery might mean.

46.   23 October 2000

I guess that most people think of Holland, if they think of it at all, as a skyscape, tulips, and a brindled cow. Edam cheese and PSV Eindhoven might also come into the homely image of this part of the Low Countries, as might Amsterdam's red-light district and a passing windmill. While it's true that the Netherlands has cows and footballers, tulips, windmills, and dildos, to this addicted writer one of the most important things about the country is that is was formed from water. The Netherlands, in its present geographical form, wasn't always there. It has been reclaimed.

Until a few months ago I didn't know what a polder was. I didn't know what a ring-dyke was for, or how windmills were originally used. They're all parts of the process of land reclamation. Stimulated by catastrophe, the process of brilliant engineering has been going on here for a thousand years.

Close to where I'm writing is an area of the country called the Haarlemmermeer. Once you've disentangled the m's and r's, the etymology is the 'mere', the lake, of Haarlem. It was a huge inland sea until the middle of the last century, when its waters were slowly pumped away, first into a ring canal ('ringvaart'), and from there, via a circuit of canals, back into the sea. The splendidly named Ringvaart van de Haarlemmermeerpolder may be difficult to pronounce, but today, it sure as hell is full of fish. While the pike angling is world-class, the canal where I hurl plugs around on a weekend is also a triumph of security and reclamation.

A polder is an area of reclaimed land, distinguished as such by its network of parallel canals, all of which function as geographical safety valves. Centuries ago, before steam-powered pumps, windmills were used to lift water into the canals criss-crossing each polder. Nor was it simply farmers who benefited from this process. The whole community was involved in the effort. Better food meant longer life; longer life meant the development of corporate utilities. Municipalities, centred on towns, invested in the reclaimed land and of course, shared its bounty. Forget the bloody tulip fields. This was a kind of agrarian banking, born from the flood.

There were floods, catastrophes driving south and east from the North Sea, ungovernable swellings from the Rhine. Slowly, patiently, these inundations were mastered, in a system of earth-works, dykes, more polders, better drainage, barrages. Eventually, even the Zuider Zee was enclosed, and became today's IJsselmeer. Ocean trade came as a result to Amsterdam via the Noordzeekanaal, while boat traffic was re-routed from inland Europe to Rotterdam through the canals that link with the Maas. The result of this engineering genius is a modest, self-reliant, quiet, independent, and very beautiful country. It's one of the most densely populated countries in the world, and yet it's full of space and light. It quietly gets on with its own business. Despite, and because of, its burgher-like solidities and civic virtues, it feels weightlessly peaceful. It's one of the most surprising places I've ever lived.

In recovery, I keep being surprised. If anyone had told me I'd be spending the autumn in Amsterdam, and enjoying virtually every minute, I'd have told them they were talking double Dutch, whatever that is. Yet the truth is that I'm living in a landscape that is almost an analogue of recovery itself. If drinking was the flood, recovery is reclamation. It isn't some heroic *put-your-thumb-in-the-dyke-now* effort, but a measured, smiling, and peopled response to the fact of alcoholic danger. Beyond alcohol, the sea-bed, the rock-bottom, of personalities is recovered, reclaimed, put to new uses, in a kind of civic enterprise. Meanwhile, Mr. Wonderful becomes a strange and drying anemone, a creature whose proper past is the fossil record – even as his existence makes possible the process of reclamation itself.

I've confessed elsewhere that I'm terrified of being thought Boring. Nor do I want to invest this recovery with the kind of epic dignity that went into a part of Europe becoming Dutch. I'm merely an alcoholic man; I can't contain a nation. Nevertheless, what I'm surprised by is coincidence. Wiser alcoholic heads have often told me that in recovery, amazing things would happen, and these coincidences seem to bring just that kind of amazement: why is it, precisely at this moment of need, I'm like the very landscape I walk through? And why is it that against boredom I can set the image of the burgher, the free, independent mind among other independent minds, and not the boring bourgeois? And why, when I would have previously thought of the burgher as meat-fed, gullible, pliant, and conservative, do I feel so weightless, so free, so independent... And so happy?

47. 29 October 2000

I said in the last piece that I keep being surprised by strange events and coincidences. Coincidence has been much on my mind this year. Three months ago, for example, I caught a dead pike. I mean, I was fishing for pike, live pike, at the time, but I didn't expect the rod to bend in to a fish that, when 'landed', proved to have been dead for several odiferous days. The pike must have been floating about underwater, in hundreds of acres of fathom, until its posthumous transition to the daylight above Bassenthwaite. One dead pike; the Lake District; and a plug two inches long. The odds against this happening must be astronomical...but I have witnesses, and both of them were as coldly sober as the eyes of that unfortunate fish.

Then again, when Monika and I first arrived in Amsterdam nearly three months ago, we'd been invited to stay at a hotel on Jacob Obrechtstraat. This is one *straat*, and one hotel, among many thousands. During the past month, as I've been researching what AA meetings are available to English speakers in this city, I discovered that several meetings each week are held in the Jellinek Centre, whose location is on...Jacob Obrechtstraat. One street among thousands. Unless Monika's new employers have an unnerving and prescient sense of humour, this must be a coincidence...mustn't it?

Stranger still, you reach Jacob Obrechtstraat from here on a No. 5 tram, which runs up the very route we first took, by accident and the map, to reach the city centre. Follow the tram line from the Concertgebouw to Spui, and a hundred metres away is Nieuwezijds Voorburgwal, and another AA meeting place. (And of course it's apt that there's an AA meeting near the tram-stop at Spui, though the near-homophony is mercifully lost in Dutch.) The place you get off the tram here is exactly opposite the ticket office from which Monika bought her unexpected ticket to Manchester, the day of her job interview. One street among thousands; one office among tens of thousands. Call it a coincidence.

Curioser and curioser. The first time Monika ever came to this city, long before Mr. Wonderful had ever chanced her eye, she had dinner one evening with her father in a fish restaurant in Amstelveen. A month ago we had dinner at the same restaurant. It wasn't difficult to find, since it's a mere half a kilometre from where we now live.

Coincidence. I can understand the feelings of déjà vu, the knowledge that haunts you as you walk, the re-occurrence of a favourite number, the third railing, the lucky stone. I can understand the familiar when it takes place afresh in a familiar environment. Known structures; the glimpse of remembered opportunities. What I can't understand is coincidence when that's transposed across time zones, across countries, across meetings and decisions and all the minutiae that bring an unexpected future close, and make it newly strange, and strangely known.

It's not even some been-here-before feeling. Of course those intuitions exist, out of some backward of time called the collective unconscious, the residuals of choosing, relicts of sensation, the same old promptings of need and regret. This, now, is something quite different. If I didn't know better, and I'm not sure that I do, I'd think that each and every local decision I've ever taken has somehow clarified a future it couldn't see. The expensive schooling, the local hurts, the travelling, the work, the faces, voices, love affairs, music, the guilts, and all the bloody words have meant precisely This, this hurtling Now, and every instant, even to the longest instant ago, was all somehow preparatory to Now, and the choices Now entails.

I don't walk around feeling gloomy and deterministic, I'm afraid. The choices of Now are more compelling and interesting, and if time's arrow did mean me, it also meant you, and meaning us both, it meant multitudes. But if I do allow myself to think of coincidence, even down to that bizarre encounter with an ex-pike, I also know that a wiser head than mine once looked at the overlaps, the gestural loops, the patterns of recurrence and need, the dreams of broken hearts, and called coincidence by a more urgent name, that of *synchronicity*. I look at that pattern of becoming, and allow myself, for once, to feel surprised.

48.   2 November 2000

I've had a cold this week. As I write, the desk beside me is littered with nauseous residual tissues. My head's so thick that the fingers are likewise clumsy, all the letters get transposed, and I have to retype every third word. It's difficult to concentrate for more than ten minutes at a stretch, which of course is playing merry hell with the productive sabbatical I'm supposed to be having. It was going to be starry, original academic papers and Optimality Theory. It's turning out to be an overflowing waste-bin and Patricia Cornwell.

So what? It's only a cold. The problem is that *only-a-cold* has brought with it a vicious downer full of bad imaginations, a preoccupation with injustice and the past, a weary hopelessness with whatever future's walking towards the feeble present. I'm an alcoholic, I want to sob, pathetically...and nobody understands. Welcome to the usual demons of self-pity and remorse. I wish they could be driven away with one of those hot lemon drinks, and that I could curl up in the corner of an armchair with a bad book and a momentarily tamed, wicked cat. I wish I could feel clean.

I think that one of the difficulties here is that an alcoholic's body never forgets. One constant in alcoholism, for example, is the fact that if an alcoholic goes back to the bottle after one, two, ten, or twenty dry years – good years, recovery years – then the effect on their body is exactly as if they'd continued to drink alcoholically *and at the same or worse rate* for all those dry years. Nobody quite understands why this should happen. Only the body understands.

Perhaps what's happening here, in this vicious downer, is somehow related to the body's understanding. It remembers – God knows, how it does remember – the retching pain, the stomach's awful, queasy emptiness, the sleepless years of vodka and craziness, grief, shock, guilt, and the hopeless, teeming silence beyond grief and shock. Remembering these things, it connects its present and very minor illness with all the psychological consequences it's learnt to associate with any physical threat, however trivial. You thought this was *only-a-cold?* It's a kind of psychological warfare, and unwittingly, disastrously, you're battling yourself. And what's the easiest way for an alcoholic to take away the pain of the battle, to make sure the scars (which I've just mis-typed as *scares*) don't ache?

I rarely think about alcohol, the substance, though I think a great deal about my own and others' recovery. But I do know, I know sneakily, I know despite myself, I know so that I wish I could forget knowing, I know that there's a bottle of wine in a cupboard in this house. It's rather like knowing that there's a mouse in the room: all that empty, peaceful space, and yet you're fixated on a tiny and momentary movement. I'm fixated on a small bit of glass with some liquid inside it, and I'm fixated on it because I know that three goes at it would make all this nonsense feel a great deal better, and do so fast, certainly, warmly. Already I can feel the effects. You thought this was *only-a-cold?* What does an alcoholic do with any kind of pain or trouble, even a sniffle into a Kleenex?

I'm a coward, I think. Bad feelings, any bad feelings, have to be fixed: it doesn't matter if it's food, the turn of a jack, a shop and a credit card, the sinuous and brassy melodic lines of Wagner played at high volume, or the stuff in that bottle in the cupboard. I want those feelings fixed, and I want that now. Maybe, among other things, this helps to explain why it has always been that I've felt terminally horny whenever I've felt even vaguely ill: it's addiction, it's acting out, it's a fix. It's also possible that my fascination with poetry has come from the same source: it's not poetry and alcohol – I could never write a line when I was pissed – but the sick, compelling violence of whatever need the hangover leaves behind. *Dr. McCully is unwell; Mr. Wonderful's writing another sonnet.*

God knows what the alternatives are. I've tried, this morning, to get out of bed and take trouble shaving. I've tried to concentrate on some meditative reading. I'm trying to write this, through all the frustrations of typing glitches and a brain that seems to have been coated in phlegm. I'm trying to remind myself that, whatever happens, today I won't have a drink, however bad the day or the feelings might become. And as for the past, it's simply standing there, like an unopened bottle in a kitchen cupboard. Its mere presence informs today, and gives today a kind of structure, but nevertheless, I have both to acknowledge that, and let it go. All the same, though I'm cut off from these homely remedies absolutely, I could absolutely murder a large hot whisky and a bottle of drowse-inducing Benylin…even though I couldn't taste a drop of either.

49.   2–7 November 2000

I was thinking about poetry. The fact is that I wrote verse continually for twenty-five years. If someone had asked me what I thought, deep down, I was put on the surface of this hot, abandoned rock to do, I'd have mumbled 'poetry'. With two collections indifferently dropped into an indifferent world, and with another masterpiece appearing from the same excellent publisher soon, poetry is Something I Do. I've also been known, occasionally, to Do It pretty well. If someone asked me to write a double sestina on the theme of recently purchased garden tools, they'd get their commission…and it would be good. Even beyond the mechanical fluency, even I see that some of the work has merited its reviewers' labels, its [modest English cough] international prizes, though I also know that the often-used word 'integrity' also means 'death to sales'.

I wrote verse. Past tense. The last poems I put together sprang messily from the drinking parts of the end of 1999, from August through October. One long-ish poem (and reader, don't get too moist, but it was a proper, formal ode) I wrote over 48 hours while drinking in two bars in San Francisco. Another was a fragment of terza rima I began and ended on a scrap of paper in a pub called something like The Golden Balls somewhere in Manchester. Both were recently published: they're immaculately polished pieces of writing. Nor did I work on either piece while I was drunk. As the lines went down, unrevised because unrevisable and perfect, I was beginning to drink, or I was hungover. Both are states of terrible lucidity. In common with many of the finest writers I've ever known, I could never write a decent line while the content was singing with ethanol. And in common with my peers, I've often looked over the lines composed that way and been horrified in the morning. Someone should write a hangover poem, to a blues rhythm, called 'Just what the fuck is *that?*'. Now I think of it, Samuel Taylor Coleridge tried this, as he tried so much else, and called his minor effort 'Kubla Khan'. I blame Pepper, the dog…and all its hairs.

It wasn't just the hangovers. Illness, however slight, seemed to bring the lines to birth. Distance, travelling, weariness, outrage, change: they all, always, brought poems in their wake, and what a wake it was. I could no more get through each day without writing a line or two, translating a phrase or two, revising, tinkering, than I could get through the same span without a drink. It wasn't real or imaginary pain, happiness, loneliness, ambition, or even other poems that made me write. It was all the above, plus the hangover. The hangover was the key. To treat the hangover was to act out, and acting out was another poem, rapidly followed by another vodka, which just about allowed me sufficient time and steadiness to correct any mechanical flaws in the preliminary effort. Verse-making was an attempt to treat addictive symptoms. I was lexically, syntactically, and often metrically administering the course of a different kind of illness. Another slug; another verbal fix; another steady correction in the process of abandonment and fatality.

It can't be accidental that as I put down the vodka, I appear to have put away the poetry. I have put by the addictive human relationships, too. I still read, and read avidly, but the reading habits have changed, into a preference for the key works of humanism (Dante, Montaigne, Erasmus), or the measured intricacies and civilities of Virgil. And of course I continue to analyse this stuff, together with Germanic verse-form(s) and the histories, linguistic and cultural, behind the evolution of poetries. Perhaps there's still a kind of service I can do, and perhaps, some teaching I could undertake. But for all the prose I manage, including this unreliable memoir, I can't write a line.

Something very profound has happened to the structure of the imagination. Civil, ironic, humorous, I have become, or seem to be becoming, a bill-paying citizen, someone who rakes leaves, washes the car, and hangs out with the easier bits of self-assembly furniture. I try to justify this to myself by attempting to find a workable distinction between the burgher (smiling, responsive, articulate, worldly, tolerant, and responsible) and the bourgeois (self-interested, self-absorbed, humourless, white, and probably American). I fail, with both burgher and bourgeois. I'm utterly and miserably aware that something, and it's something called recovery, is keeping me from the most profound sources of creativity and disturbance. The vision, the compelling way in which fragments of seeing and hearing would speak to each other, the need to express, the ambition, the pride, the way a line fell inevitably right, and all the dislocated happiness of that form of making… These are, these seem to be, no more. Despite the assurances of friends that the Absent Muse (ha!) will return in triumph, and soon, I know beyond their, and beyond all, knowing that without alcohol, I may never write another decent line. And this in turn leaves me wondering what all the fuss and all the writing was all about. Was it just some infantile form of verbal need? Does writing come from the childhood of the race, with all its violence, integrity, and freshness? Was I merely trying to fill the void of anxiety and headaches with structures I could compose into my own implacable and disconsolate shapes? Was the poetry, at its dis-eased root, simply a substitute for another drink? Perhaps. It's all the country of Perhaps, where Mr. Wonderful is drunk again with words.

Put down the alcohol, put away the verse. It's like losing a sense, a method of orientation, a means of seeing. In my often unacknowledged but deepest and most secret heart of frantic hearts, I want to drink again in order to write out of that sick and compelling violence. I want the woman, the chaos, the notoriety, the never-forthcoming money. Part of me despises this burgher-like, ironic, and polite alternative where everyone is some kind of civil expedience and where useless pleasantries are traded over the garden fence as if they mean peace, and security, and happiness. 'Good fences make good neighbours'? Good fences mean boredom, bucolic safety, an evening with Scrabble, and someone from, God help us, Wales. Writing, by which I mean writing poems, brought on a solitary, savage, and reckless joy, and although I'm surrounded by different kinds of joy, some of them quite new, I miss that primal sense of becoming, and miss it continually, however I contrive to be differently creative within the civilized boundaries of a recovered life. Perhaps I was mistaken, all my adult days. Perhaps I was wrong about writing. Perhaps the poems, for all the training and discipline, were as pre-pubescent, as thoughtless, as instinctive, as the vodka, and came from the same awful source. I know I was Mr. Wonderful, that bastard, but I miss his reckless brilliance, I miss the words, the laughter, the structures that went 'click', the compulsion, the reading, the pride... And I miss the fractured, truthful understanding of the years of words. The truth is that missing these things, and knowing they may never come again, I'm frightened, and lost, for all the love, the recovery, and the second-hand analysis. I'm still alive, true, but it sometimes feels like being only half-alive, in some weird dream of soup and ironing, and unlike Mr. Wonderful, I don't have a ready answer to the question 'What are you for?'

I remember the process. Often enough, it would begin with another poem, some finagling excitement, something akin to anxiety. It was an anxiety to put right, to set unchangeably in order. It was seeking after per-manence, a perfect, cold, hard, clear structure, something inescapable, with edges and corners and closures. Doing this, attempting this, was a form of self-justification that became a habit. If I could do that, maybe I wasn't the shambling mess of might-have-beens that couldn't even please their own childhood. Writing was a form of ever-renewable relationship, inevitable, necessary. The turn of a good line was like turning a street corner and finding the smiling, vital face of a lover. Yes, of course this sounds fanciful; if it sounds pretentious, you've never been there. Imagine walking out of your expensive patio doors (IKEA self-assembly, flat-pack furniture, double glazing extra) into some kind of steel garden, burnished in the sunlight, blue in the moonlight, vivid with meaning and conquest, blazing darkly with all the poisons of happiness and reciprocity. Every-thing here connects; everything speaks to everything else; bizarre streaks of rain fall like light, and the falling, the sense of intimate distance, is inevitable, vital, appropriate. And this is where I want to be, falling, awake, aware, and *making*, out of history and anger, also called time. This place is where I know how to be, even as time passes as if it's been bereaved, and there are shadows of clouds, and dissolving fragments of faces and voices that have turned or are turning into time and rain, and the stricken sun-dial is streaked with Roman, chosen, implacable, and unreadable writing, or the further shadow of a lifted, and greeting, hand. Out of necessity and damage, we made language in this time out of time, and it was very beautiful. But we needed, and some of us still need, to be there. *Here* is a compound alloy, the pewters, rusts, and bed-linens of the *burgerij*; here is the rustle of misery in the bedroom curtains, here is the inhaler and the catalogue on the living-room chair, here is the hot water bottle, the cheque, the one-stir instant soup, and the morphine.

And then there were the drafts, the re-drafts, the hopeless quest for perfection, for the line to be right, for the image to be multiply resonant, the stanza to be open or closed. And I always asked myself, at every uncertain step, could this be put any other way? Is it inevitable as it should be? What is it asking? What does it want? What does it need? I could please the emerging structure of a poem even though I could never, apparently, please any of the structures of real life. I could become its instrument, and only I could be useful. There was a kind of power in this, called hunch, awareness, a form of flawed brilliance. I would back my knowledge of, and instincts about, writing against that of this year's – or any other year's – Nobel laureate. It came out of effort, reading, the cerebral shocks of literate discovery. It was almost perfect. I'm not stupid enough to believe that every outcome was flawless, but the processes of writing verse involved almost the central, most difficult, and most absorbing relationship of my working life. I would look at a manuscript of my own poems, sheets of paper torn out of time and need, and think that this, and this alone, was what I was for. It was a careering excitement modulated by words; it was all momentary want pressed into the service of a structure; and since the paper and ink endured, in journals, in archives, singing inevitably and forever into other people's heads, it was the illusion of nothing less than immortality. *So long lives this, and this gives life to thee.*

You scoff. Yet I'm writing the truth. It's the more true because it's grandiose, it's absurd in any human terms. And the absurdity is that I was trying to find a relationship where there was none. The bottle doesn't exist to form a relationship, and at the deepest levels, the poem doesn't live to form a relationship *with its maker*: having had, having used up, the instants of its making, it exists thereafter only to be consumed. At this level, the level of consumption, there's little difference between the addictive writing of a poem or an alcoholic drinking from a bottle of vodka. In both, there's the illusion of relationship, when in truth, both – perhaps, all – are commodities. They fix feelings. Addicts finish a bottle, and want the next. It's something they do, because it's something they are. Thus poets, even failed poets, with their fatal, inglorious, vibrant, and necessary words. And poets and addicts will do anything, anything whatsoever, in order to sustain the relationships that *to them* are the most profound of their unspeakable and ungovernable lives. One of the tragedies of verse-making is that any society, in order to be a society and not a collection of psychopaths, needs that creative and singing insanity in order to remember itself, and in remembering, to define itself. Plato didn't see shadows on the wall of the cave: he saw the odious, affirming penumbra of human creativity. Unreliable, evanescent, chaotic. A narrative written by smoke. Writing out of this awareness is like bringing back perfectly structured reports from all the smoky, dripping cerebral mess that has ever existed. Poets have been urgently awake since the fontanelles were soft. Legislators of the first conscious world, they define the present, and the yet to come, down to the last slurred syllable of recorded time.

Failed poet. D'you have any idea what merely typing these words is like? I look into the teeming, messy, and hurtful past and find failure spread over it like the stains of red wine spilt ineradicably on a living-room carpet. As a husband, I failed. As a lover, reader, writer, colleague, and friend, I failed. As a thinker and analyst, I failed, though I was maybe good enough to write a textbook or two… I was a generalist, an intellectual butterfly, restless, talented, too ambitious for his own good. I was an addict, and I still am. Perhaps, since I'm still, perilously, in recovery, I'm a failed addict. I couldn't even do that with grounded, burgher-like conviction. I'm sick of myself…and despite syntactic appearances, I'm also sick of starting every fucking clause with the fucking first-person pronoun.

If there has been a profound change in the structure of the imagination, or at least, in how that imagination manifests itself, it may be that I have to adjust my own attitudes to writing and to 'creativity'. I sense, somewhere, that there may be a way of handling recovery in, or better, through verse, but it will be an instrument of exile, defeat, and humour. It may be sardonically civil, viciously funny. It may be built out of clear-eyed satire and the demotic guilts. It will aspire to the condition of prose. And it will never be what I could or should have written, but it will be something. It may be something.

I may never write that Could and Should ever again. I have to face this, as I have to face my own wrongs. I feel sometimes completely hunted, as if I've turned and am finally at bay. Actaeon. Myth has power because it is invention about truth. I saw the nakedness and terror, the shadow and the rain-streaks on the sun-dial, the purity and destruction of sheer beauty, and I'm being torn apart now by my own creatures. Memory, desire, need. Would I be able to write that failing masterpiece, one last, one almost-final, one great, lasting structure if I had the help of ethanol? Sickness and clarity: give me a hangover, and I'll give you the best words, in the best, unthinkable, inevitable, and fatal order. Before I finally slip into unconsciousness...something perfect, unshakeable, something that will live in your head forever, and despite ourselves?

'God grant me the serenity to accept the things I cannot change...' Oh, please. I'm not serene. What? To accept the failures, the lack of known forms of creativity and compensatory illusion? I have to stay sober if I want to stay alive, and these...consequences, together with the words you've just read, include my deepest fears.

50.   8 December 2000

It's been a year. A year ago I was poured, or poured myself, into a taxi, assisted by my ex-wife. Three hours later and I'd been diagnosed – again – as a chronic alcoholic; another hour or two and a patient Iranian houseman was taking my blood pressure and administering the first in a series of anti-death Smarties. Life and work were in chaos. Friendships, peace, family, and love were in ruins. I'd hung off the mountain for so long that I had no fingernails left. I think another day or two would have meant the extinction of Mr. Wonderful, and he would have taken Chris with him. It was as close as that. At the time, I didn't care.

I need to find the words for gratitude, and they won't quite come. I sit here in front of this bloody computer, surrounded by peace, and some precious stability, and a love I didn't expect, and instead of the thank-you the day and the hour merits, I just feel empty, and slightly sick, and angry that no one is here to pat me on the back, give me a certificate, and tell me it's the Best Recovery they've ever seen. I would also very much like someone, anyone, to tell me that I'm cured, so that I can celebrate with Dr. Vodka over the glass that cheers, and go down as Mr. Wonderful in all the annals of medical science.

I'm used to, and I have even worked to deserve, at least some of the glittering prizes. The starry first-class degree, the doctorate, the shy smile at the awards ceremony, the congratulations turned away with a squint of false self-deprecation... I can do that stuff. I can also do the coming home afterwards and framing the certificate, or placing the trophy plinth somewhere visible on top of the piano. Oh, look: the gongs of Success, the ribbons of praise.

It's all nonsense.

Last night I went to one of the warm, messy, wonderful AA meetings here in Amsterdam. Ostensibly, I had gone, on the eve of this first birthday, to say the appropriate Thank-Yous. But deep down I knew I'd gone simply to be congratulated. There, once more and yet once more, was the big *I Am*, the Mr. Wonderful ego, coextensive merely with the size...well, shall we say the size of a non-trivial continent? I said as much, feeling ashamed of my own squalid self-centredness. And d'you know what those good people, those good friends, did? They broke into applause anyway, while I was feeling so selfish and wretched. A group of drunks. And each one of them, whether on a month's or twenty-five years' sobriety, was a fucking miracle. I could have cried – and but for the terrible training of an English stiff upper lip, I would have done. Group Of Drunks. What d'you think the letters G-O-D stand for, anyway?

There are no medals, no certificates, no gongs, and the ribbons of Success are just society's tatters. Today's a day like any other, but it's filled with all the surprises of Now. All those Nows have made up the most remarkable year, a year of coincidence, and listening, and change. Almost despite myself, I've travelled to different continents, and seen them. I have worked in five different countries, and even been paid for it. Somehow, the words have come out, have been produced as well as I can make each piece. And they have been done pretty much on time. I have used this sabbatical to catch up on some necessary writing projects and books as well as on some even more necessary rest and sleep. There has been some teaching and some new responsibility. And above all, there has been love – surprising, generous, warm, real, grounded love. For an addict, recognizing this is possibly the most difficult part of the process of re-integration. You don't trust the love, particularly when it's offered for nothing: they can't, he can't, she can't mean you, you're not worth it, if only they knew, it won't last, it will, it won't, I am... The baleful litany of a mind and spirit that learnt so radically to mistrust themselves.

Not drinking has been the easy part. The horrifying shock comes as I continue to discover how all the addictive patterns had slowly configured around the fact of the bottle. It's these, the Gordian knots of self-absorption and manic energy, that are so hard to unravel. And along with the painstaking unravelling, there's also been loss – loss of faces and voices, loss of verse-making, the loss of friends. There's grieving in this as well as joy. I have tried to put right what I can. And some things I am learning I can never put right.

No medals, no certificate. But a face and voice I'm coming to love ever more closely, and a crazy family I'm beginning, clumsily, to rediscover. Some great fishing, some teaching and writing, some peace and quiet, a little bit of truth, laughter, and self-respect... I'm still alive, with a measure of hope, a sense of humour, and all the choices of Now. The other stuff... Thanks, but you can keep it.

51.   18 December 2000

I don't know whether you've ever been on a Hull to Rotterdam ferry while it was in the grip of hurricane force winds, but it's not altogether an experience I'd recommend. Walking back from the restaurant, past the signs to the Sunset Lounge ('entertainment cancelled'), was eerily like being drunk, as the boat veered and ducked into the teeth of a south-westerly from hell. Still, I had been there before. My name is Chris, and I'm a professional alcoholic.

In the first year of recovery, the theory goes, you shouldn't try to change too much. House, family, job... As you were, if you can. Take it easy, take things steadily, have patience.

I didn't quite get it right. I have tried to do too much, and this past week has seen a partial relocation, from the UK to this surprising and beneficent country. This is why Monika and I were on the inbound ferry yesterday. Other people take their honeymoon cruises to Venice. We held hands in the rain on the way to Rotterdam, and there was a double futon strapped to the roof of a Mazda.

No one was waving, since there was no one to say goodbye.

I'm lucky that the university think this plan is workable. And the plan is to remain in post, Monday through Thursday each week, while Fridays, most weekends, and every university vacation I aim to spend here in Amstelveen. This will involve a fierce amount of travelling, and I'll have to be fit, mobile, and wired to a laptop. It will also involve money spent on airline tickets – but what I save on rent and utilities in the UK should more than cover that (the theory goes), and the new, planned life should allow more working time as well as time for rest and relaxation (the theory goes).

I can work a 50-hour week. Come to that, I can work an 80-hour week, and I often have done. But I guess the trick here is to find something sustainable. If I work too hard, like the rest of the addicted world I get tired, depressed, moody. And what does an alcoholic do with excessive tiredness? Exactly. So the working life has to be planned: nothing too ferocious, nothing excessive, nothing too much. Just some teaching, some research, some administration; two books to finish; half a dozen papers to complete; some editing work; a couple of international conferences; a new degree programme… It's more than enough.

I'm still worried about the changes. I don't really want this life to blur past in a series of anxieties, airport lounges, and expensively avoided optics. I'd rather grasp, however slowly, at all the moments and connections that make up Now. At the same time, I'm haunted by a partially wasted past, by the wreckages of ambition and professional trust, and I want, I need, to catch up. (I grind teeth as I write.) The terrible truth is that I can only catch up slowly. All this reconstruction is going to take time, and time takes patience, and patience is a virtue I have never learnt…until the enforcing, difficult lessons of Now.

Impatience is a threat to recovery. As any addict will tell you, addiction is a fix of feelings, and the fix is necessary *at this instant.* 'I want it done, and I want it now' could be written on a million tombstones. And I find myself getting irritable with how slowly the reconstruction is moving – irritable with Monika, with friends, with colleagues. I want them to see it my way, to pull their fingers out, to be the exact analogues of, and answers to, the need I feel at the present moment. God knows where I learned this kind of behaviour – or from whom. Still, I think I can guess.

At the same time, I also know that the plans are real, and grounded, and lucky. It doesn't matter if anyone sees them as slow, or average, or mediocre. Average and mediocre are words that belong to other people's opinions, and they're welcome to think what they like. Nothing too much, patience… These attributes are very different from the ceaseless and restless grandiosity of Mr. Wonderful, who was working and drinking through his crazy, driven 80-hour weeks. Now I can no longer afford them. I can no longer afford him.

This, also, is very well, because as I write, the former house in Manchester stands empty, gathering dust and money and expecting some hapless new tenant. The ferry plies from Hull to Rotterdam and back again, and there are no tear-stained handkerchiefs and no farewells. There's only a bored, unemployed docker and a squall of seagulls with something better to do than to watch the absurd posturings and all too real illusions of Mr. Wonderful, who as of this moment is of No Known Address.

52.   4 January 2001

Addicts fear Christmas and the New Year. At this juncture between old and new, between parting and resolution, there are both the memories of drinking and fixing – memories of the parties, the posturings – and the immanence of change. Both are opportunities for using, and offer the familiar illusions of promise.

At the same time, there are families and contacts, with all their moments of misunderstandings, resentments, and mute hostility. Why was she like that? Why does she…? Can't they…? And what about…?

Even when Christmas and the New Year have come and gone, and as the fireworks go sodden in January's gardens, then comes another danger

– complacency. 'Well, I got through all that, even my mother's visit,' says the dry drunk, clutching onto the chair with a set of white knuckles. 'Must be okay now. I think I've deserved one for the belated bloody New Year…' Mr. Wonderful spits the party ribbons from his mouth while staring at a balloon – a glass one, full of leftover cooking brandy.

Complacency can be – in my case, it is – accompanied by resentment that I Wasn't Invited. People don't invite Mr. Wonderful to the party any more because these good, well-meaning people know that Mr. Wonderful is on the wagon and other clichés, that he's gone serious and threatens to be preachy or disapproving, he's not the same man, he's no fun. Thanks, folks. Sometimes I feel like Mr. Bean, posting his own Christmas cards through his own front door, finding them with a forced smile and a rictus of feigned surprise. No invitations this year? *Poor me. Poor me. Pour me a drink.*

I have been through one other Christmas, New Year, and birthday almost dry, back in 1998. I drank on the night of my fortieth, then stopped again until early March. Then I was ready for a drink, came out of retirement – or so I put it to myself and anyone who would listen – and not only alienated and insulted my dearest and oldest friends, but was arrested for drunk driving the same night.

Last year, I was dry because I was in hospital, undergoing treatment for chronic alcoholism, watching the millennium fireworks from bed, feeling sick.

This year, I have had to go it alone, in the pages of the Big Boy's Book of Recovery, and not quite alone, because there has been plenty of merciful, graceful contact with other addicts.

I can only tell you what it's like, and the things I try to do.

There has to be the feeling that today is just a day like any other floating island of 24 hours. Since it's like any other day, it's not a day off – there are no days off in recovery – and there are the normative small disciplines of reading and meditation.

There has to be contact with other addicts. This means the phone, making and receiving calls. And it means keeping up attendance at whatever after-care or AA group you've chosen, or been chosen by.

There has to be real communication with the people around you. This may mean simply saying, 'Look, this is what I'm trying to achieve today.'

It may mean forward planning, being complicit, creative, and adventur-
ous in allowing yourself to find a polite escape route from a social
function or one of those bloody awful parties.

There may have to be minor change. I don't think, for example, that I
could spend Christmas dry in my own house without rearranging the
furniture or the pictures from the way they were when I was last pissed
there, last Christmas. I need the smallest of new perspectives; I need to
feel cleaner. And I don't think I can or should spend three days slumped
by God-awful television with a bag of chips and a box of suspect chocolates.

This year, despite the ice and snow, I worked in the garden with a
chainsaw, and transformed the view; planned some spring planting in the
same garden; kept in touch with recovering friends. I wrote to each
member of the family, and sometimes told some of them explicitly that I
loved them and hoped we could get to know each other better. I tried to
find hope, and told myself that the faith I needed to get through each day
wasn't a matter of *Why?* but a matter of *How?*.

How could I be a better…? How could I sustain…? How could I let
go…?

It wasn't easy, and it sounds serious and high-minded, put like this.
There has also been laughter, failure, mess. But I know surely, and feel
surely, that in this life there are people who love the reality of the mess
that happens to be me. And there – not in the Why? of alcoholism, but in
the How? and the Here of recovery – there is some kind of feeling of
homecoming, even if it's a homecoming that will mean another set of
departures, and their consequences.

But those are for tomorrow. Today, I merely wish us, including
myself, a happy, peaceful, and connected year.

53.   4 January 2001

When my prospective mother-in-law let slip that she thought alcoholism
was 'a weakness' it was a cue for hyper-sensitivity to kick in. What she
had actually meant was that in her view, alcoholism was a *Schwäche*. This
translates as 'a partiality for, a soft spot for…'. But I didn't hear 'partial-

ity'. I had heard instead: 'You are a weak-willed lush, and I'm horrified
that you're marrying my daughter.'

She visited a couple of days ago, and during the progress of the afternoon asked me what it was like to go through the holidays without
drinking. Since it was a serious question, it drew a serious, and no doubt
an overlong, response. It was during the course of this that she let fall her
view that alcoholism was 'a weakness'.

At first I thought she was being ironic. It's the kind of thing Jud
would tease me with, while shooting a meaningful smile and a wink.
Then I began to construct a bizarre dialogue in which I had been accused
not merely of *Schwäche*, a weakness, but of character deficiency. I add here
that I had heard nothing of this dialogue: I simply made it up, out of
panic, fear, and epic touchiness. Matters became worse when she an-
alogized my *Schwäche* with her weakness for chocolates – but of course,
she can these days have just one or two chocolates, and then choose to
stop. That was quite a reasonable thing to say, but I hadn't actually heard
what was said. I had heard 'my self-control is fairly perfect, yours isn't;
you're a weak-willed lush, and I'm horrified…'. And so on. My touchiness – amounting to paranoia – construed something entirely well-
meaning as nothing less than a deep-level accusation.

Like any other recovering addict, I'm used to handling other people's
attitudes to alcoholism, which range from the miraculous to the ignorant.
These attitudes are entirely outside my control, under every normal circumstance, and usually I don't take much notice, since I'm too busy with
all the Hows of today's recovery. It's not easy to maintain this…this…it's
not indifference, it's a studied neutrality. I'm so keen for people to like me,
and to applaud and approve everything I do, that critical or unthinking
opinions can hurt, however momentarily, until I regain the neutrality that
comes from the realization of powerlessness. But my prospective mother-
in-law's attitude cut deep. If she thinks this about alcoholism, I reasoned
(with the entire lack of reason that my paranoia was encouraging), then
what must she think about the fact that her daughter has chosen to marry
an alcoholic? I also felt that for her to express such an opinion in this
house was…intrusive. Guests, in the Alcoholics' Book of Total Perfection, shouldn't behave like that. By now I was walking on stilts, ready to

get onto the high horse. Then I went inwards, into a silent anger that poisoned my forty-third birthday.

I am ashamed of myself.

I know that I can't afford to hang on to any kind of resentment. If there has been any single factor in recovery that has been ultimately difficult, it's this, the letting go of real or imagined hurt – and this incident fell very much into the category of 'imagined'. A need to be approved holds hands with an intense and destructive over-sensitivity. It's this combination that broods, until it's exhausted, defeated, drunk.

I slept on it, uneasily. If the anger was gone in the morning, I'd apologize simply for being distant and 'having things on my mind'. But the anger wasn't gone, and I didn't want – couldn't afford – to retreat into polite half-truths. Behind the anger, there was also (paranoia told me) the fatal hint of power-playing. My prospective mother-in-law is what the world would call a strong woman, someone used to being In Control, and I don't think I was emotionally unreasoning to sense someone else's need for control in this context.

Well, I was quite wrong.

I can count on the fingers of one hand the times in my life when I've sat down and said, 'Look, this hurt me.' It's something I find almost impossibly difficult. If I have ever done it, I've done it heatedly. This helps no one. I resolved, shaking inside, to sit down and point out, as calmly as possible, that this 'weakness' remark hurt. It hurt not because I found her attitude to addiction wrong – whether I found it right or wrong was irrelevant – but because it coded another feeling she'd never talked about, and that was how she felt about her daughter marrying one of these 'weak' people. I tried to stay as calm as possible, and acknowledged the truth – that I was powerless to govern, alter, or affect her opinions in any way. I could only live recovery. But that wasn't to say that I didn't find other people's judgements hurtful sometimes.

Her reaction, which was thoughtful, and generous, made me feel all the more ashamed of my own destructive touchiness, particularly where these involve alcoholism… More truthfully, perhaps, 'particularly where these involve *my* alcoholism'.

I don't know whether I should have acted in the way I have acted. For two days I have had to work, every hour, and sometimes every minute, on my own powerlessness over alcohol and over other people, since it is, as always, this acceptance which holds the keys to continued recovery.

There is a problem here, though, a real problem. In early recovery, addicts who have been lucky enough to obtain treatment and counselling will have been taught, as I was, that there is no conceivable way in which alcoholism can be a 'weakness' or 'partiality'. It is a condition that is unchosen, progressive, and often fatal. Yet, emerging into the real world beyond treatment and counselling, addicts will find that even people close to them may well hold, and express, the view that alcoholism is exactly the weakness they, the addicts, were told it wasn't.

If other people think alcoholism is 'a weakness', so be it. Persuasion, power, argument, reason – the intellectual arts that I am so accomplished in, that have so often betrayed me – are of no conceivable use here. The only interesting and sustainable attitudes are those belonging to the truth, and those I have to get on with living, hour by hour, without approval – even the approval of people whose love and respect I would dearly wish to have.

Then again, I can't get recovery on approval, since I haven't hired it from anywhere or anyone in order to give it back.

54.   9 January 2001

It was somewhere in Arnhem – a dim-lit Indonesian restaurant just off a dull town square – that I realized the dangers of liqueur chocolates. One came, wrapped in foil, with a pre-emptive cup of coffee. It looked innocent enough. I unwrapped it, I was starving, I bit. My mouth filled with neat brandy at exactly the point when Monika said, 'Look, sweetheart, don't you think that might have alcohol...' I spat the whole lot into a passing tissue. '...in it?' Since then I've been careful about what I eat, and about what we buy. Or rather, and more truthfully, I've borrowed Monika's habitual care.

The same problem showed up when I tried to buy Jud a quarter of expensive chocolates from one of those chi-chi handmade-chocolate shops somewhere in Cheadle. As an afterthought, and when the bag had been almost filled with soft centres, I asked whether any of these luscious bites had alcohol in them. It turned out that even innocuous-sounding pieces – Lemon Crème, Belgian Fondant Fancy – had been laced with booze. You wouldn't have guessed from the names alone. I would have been handing Jud relapse as a gift. You may think 'only a minor relapse', but in this game there's no minor relapse. You might as well claim that there's such a thing as a minor Ace of Spades, or a minor lie. To take alcohol in any form knowingly into one's system is a grave mistake, the black and disastrous card. It's an invitation to self-deception.

On my forty-third birthday my lovely sister had sent a food hamper of sorts. In it was an individual piece of crisply white-iced birthday cake. It looked wonderful. Then I looked at the ingredients. The raisins had been soaked in rum. True, all the alcohol had probably been baked out of them, but they would taste of booze, and the taste of booze is like the taste of lying. Sooner or later, and probably sooner, it's poison.

I can only write about what I do now. I have learnt to steer clear of most forms of alcohol, in whatever form it comes. Here's a list of everyday shopping items, courtesy of the last three months, and supermarkets in both the UK and the Netherlands, each of which may contain some form of alcohol: *cakes, chocolates; pâtés; ice creams* and *desserts,* especially *frappés; certain kinds of soup* (some are finished with sherry); *wine vinegars; rich, flambed sauces and gravy; boeuf Bourgignon; cocktail sauces* (e.g. bottled prawn cocktail sauce); *bottled salad dressings.*

If you keep stuff in the fridge forever, *fruit juice,* once it's turning bad, makes naturally fermented alcohol.

Then there are the personal hygiene items: *mouthwash, aftershave, body spray...*

And there are very many forms of *cough medicine* and *cold cures* that contain alcohol – sometimes more alcohol than you might expect, up to 23 per cent. No wonder I used to love the drowsy semi-smashed feeling of having a residual bad chest. Hot whisky and lemon? England Expectorates, so make mine a treble, and pass the lung-syrup.

In fairness to the supermarkets and chocolate-makers, you can easily obtain alcohol-free substitutes. But often you have to look carefully at the small print on the label, or worse, you have to ask. This curdles me with embarrassment, and I don't quite know how to do it. Do I tell the truth (the bare-faced 'I'm an alcoholic'), or do I resort to the kind of minor lying I wouldn't normally allow myself ('it's for a sick friend')? Usually I compromise, and ask via a justifiable manipulation of the truth: I'm allergic to alcohol in any form, so please could you check? You may, one time in a hundred, get a knowing look in return, but the chances are then that you're looking back at another alcoholic, who's heard and used the 'allergic' line themselves.

The 'allergic to alcohol' tactic is also useful at parties among strangers. Most people don't understand, and don't want to understand, alcoholism, and I'm not really interested in answering badly put and insincere questions about it. On the other hand, most people understand the word 'allergy', and it's a word that's neutral enough to deflect further questions. It also involves the curiosity and phlegm-like sympathy that the word 'illness' might generate. Besides, I *am* allergic to alcohol; it's a metaphor that practises on fact.

I have sometimes wondered whether to tell doctors, hospitals, and dentists that I'm an alcoholic. My doctor knows, since CHRONIC ALCOLHOLIC is written for all time, in shaky capitals, across my notes. How that has rankled – you can tell it's rankled, because it's the third or fourth time I've mentioned it. But hospitals? Maybe the most appropriate moment of disclosure comes at the point of admission, when you're asked about your religious beliefs.

Faith? *Recovering alcoholic.*

55.   11 January 2001

I'm trying to identify what's wrong. Something is amiss. I woke up yesterday and had dreamed of murder. There was a body cut up in a suitcase, and somehow my life would be hunted down, changed forever from the calm look of today into hurtling instants of cries and malevolence. I recognized that feeling of guilt and shock only too well, and knew again that 'normal' life is just the thinnest of veneers on a different, far more savage kind of underlying reality.

I have missed even the veneer, the welcoming reality of passing time, and the days pulse with difficulty and technical failures. I don't seem to be joined to the hours. I'm either living through the remorse and problems of the past (sometimes, of the very far past), or agonizing over the real or imagined errors and difficulties of next week, the week after that, and the whole coming year. Will we actually get married? How will we stump up the mortgage for this apartment? Where will we go on our honeymoon? Do we really have to organize all this for everyone else...and for each other? Tomorrow, and tomorrow, and tomorrow.

Life's not helped by the fact that I'm shortly due back to work in the UK. The sabbatical is coming to an end, and with it, the relatively peaceful days of writing and reconstruction. I can tell from e-mails that as the academic pace picks up once again after the winter break, the tensions in the department are also building up. They're as palpable as the pressure in a tyre. There's so much, always, to be done that I can feel my body clench as it anticipates the shocks, the weariness of travelling, trains, faces, briefing papers. Everything takes too long, no one seems to know what they're supposed to be doing, the students complain, colleagues complain, I complain. Grudge, resentment, remorse: it's a culture of fear. Facing it once more, I'm filled with nothing short of panic, and dangerous energy. Nor can I say 'This too shall pass'. The pressures and the deadlines don't pass. They seem to increase.

I have often wondered whether to change my job. I say this to myself with the utmost reluctance, because I've been privileged to work with some of my colleagues, and have been lucky to have had the chances I've had. I've loved a great deal of my work, and it's been a real love, even through the over-identification with the department's problems, the problems of British Higher Education themselves, and the mysteries of getting the system to work at all. But perhaps it is time for a change. Perhaps I'm simply not strong enough to face down all the present challenges. But perhaps, also, this is sheer cowardice, and pathetically, I want to run away and hide, probably in the nearest passing bottle of Wonderful. Instead of this abjection, why don't I simply refuse to think of myself as the powerless and worthless object of friends and co-workers? I must alter some attitudes. Powerless over 'Work', this at least is in my power.

What's the right course? How do I ease the troubled sleep and the terrible dreams? How do I live with myself peacefully today?

I have prioritized. I've made the high-pressure lists, and the most important and troubling items are listed first. One such To Do list runs to a full side of A4 file-paper, and today, I can just about get through point No. 1. Everything takes longer than I expect, longer than it should, long enough so that I panic and make mistakes, try to cut corners. Or I forget, in the middle of a complex job, where I was and what I should have done when I started. Whirl, whirl.

I have gone for a walk, tried to quieten things. An hour in the cold winter sunshine. Maybe that helped, but I'm writing this soon after coming back, and I don't think the walk has changed any perspectives or fears. 'I can't manage this,' I want to say, silently screaming. 'It's too much. And if only everyone else would do what they say they're going to do, if this computer wouldn't keep screwing up...' Whirl, whirl.

Of course, I recognize the addict. 'It's other people's fault, I'm so hard-used, I have to do this, that, and the other, there's never any rest...' It's all nonsense. But I still find it difficult to cope with the different atmospheres of the academic year, the tacit howling of colleagues in bewilderment, the incessant neediness of students. Where do I go, when life's full of pressures? Is there anywhere I can go?

I can go to an AA meeting. There's one scheduled for tomorrow evening. I could use the phone, keep in contact. I could sit down with a cup of ersatz coffee and tell myself, if necessary ad infinitum, that all I can do today is all I can do, and that will have to be enough for everyone, including myself. At least it's an attempt to stay in the moment, in the Reality Factor, and not escape onto Cloud Nine (which is bringing a local thunderstorm). Easy does it, I tell myself. 'Altered attitudes.' Gently.

56.   22 February 2001

It's been nearly a month since I picked up the usual duties of teaching, administration, and research. It's been a month of largely lapsed disciplines, a month since I've written in this unreliable memoir. There have been danger signals scattered all over the days – tiredness, hunger, loneliness, and the kind of grinding anger that wakes you up at evilly small hours.

I am learning again that my attitudes to work were almost exactly aligned with my attitudes to alcohol. With ethanol, even after two detoxes had left some casual shatterings in their wake, back I went to the bottles, the faces, and the places, thinking to concoct the old heroic bang. Even after the losses, the sickness, and the miseries, I kept going back, expecting a different result – the heroic bang – when all the evidence suggested fracture, illness, and disaster. I'm reminded of the story told by one of my patient, skilful alcohol counsellors. The story's set in Halifax Prison, and involves a group of two dozen women inmates. 'How many of you are in here for offences that involved alcohol or drugs?' A couple of dozen hands shoot up (as it were). Next question: 'D'you like it here?' Furious mutterings. Last question: 'And what's the first thing you're going to do when you get out?'

Right.

Expecting a different result, when all the evidence suggest that the result will be the same poverties of humanity, is one definition of insanity. But it is exactly that set of expectations that I have characteristically – and somewhat touchingly – brought to my working life. These expectations began as a naive, public-schoolboy dream of playing for the House, the side, the School. They endured through the painful creativities of adolescence, and into adult life as a professional academic. Always I expected that this self-regarding naivety would be noticed, applauded, rewarded. It was not. Always I hoped that there would be the support for this crazy, worthless, self-generated programme. And although there was support, it wasn't what I craved; nor was it what I expected. Always I was starved for the company of the like-minded. They weren't there. Always I had faith that abject form of self-aggrandizement would somehow protect me. It did not, and instead, I gave myself – perhaps, once again, that should be my Self – away.

Faced now with the stringent demands of work, down to all its responsibilities, its whisperings, and its overloads, I feel the same pull towards the next fix. 'Chris will fix it.' And I have to understand – how much more do I now have to understand – that I can fix nothing, fix no one, and that the attempt to bring about that kind of fixing will only mean that I fix myself fatally on self-aggrandizement, power – and finally, on alcohol.

It's the ability to say No that I'm trying to talk about. *No* can be said quietly, politely. It doesn't have to be a matter of furious rejection and counter-argument. It's merely a matter of calculated but generous self-protection, where the single word *No* is interpreted as a full sentence.

The Stoics, and, in a slightly different sense, the Epicureans, had this about right (as, above all, did Montaigne). *No* embraces the quality not of rejection, but of detachment. Nowadays, in this flawed recovery, it's neither rejection, heroism, nor even love that I crave: it's the capacity for detachment. And finding that – if I can find that – will feed the professionalism I need not only to do my job, but to endure it happily.

I don't think I'm succeeding particularly well, but I'm aware of what needs doing – of how the small, ignorable disciplines of readings and meetings actually do feed the process of detachment; how a community of recovering drunks embodies this quality of insight; how a phone call, or a well-put, well-aimed joke, can neutralize the destructive self-obsessions that come with over-involvement in work, alcohol (or even with recovery). In this context, Monika came up with a wonderful apophthegm last week. After I'd fulminated for far too long about the iniquities of the DVLA, the Dutch bailiffing system, and the department, she looked at me rather calmly and Germanically and said, 'Darling heart... However triumphant the triumph, and however deep the defeat, it's good to remember that there are one billion Chinese out there, and they don't give a shit.'

That's made me smile all week, in a detached kind of way.

57.   22 February 2001

The girl behind the check-in desk for the flight from Manchester to Amsterdam was clever, pretty, helpful, and sympathetic. 'Dr. McCully,' she breathed, 'you look exhausted.' I confessed – to her and a passing gallery of imaginary sympathizers – that I was, that I'd had three weeks from hell. I attempted to look haggard, strong, and interesting, and looked merely middle-aged, pouchy, and haggard. 'Would you like an invitation to our Executive Lounge?' An Executive Lounge, whatever that was, sounded good. 'Go on, relax, put your feet up. We'll call your flight.'

Off I stumbled, carrying a non-executive briefcase and a cheap plastic shoulder bag, both full of junk and nonsense, tiredness, resentment, and worry. Anyone less like an 'executive' would be hard to imagine. For the record, my jeans were made by a German street-market; my green overcoat came courtesy of the second-hand merchant adventurers of

Waterlooplein (25fl., or around £8); my haircut was by someone called Frank, and the make-up generated by that well-known manicurist, Fate. I called in to the Gents, splashed on some highly expensive aftershave gel (Gillette, £2.50 in a Dutch supermarket sale), and gatecrashed the Executive Lounge.

Unlike most airport waiting areas, it was quiet. If large leather armchairs could steam with relieved stress and money, these would have been steaming, expensively. Newspapers and current issues of journals (*Newsweek, The Economist*) lay in racks. There was silver cutlery, there were cloth napkins. Someone was working, inevitably, on a laptop. A pair of rimless eyeglasses briefly looked round at the disturbance provided by the entry of a plastic shoulder bag. The cheese, the biscuits, the things-you-nibble-before-a-Martini – all these were complimentary, Dr. McCully. And there, last Thursday evening, there on an immaculate white tablecloth were open bottles of chilled Chardonnay, of warm and full-blooded Chilean reds. There were cold beers in the coolers, grapes in bowls. It's complimentary, Dr. McCully. Please help yourself, and make yourself at home.

It's hard at this distance to reconstruct the thought processes of those moments. The first thought was something like 'Christ…'. It was rapidly followed by 'Well, you *are* exhausted'. This brought with it a leer towards the booze: '…and you deserve it.' That was backed up, supported, and loved by the following sentence: *'No one would know.'*

The passenger route to the coffee led past the open bottles. It was a straightforward thoroughfare – but not for me. I went on a detour of the room's perimeter, pretending I was looking for a seat; pretending I was looking for a friend; pretending I was looking at the nice parked aircraft; pretending. Eventually I grabbed some fresh coffee, loaded a plate with cheese crackers and a napkin, and hurtled towards a vacant table where I could smoke.

Perhaps I should simply have left. My friends in recovery do this well, and do it invariably, if they feel they're in an uncomfortable situation. They check out of hotel rooms at 3am because they're bothered by the hum of the mini-bar; they leave the ceremony, the dinner; they always and forever find good escape routes – even after many years' sobriety. Perhaps I should have done the same at Ringway, but then again, to escape the dubieties of the Executive Lounge would only have landed me in another noisy and noisome shed – the smell of stale, spilt alcohol, and yet another bar.

After I'd exhaled, I looked round. I expected to see my fellow non-executives merrily tipsifying on Chardonnay. One was sipping designer water; another was drinking coffee; another was bravely raising his eyebrow over a grapefruit juice. Not one of these travelling souls was drinking. Maybe it's only drunks who are so self-absorbed and habituated that they expect the ambient world to be drinking deeply too. But, as I'm learning, many people choose not to drink, because they like it that way. They are social non-drinkers.

The flight was called. I finished a cigarette, swallowed the rest of the Perrier-equivalent, and had a thorough wash before making the plane. On the way out of Ringway's Executive Lounge, I had no need to skirt the booze on the way to the door. There were the chilled bottles, and the beer in the cooler. But somehow, in this minor accident of momentary distance and attitude, they had entirely lost whatever power they had once had. Perhaps, at last, I am learning to discriminate, or at the very least, to choose my own enemies, and my own disasters. As the wheels of the Fokker folded up as we lifted towards Amsterdam, I was glad.

58.   4 April 2001

It's been more than a month since I've written in this – what is it? A diary? An unreliable memoir? A dialogue with myself? The lacuna suggests that March was a bad and difficult month. It was. In fact, I'm finding that the second year of recovery is in many ways far more difficult than the first. In the first year, recovery is a satisfactorily impressive novelty. You learn new ways of navigating reality, and those few friends interested in the new navigation think you're Doing Well. You get the kind of plaudits, even silent plaudits, that addicts crave, and to some extent, you are yourself a novelty, and a centre of attention. For an addict, this is a much-desired state of affairs. And yet admiration and novelty are themselves a dangerous illusion. Deep down, you know you are just yourself, and that precarious self can't survive on other people's good opinions (though it will try to do so). In the first year, there is too the immediate satisfaction of overcoming difficult or tricky situations – pubs, dinner parties, Friday nights. Handle enough of these, and you begin to think you're cured.

Into the second year, and the novelty has worn off along with the immediate satisfactions. Your handful of friends no longer think your sobriety and recovery is interesting. They take it for granted, without realizing (and why should they?) just how bloody difficult it continues to be. The adroit beckoning of situations, the dangerous play of parties and receptions, is all old hat. Meanwhile, the addicted Self is largely intact, and to that Self, as novelty wears off, the tired, used, inappropriate ways of thinking and being seem more and more attractive. They are, after all, what you know how to do. The effort of staying in recovery – as opposed to the non-effort of staying merely sober – begins to seem like too much, and it seems that way because accepting recovery means accepting continual change, and continual reconstruction. You never stand still. You can't afford to. Stasis eventually will mean relapse. And yet the continual questioning that underpins the acceptance of change is very tiring. Without meaning to, you become tired of your own agony. It's not an agony caused by the absence of a drink. You rarely crave. For me, the agony is simply that I have to live each situation as a recovering drunk, morning, noon, and night, and crucially (though this is hard to admit) there's no one to pat me on the back and say Well Done. The ones who could, have done all the Well Dones already. I could of course speak more to the recovery group(s) I attend, but that would seem like a cry for attention, not a true sharing of experience, strength, and hope. And I would despise myself for craving attention, since to get it would mean I was merely preening the Ego. Self, self, self.

The way to avoid the pernicious beckonings of the Self seems two-fold. One is a kind of slow meditation. The other is service to others. I am very bad at both, although I'm trying to learn. On the one hand, I still begin every day with some meditative reading, not in order to surmount problems and to feel a spurious, self-constructed Peace, but in order to have the truthful capacity to circumvent or to confront the problems and the changes that will inevitably occur. Yet even here, I find myself being critical of the readings I do. I read through them with a kind of fierce disdain, driven by the shame that I have to undertake this dumb…stuff…in the first place. Then again, and on the other hand, there's service. In a small way, I tried to offer service to the AA group here in Amsterdam, and said I'd operate as their 'literature person'. (*Chris, the literature person.* No, the irony wasn't lost on me.) It took me six weeks just to order the relevant literature, the books and pamphlets, because I was nervous about possibly having to use Dutch over the phone. Then when I had laid my hands on these valuables, I arrived too late to set them up for the meeting. Some 'service'. And there was my driven, perfectionist head again: you always screw up, you're never reliable, so why not give up now? What's the point?

I guess the point is that despite an awful past month, with its illusions, its addictions to coffee, satire, sarcasm, and bad temper, despite all of that I still haven't picked up a drink. That must mean something. Perhaps sobriety itself has become a habit, much like drinking used to be. But if so, least among equals can I afford to take that habit for granted. And it seems that beyond the clinical facts of this relationship with alcohol, there's a great deal of reconstruction still left to do.

59.   4 April 2001

There's one big problem that's been troubling me, and that's my paid work. I have been trying to reconcile what I understand as the principles of recovery with what I understand to be the working principles now operative in UK universities. And I can't reconcile the two. Recovery seems to be about continual truth, to the extent that a recovering addict has to develop a changed, more positive and realistic relationship with himself, where that relationship can only be sustained by honesty. University work now seems, to me at least, to have abandoned any pretence that research or teaching exists to investigate even contingent 'truths'. Instead, it pretends – fine, let's use a more neutral word, it *assumes* – that education is synonymous with instruction, and that instruction, and its value, are measurable commodities. Universities in the UK are now, and have been for more than fifteen years, awash with the dubious rhetoric of consumerism. We are urged to think of our students as consumers, as customers. Our customers, we are told, consume our product, 'education'. If they don't like the product, they will vote with their feet by staying away or going to test a different product somewhere else (if they can). Or they will try to change the product. Or if they don't like the result of their consumption of the product (a second class degree, say, rather than a first), then they'll sue. The consumer rhetoric: education as a comparative commodity. That is, higher education is no longer about the disinterested pursuit of knowledge. It's at bottom about providing stuff for people to consume, i.e. like any other business it's in the business of money.

Follow this through, and it becomes clear that difficult or unpopular subject areas (like physics, like Anglo-Saxon) will fail to attract the interest of many consumers. Consumers like easily-digestible fare. Just as television stations rely on a diet of soaps and quiz-shows, so universities have come to rely on intellectual materials that are often (it seems to me) the cognitive equivalent of *Holby City*. They are the mirrors of the fashionably current, and deeper lessons, hauled from the generous and terrible structures of our narratives of history, are untaught and therefore unlearned. In this environment, subjects perceived by consumers to be less 'relevant' will be disfavoured (so fine, let's scrap them). Subjects perceived to be 'relevant' will be favoured (so let's keep them, and expand them). But let's try to be clear about what's happening: the disinterested pursuit of knowledge has given way to a consumer-driven drama in which the 'weak' (the unpopular) go to the wall, and where the 'strong' (the fashionable) appear to prosper. It's all about prosper-ity. Money.

Like any other business, university accounts are audited. It's quite proper for that to be so. Higher education in the UK eats £6 billion of taxpayers' money each year (roughly one third that of the defence budget), and of course taxpayers should know what their money is buying. In essence, in the present circumstances, that money is buying an expensive screening process: Anna has a 2:1 degree, therefore (it's assumed) is a more viable human prospect to a prospective employer than Isobel, who has a handful of GNVQs. But what does 'viable human prospect' really mean? Right: someone who's capable of generating yet more wealth. But the economics of this – a judgement on the potential 'productivity' of Anna or Isobel – are shaky, and have never been proved (see for example the two Annexes to the 1997 Dearing Report).

Still, university accounts are audited, properly. As a consequence of those audits, the research produced in individual departments is assessed, and the 'delivery' of teaching is likewise assessed. The ostensible logic of these audits is that when the results are made available to consumers, they (or their parents) can choose which business is the most 'productive'. The problem here is that the scrapping of student grants, and the introduction of fees, has made it less likely that Anna or Isobel will be able to afford to move to Manchester, or Brighton, or Aberdeen. They'll be far more likely to live cheaply at home, and attend their local college. Meanwhile, the audits continue. Their logic is at least faulty.

A result of one auditing process is that I have to complete a 'diary sheet' in order to account for how I spend my time. The spread-sheet runs from Sunday to Sunday, from midnight to midnight. In other words, I'm asked how I spend my time 24 hours a day. Sometimes it's Research. (I tick a box.) Sometimes it's 'Research Support' (what does this mean?). Sometimes it's Teaching, or 'Teaching Support' (?). Sometimes it's 'Other Activities'. But what does this heading mean? Sleeping? Attending AA meetings? Doing recovery reading? Gardening? I don't know. (I tick some boxes anyway.) Yes, I think it's proper that I should account for how I spend my time, but surely, the results are publicly available in the forms of books, articles, papers, essays. They're available, again publicly, in the contact hours I spend in the classroom, in student reports on my teaching, in the papers I grade, and the preparation I do. They're available, publicly, from peer assessment of teaching. They're available, again publicly, in records of my development work for the subject, both inside the university and outside it. Why, then, do I have to provide a separate account of how I spend my time? The fact that I have been so asked, in terms that I don't understand, seems to me like an insulting lack of trust on the part of the money-men and the bureaucrats.

In terms of this particular audit, I can't give an honest account of myself. Recovery tells me to try above all to be honest, yet the current ethos of the university, and the process of fulfilling its requirements, oblige me to be dishonest, to construct an entirely fictional working Self. Truly, ideas may speak to other ideas in unexpected ways, at strange times. I sometimes think I've learnt more about the concept of 'underlying structure' from fishing than from Plato (or from linguistics). I have learnt to read John Donne's *Songs and Sonnets* because I was once impotent. I am learning again to read Chaucer because I acknowledge, and share, the inward nature of my fellow pilgrims on this erratic, funny, and messy journey. I have learnt more about the archetypal pattern of descent and ascent in Dante from a diagram given to alcoholics in treatment than I have by studying Dante's models and the *dolce stil nuovo*. I have learned more about language by learning to listen to music...or to silence. And I often think I've learned more about the *disinterested* pursuit of knowledge from alcoholism and recovery than from a first class degree, a doctorate, and all my official, badgered, harassed, over-audited university work. And how can that learning – my own learning, my own progress as a thinking human being, a creature who is continually, and often anew, learning *how to think* – how can that be audited? And by whom?

2002 RETROSPECTIVE

The Changes

I t worried me. It worried me for a year, for more than a year. I look back now into
these entries – it's not easy, re-reading them – and know that behind the anxieties
about work a decision was forming.

The nature of my paid work was becoming incompatible with the imperatives of
recovery. I did not wish the two to be irreconcilable. Behind, and yet closely aligned
with the writer, was the academic. I had always, rather unthinkingly, expected to be
somehow a part of the university system throughout my working life. But as the university system had changed, I too had changed. It was becoming clear that it was time
to say a mutual goodbye.

In any conflict between life, personalities, work, and recovery, recovery must
always come first. Always. If the relationship doesn't allow recovery to prosper, it's
the relationship that has to change, or to go. If the work doesn't grant recovery its
dignities and freedoms, then it's the work that has to change... Or you must recon-
sider your position, as they say, and leave your work.

There were other forms of truth – truth at work, I mean – that clarified my
thinking, but which at the same time made me outraged, or just plain scared. One
truth was that my working record seemed to have been, carelessly or wilfully, misrep-
resented, partly via the wretched 'diary' entries – whereby I felt I had to construct a
fictional working persona for myself – and partly through the introduction of a
'profiling' system for individual staff. 'Profiling' promised to record individual

workloads via the allotment of some kind of points system, and thereby to make the distribution of administrative responsibilities more equitable.

I wanted nothing whatsoever to do with the introduction of such a ridiculous system. I saw it as divisive, and, like many of my older colleagues, I had already lived through almost two decades of that crudest and most common of all governmental, administrative tactics, Divide and Rule.

'Fairness' is all very well, except when its jurisdiction falls into thoughtless (or possibly, unscrupulous) hands. To the end of my life I will find it difficult to forget – though I will try to forget – some colleagues waving their order papers in a committee meeting, turning crimson with anger, and claiming to have 'three times as many' profiling points, the implication being that they were working 'three times as hard' as...well, as me. Perhaps they were trying to be helpful. Perhaps it was kindly meant. Perhaps it was very kindly meant. Or perhaps... Well, there's little use now in rehearsing all the Perhapses.

There was a large part of me that wanted to reply to these spurious charges, these unbidden skewings, by saying it was a matter of public record that I had been undertaking difficult and creative work within the university system when my most accusing colleagues were still at school. But what would have been the point? Whatever I might have said or done, I was becoming dispensable. The face didn't fit. I was the unlucky place. The wrong railing.

Through it all, I was also acutely aware of my touchiness about criticism – any form of criticism – and my capacity for selfish hyper-sensitivity. It was difficult to maintain any kind of good-humoured balance.

I couldn't afford to lose my temper. I couldn't afford the worry or the resentment, though I lived both the worry and the resentment, and behind them was another anxiety – about money, about Monika, and about how we could possibly manage if I did eventually leave a job at least part of which I had loved. There was also – hard to admit – a worry about prestige, a residual competitiveness with the world...and even with Monika. I quite liked being the centre of attention, and would surely find it difficult to take a back seat, to live anonymously, quietly.

Recovery told me that quiet and creative anonymity was pretty good.

Recovery told me I was lucky to be alive.

I wanted to tell recovery, and the rest of the world, to fuck off and leave me alone, so I could be lonely with the known illusions.

Throughout this period, I was also, and on several different occasions, informed that I was having 'an easy time'. Perhaps that, too, was kindly meant. 'You are having an easy time.' You have heard my nervousness about this, if you've read thus far: here and there in the present text there are references to the extent of what I was trying to do – this conference, that paper, this international trip, that degree. I read these insistencies now in two ways: first, I'm slightly sickened by these attempts at self-justification, and second, I'm touched by them. The truth was that I was both scared, and increasingly invisible to many of my colleagues. Whatever I was doing, whatever I might have achieved, they weren't interested – or were only interested insofar as they could assign blame. The blame came from a bad place, from a tacit and unacknowledged anger. This didn't really surprise me: deep down, many people around recovering alcoholics are bitterly, furiously resentful.

The 'easy time' I was allegedly having can be found in several places: my curriculum vitae; the medical, financial, and criminal records; and finally, this writing.

ANOTHER THING THAT hurt was the verse. After many, many false starts, after crossings-out, hints, hatches, beginning again at the tops of pages, I did attempt to write verse once more. Or at least, it was a kind of verse. I don't know whether it's any good, though it seems to insist on itself in the ways that a poem should – in order to be a poem.

I'll try to show you what I mean.

The first text is lifted from The Country of Perhaps *(Manchester: Carcanet, 2002). It's a curious book, in two parts. The first part is filled with a handful of shorter, lyric poems. They were the only ones I could bear to keep after the chaotic years of 1996–2000 – that is, they were the only poems that stood up as poems, that could be said no other way. And so here, from the drinking time, is a piece about Icarus:*

Icarus

He was mad with it:
    the intricacies of construction,
    the wax that sealed each joint
    to a workable point,
    the local clarities of angles,
    feathers, whatever could explain
    the assemblage and harness it
    to the dynamics of the sky.

He was mad with it,
    and as the air glazed
    without effort under the beating wings,
    as the olive groves and the blue zoo
    of the sea receded merely
    to hillsides and ocean,
    a disarticulated view,
    he had succeeded.

He was mad with it,
    the whole beautiful engineering.
    But turning westwards, higher,
    becoming pressure, becoming weight,
    he had forgotten the sun.
    And strange that when there was
    that endless sense of falling,
    he was glad of it.

(Reproduced from McCully (2002) The Country of Perhaps,
Manchester: Carcanet Press, with kind permission.)

I can't remember precisely when that was written, but it was during 1997 or 1998, at the height – if that's the right word – of the alcoholic nullity. Read it as a poem about alcoholism, if you will, or about the obsessive perfectionism of making any form of relationship – but I guess the piece is really about the addictive nature of ambition and creativity, and about its fatal, necessary weakness.

At the time, I think I saw myself still as the hero, the doomed victim, the mythic creature. Even in this present text, there are scattered references to the gestural and perpetual largeness of myth. Perhaps I was trying to dignify my own folly by dressing it up with literary references – Icarus, Orpheus, Actaeon.

But there was something else behind these references to myth, to archetype, and it's not something I'd confess to a reviewer, nor is it anything a reviewer would ever find out.

During the terminal drinking phase, I tried to translate Virgil – specifically, Book IV of the Georgics. *This text spoke to me because it concerned Orpheus, whose pattern of mythic, recovered, unrecovered descent I would claim to recognize. It wasn't just that famous moment of loss – the loss of Eurydice – that spoke to my condition then. It was what happened after the darkness of the estranging, final glance – the disconsolation, the continual poetry, the dismemberment by an outraged society, the singing head tossed casually into the river.*

It all sounds pretty silly now. But it spoke to me then. Somewhere, I bribed the bar staff to keep my glass filled up, and sat down in the middle of a Manchester heatwave – dressed in nothing but a stained pair of boxer shorts – with my old Latin grammars and vocabularies.

From this distance, I must somehow try to pity myself. But I can't.

In the alcoholic hallucinations I had seen birds, humanoid birds. They somehow were part of this insane creativity, part of this drunken, appalling, self-pitying myth of Mr. Wonderful. They followed me about, and I sang to them, out of distraught alcoholic chains. They did nothing. They were, it appeared, merely waiting.

Months later, I was visiting the British Museum. In one of the 'early' rooms of the BM there is a reconstruction of a Greek tomb. It is called the Harpy Tomb. Though I'd visited the museum several times, I had never seen this particular reconstruction before 1998.

The harpies, in myth, are humanoid birds whose unpleasant habit, among other things, is to carry away the souls of dead and dying warriors. You will find these creatures, harpies, first in Homer.

If you ever visit the BM, look – however briefly – at the Harpy Tomb. You will see the harpies, carved in stone. And you will be looking at the exact structure of the creatures who peopled my hallucinations back in 1997.

Dressed in stained boxer shorts, sitting at a table among Latin grammars and spilt beer, I had become...

I was about to write 'I had become my own, pathetic myth'. But it wouldn't be true. I had become merely a middle-aged man who was about to die of alcohol poisoning.

I can't find the right words of pity for this.

But I was showing you the difference, and the distance between the vaguely grandiose, acutely sick drunk and the recovering Self of Now.

Here's another piece, slightly longer, from less than a month ago. It, too, is about a kind of illusion, but the poem itself doesn't just carelessly invoke 'local clarities', it tries to notice them, to use them. It's outward-looking, to the same extent that the 'Icarus' piece is perilously solipsistic. It's a piece that is trying to take an interest not in its maker, and not in itself, but in its fellow travellers, and in the landscapes the poem and its people are imaginatively inhabiting:

An Auction for Amsterdam[1]

That man, who recently acquired –
    for an astronomical price –
    the old Dutch master,
I wish him well, I wish him well.
It turns out that this hitherto-neglected, until-now-
    unattributed piece of transcendent
    Biblical hokum
wasn't anyone's to sell.

Imagine avarice, locked in
    its 22nd floor office with its Dic-
    taphone and its cruel secretary,
its bank of screens, its plasm of phones.
Hands crook round the Eagle atop the walking-frame,
    but nothing moves except the brightening eyes
    that get their promises to keen
among a nest of deals and bones.

And what's he bought, that man? A prophet
    in a 17th century, Thank-God-I've-made-it pose:
    'I travelled, then studied Greek; then put that by for guilders.
'Now here I am. Now here I am.'
Nonesuch, I sit and watch them every day. They move in
    rimless glasses, architects of coffee, raincoats, air,
    on any street that crawls the smell of drains
in Amsterdam, in Amsterdam.

---

1   To my surprise, this poem was among the prize-winners in the 2004 Academic Cardiff International Poetry Competition. I am grateful to the Welsh Academy, the Welsh National Literature Promotion Agency and the Society of Writers, and the judges and organisers of the competition, for permission to reprint the poem in this context.

To the last most intricate detail, they too
      have wives wear sharpened scissors, dirty toenails;
      down to the valves and palp, breasts and bush consumed:
mute need; burnt night. And then the night
whose ochre grumbles as it pays, or scratches
      stub-ends of its brush. The technicalities of skin admire,
      geometry of moon betray –
and bleed them white, and bleed them white.

And what the eyes just paid for is this
      culture that means everywhere, yet is no one's –
      a finicking insistence on the peripheral, pathetic, over-obvious bowl
of withered flowers; the abandoned dog.
These things are home, they nag between the tapestries,
      dust falls and lies, whatever light. While outside… Outside…
      Perhaps he knows, the man who rooked the master. If so,
he bought the fog. He bought the fog.

I hope you can read the difference. The second piece is writing that somehow 'aspires to the condition of prose'. Exile, humour. It affirms my own fears, but manages to overcome them simply by being itself. It seems… better grounded, more clearly constructed, larger, more generous, than the earlier piece.

Who knows? Perhaps I will write again.

I have to trust that this may be so, though I have no trust except in the immediate veracities of Now.

But now, at this moment, appalled by the remembrance of a man trying to translate Virgil while surrounded by chaos and the end of one phase of his life, despite time, despite re-marriage, despite the realities and the joys, for the present face and voice there is still no pity in it, and I'm still, deeply, destructively, ashamed.

April 2001

60.   17 April 2001

Something's fairly badly wrong, and I don't know quite what. I'm finding it difficult to work. The sleep I have seems limited to six hours of coughing and worry. During the days I can't settle to much. Concentration and peace seem equally at a loss, and I'm fighting myself into enervation and standstill. At the same time, I'm beating myself up for being lazy, lousy, and lost. The deadlines come and go. I meet some.

None of this is taking me close to the first, last drink. I don't think any of this is about alcohol, *per se*, though I could be wrong. It's more to do with the continual shocks of adjustment, of coming to terms, and of letting go. This coming to terms sometimes feels like a daily reinvention of the personal wheel.

What seems to be happening is that, this far on in recovery, the allure, the promise, and the novelty has worn off. When that's worn off, what's left is the world, the tired, addicted, small, stained world, and the strangeness of myself – a self I never quite learnt to know, and much more certainly, never learnt to care about. Real life hurtles in through work, through continual news reports. Fixes are not available. In the recovery jargon I learnt many months ago, this is 'Life on life's terms'. Whether one likes the terms or not is irrelevant. *Deal with it, and let it go.* And if that sounds easy, you've never been there.

I was looking back, into the weary past and the weary self. This retrospection wasn't really a matter of grief or regret. Grief and regret there are, of course, but somehow they have lost their savagery: they are just grief and regret. Tough. This face, this nonsense, this piece of hurt, this or that city and their blown, cigarette-streaked memories... We all have them. But behind and beyond them, what is there? The face – the serious, moonscaped, bespectacled face – of a boy. This boy has a school nickname, and that, unbelievably, is Mr. Responsible. Mr. Responsible has two sworn duties: one is to be, er, responsible; the other is not, ever, to hurt his mother. These duties amount to a drive – for success, urged on by ambition, competition, pride. These disasters constitute his world, and he thinks these things are very good. In fact, he is taught that these things are very good. Never to fail. Never to be impolite. Never, in all truth and conscience, to say 'I need...' Stupid, inarticulate, insecure boy, streakily brilliant.

This boy is so afraid of the present that he learns continually to reinvent it. There was no one to explain the rules of cricket, the possibilities of fishing, the off-side law of the football that was considered to be a game fit only for the council estates. This boy had largely to work them out for himself, borrowing books from the Public Library, making mistakes.

Well, well... The huge, bizarre construction of a life. And why construct? Fear. Self-centredness. More fear. Not to get caught, not to get found out, not to seem stupid... And from there, an easy step through adolescence to the failed glamour of Mr. bleeding Wonderful. It was all fear, Chris. It was mostly illusion. It was about selfishness and pride, deep down. And deep down, the fragilities, perfectionism, and shocks of something that can only be called loneliness.

Listen, please. This isn't the bleeding heart. It was all long ago, in a lifetime that seems only precariously joined to this. There were good things. But these malevolent tinkerings, the solitary conundrums of Sorry, these were the places where the self-accusations began, and the fishing, and the poems. And to get on with this recovery, I have to hear the self-accusations again for what they are, and learn the fishing and the poetry again. I have to arrive at where I started, uncertainly, and – as someone once said – know the place for the first time, without apologizing for being there.

Any recovering addict will tell you as much, and do so with more truth and humour than I can muster at the moment. And today, yes, life is better. Amsterdam, home, Monika: these places, this face, are certain priorities, with their certain separateness. And yet I feel uncertain, being included here. It's a kind of loss, because when addiction was active I learnt for so long to be non-included everywhere. And yet it is also a kind of blessing. Thank you, I want to say, followed by the one endless word, Sorry.

Perhaps the smart thing to do would be to live the Thank-You, and consign most of the Sorries to the past, where I can do little about them beyond what I have already tried to do. It seems rather better to think with a smile through the whole human comedy than it does to weep crocodile, selfish tears over the brazen, unavoidable tragedies of one small, scared life.

61.   17 April 2001

We're back from Denmark, and four days of non-holiday. I have to learn again that it's entirely possible to get through the days of fracture and bickering without a drink. Not that there was too much fracture and bickering, but there was some, and that 'some' was enough to have marred one Saturday in Odense.

Holidays are supposed to be for relaxation. They aren't supposed to be about sitting for hours in traffic jams in or around Hamburg. They aren't really supposed to be about ten hours' drive to get to a rain-streaked, gale-swept Fyn that has become nailed to the north wind.

I felt guilty, because I wasn't driving (still can't drive, since the DVLA are making it more than usually difficult for me to regain my licence). I felt guilty because I'd miscalculated the time it was going to take, at Easter, to drive from Amsterdam to Nyborg. (For the record, it is the best part of 800 kilometres, and a ten-hour stretch in a cramped Mazda.) I felt guilty, because I'd taken the fishing rods and wanted, if possible, to get in a day or two's sea-trout fishing, and this wish seemed to conflict with spending time – what Americans so glibly call 'quality time' – with Monika. And then I felt guilty about feeling guilty.

If I feel guilty about the quotidian demands, it translates very unfortunately into a grim dose of withdrawal. Okay, let's call 'withdrawal' by its weekday name: it's sulkiness. It's also hostility, faultfinding, exasperation. It makes me awful to be around, despite Monika's gentle and loving protests – a gentleness and lovingness that made the sulking worse.

I sulked. No adolescent could have behaved worse. Then Monika sulked, and there were tears. Then, just for the hell of it, we sulked together.

If there is a good thing about any of this, it is that we tried to talk it through, and out. It was at the trying-to-grow-up-and-talk-it-through stage that I wanted to run, and hit the nearest bar, and drink Danish beer at 40Kr. a bottle. It's not that I was particularly disappointed in the weather, the conflicts, or the company. I was disappointed in myself – for being less than perfect, for being an addict, for feeling that I wanted an immediate fix… Anything, just to get out of where I was, what I was saying, and how I was behaving. I was disgusted with myself.

For an addict, what does self-disgust mean, and where will it lead? Right.

Was I hungry, angry, lonely, tired?

Right.

By some miracle we avoided the worst. We went shopping. Even outrageously priced, imported Danish strawberries began to seem better – not much better, I grant you – than a skinful of hops and flatulence. We drove back to the house we were borrowing, wearing a brand of sullen quietness. We read, separately, retreating into comfort stuff like John le Carré, and bloody Harry Potter (in Dutch translation). We cooked.

The strange thing, the good thing, is that all this nonsense – and it was nonsense – did pass, and even in the home-bound Hamburg traffic jams we were happier and closer than we might have been. The alarming thing was that the long instants of sulking had taken me near to the beer, and near to the schnapps that go so well – that used to go so well – with Danish meat and sea-food. But that passed, too, and Sunday passed, and passed fishing-less but peacefully, a kind of negotiation, a kind of wary hope. But if I needed any lesson to make me realize that I am in no way 'cured', this was one. And I suppose, as a lesson, it was almost welcome.

I have to learn that it's entirely possible and desirable to get through the tough times without resorting to drama. Drama, crisis – the known landscape of the addicted heart. But yes, it was much better, driving through eastern Friesland, into the empty horizons, and then crossing the Noord Holland border, travelling always westwards, past the wind-farms, the white horses of the Markermeer, and driving together, until we had reached ourselves and each other. This also, for all its faults, is called home.

Some Diagnostics of Alcoholism

I was thinking about how much in common alcoholics seem to have with those most closely around them. I'm puzzled, to be honest, about the extent to which my own addictive behaviour seems to overlap with those characteristics shared by those not addicted themselves, but who have been, or are currently, exposed to others' addiction(s). Recently, I went back to the diagnostic set repeated below, which I have found increasingly, and usefully, thought-provoking:

Did You Grow Up With a Problem Drinker?

Al-Anon is for families, relatives and friends whose lives have been affected by someone else's drinking. Many adults question whether they have been affected by alcoholism. If someone close to you has, or has had a drinking problem, the following questions may help you in determining whether alcoholism affected your childhood or present life and if Al-Anon is for you.

1. Do you constantly seek approval and affirmation?
2. Do you fail to recognize your accomplishments?
3. Do you fear criticism?

4. Do you overextend yourself?

5. Have you had problems with your own compulsive behavior?

6. Do you have a need for perfection?

7. Are you uneasy when your life is going smoothly, continually anticipating problems?

8. Do feel more alive in the midst of a crisis?

9. Do you still feel responsible for others, as you did for the problem drinker in your life?

10. Do you care for others easily, yet find it difficult to care for yourself?

11. Do you isolate yourself from other people?

12. Do you respond with anxiety to authority figures and angry people?

13. Do you feel that individuals and society in general are taking advantage of you?

14. Do you have trouble with intimate relationships?

15. Do you confuse pity with love, as you did with the problem drinker?

16. Do you attract and seek people who tend to be compulsive?

17. Do you cling to relationships because you are afraid of being alone?

18. Do you often mistrust your own feelings and the feelings expressed by others?

19. Do you find it difficult to express your emotions?

20. Do you think parental drinking may have affected you?

Alcoholism is a family disease. Those of us who have lived with this disease as children sometimes have problems which the Al-Anon program can help us to resolve. If you answered yes to some or all of the above questions, Al-Anon may help. You can contact Al-Anon by checking your local telephone directory or by writing to: Al-Anon Family Group Headquarters, Inc. P.O. Box 182, Madison Square Station, New York, NY 10159–0182.

(Reproduced from www.recovery.org, with permission.)

I am interested, too, insofar as none of these diagnostic sets include mention of the amount of alcohol, measured in units, that the alcoholic may be, or may be seen to be, drinking. As far as I know, 'units' – gauged whereby 1 unit of alcohol equates to a half-pint of ale, a medium glass of wine, or a pub measure of spirits – don't figure in the acute-admission procedures at those hospitals and clinics specializing in the treatment of alcoholism. You can't do alcoholism in units. First, individuals differ in their susceptibility to the drug ethanol (and how I seized on this fact – Mr. Wonderful would have claimed to be entirely non-susceptible to alcohol). Second, the consumption of units is, I guess, invariably under-reported. What does an alcoholic say, when the doctor asks 'How much are you drinking each week, measured in units?' 'Well, I gave up counting when I approached three figures. . .'? I don't think so. You say – that is, I used to say – 'Actually, it's around 27 units a week, a bit on the high side I know, but. . .' 'You're a social drinker, then?' 'Oh, yes,' replied Mr. Wonderful. And third, no one I know drinks in units, or thinks in them. Drinking – by which I mean alcoholic drinking, addiction – is primarily a matter of behaviour, not units. And GPs, however concerned, however professional, simply do not have diagnostic time in the surgery to begin to analyse the complex of behaviours that characterizes the souls who sit in front of them.

Behaviour, not units. In 2001, as I was listening in the small hours to late-breaking stuff from the Balkans, I heard alcoholic behaviour very well summed up in a BBC World Service feature, whose analogy I have never forgotten, since it struck me as profoundly true, and therefore profoundly useful. 'Alcoholic drinking,' the feature said, although I'm paraphrasing from memory, 'is like pushing again and again at a locked door. At some point, you burst through, breaking the handle and the door-frame. And you will know – you will just know – that you've gone through. You will also know that you will never again be able to stand on the other side of the door.'

Behaviour, not units. The thing that characterized my own alcoholic behaviour, which extended everywhere, and to everyone around me, was increasing chaos. Unmanageability. And so, confronted by diagnostic tests for alcoholism, and as the locked door of addiction bursts open forever, one thing anyone might do is to sit down and analyse not the units of alcohol they consume, but those aspects of life they find so unmanageable. . .beginning with the stricken claustrophobia of the drinking self.

It's worthwhile remembering, as one begins to penetrate the structures of alcoholic behaviour, that what exists at the end of addiction to alcohol is not a neat summary, judged in units. If the chaos of your condition continues, what exists on the other side of the door is an institution – a hospital, a jail, a courtroom; or insanity ('First you won't be able to walk; then you won't be able to think'); or death.

April to May 2001

62. 30 April 2001

One of the most helpful descriptions of the deterioration experienced by an alcoholic, together with the new hope that can be generated by recovery, comes in diagram form. Because I have lived through almost every one of its descending stages, the diagram on the next page speaks to me of my own past. And because that past was real, there is also the hope that a recovered future can be possible, too.

63. 31 May 2001

It's been bothering me that it's been over a month since I've written in this unreliable and educative chronicle. It's been a month where a great deal has happened – my mother's bereavement, a working trip to Edinburgh, flights home to Amsterdam, the responsibilities and work of student exams – and I'm conscious of just how easy it is to let the small disciplines of reading and reflection lapse. Still, first things first, as they say – that is, as alcoholics say, reaching for one of the enduring clichés of recovery.

And the first thing is that down this distance of treatment and recovery, I bought my first alcoholic drink a month ago. It wasn't – mercifully it wasn't – for me, it was for a just-graduated PhD student

The Cost Time Lag

The cost time lag to recovery from his drinking problem may be arrested at any point noted on the Addiction Chart. The 'rock bottom' level is an individual experience and may be the place at any point in the development process of the individual's alcoholism. Three examples of 'rock bottom levels' have been indicated on the Chart. The time lag is due to several factors: e.g. finds himself unable to accept the fact that he has a serious drinking problem discovering or inventing a host of events or other persons as 'scapegoats' responsible for his plight, and on the other hand society lacks understanding for his needs and his condition (stigma) and is not prepared to help him towards recovery.

Recovery, through total abstinence, is a life-long process. The steps toward rehabilitation charted here average 2 to 3 years.

Left / downward slope (progression):

SOCIAL DRINKING

PRE-ALCOHOLIC PHASE

OCCASIONAL RELIEF DRINKING

CONSTANT RELIEF DRINKING COMMENCES

HEAVY HABITUAL SOCIAL DRINKING

ONSET OF MEMORY BLACKOUTS

INCREASE IN ALCOHOL TOLERANCE

INCREASING DEPENDENCE ON ALCOHOL

SURREPTITIOUS DRINKING

REPEATED 'UNDER INFLUENCE' DRINKING

URGENCY OF FIRST DRINKS

MEMORY BLACKOUTS INCREASE

UNABLE TO DISCUSS PROBLEM

DECREASE OF ABILITY TO STOP DRINKING WHEN OTHERS DO, LOSS OF CONTROL

DRINKING BOLSTERED WITH EXCUSES

PERSISTENT REMORSE

PRODROMAL PHASE

GRANDIOSE AND AGGRESSIVE BEHAVIOUR

CRUCIAL OR BASIC PHASE

PROMISES AND RESOLUTIONS FAIL

EFFORTS TO CONTROL FAIL REPEATEDLY

LOSS OF OTHER INTERESTS

TRIES GEOGRAPHICAL ESCAPES

WORK AND MONEY TROUBLES

FAMILY AND FRIENDS AVOIDED

NEGLECT OF FOOD

UNREASONABLE RESENTMENT

TREMORS AND EARLY MORNING DRINKS

LOSS OF ORDINARY WILL POWER

DECREASE IN ALCOHOL TOLERANCE

PHYSICAL DETERIORATION

ONSET OF LENGTHY INTOXICATIONS

MORAL DETERIORATION

IMPAIRED THINKING

INDEFINABLE FEARS

PHYSICAL AND MENTAL

UNABLE TO INITIATE ACTION

OBSESSION WITH DRINKING

ALL ALIBIS EXHAUSTED

VAGUE SPIRITUAL DESIRES

CHRONIC PHASE

COMPLETE DEFEAT ADMITTED

stops drinking —
Prelude to recovery

stops drinking —
Prelude to recovery

Detour recovery

Bottom:

OBSESSIVE DRINKING CONTINUES IN VICIOUS CIRCLES
(possibly to point of no recovery – irrevocable mental or physical deterioration)

Development period for addiction can be 5 to 25 years. Average 10–15 years.

E. M. Jellinek

Right / upward slope (recovery / REHABILITATION):

INTERESTING, HAPPY, USEFUL WAY OF LIFE OPENS UP

CONFIDENCE OF EMPLOYERS

GROUP THERAPY AND MUTUAL HELP CONTINUES

INCREASING TOLERANCE TO FRUSTRATION

CONTENTMENT IN ABSTINENCE

FIRST STEPS TO ECONOMIC STABILITY

FAMILY AND FRIENDS APPRECIATE EFFORTS

RATIONALISATIONS RECOGNISED

INCREASE OF EMOTIONAL CONTROL

RETURN OF SELF ESTEEM

APPRECIATION OF REAL VALUES

FACTS FACED WITH COURAGE

NEW CIRCLE OF STABLE FRIENDS

SPIRITUAL NEEDS EXAMINED

REBIRTH OF IDEAL

CARE OF PERSONAL APPEARANCE

NEW INTERESTS DEVELOP

THE DESIRE TO ESCAPE GOES

ADJUSTMENT TO FAMILY NEED

NATURAL REST AND SLEEP

DIMINISHING FEARS OF THE UNKNOWN FUTURE

REALISTIC THINKING

ONSET OF NEW HOPE

APPRECIATION OF POSSIBILITIES OF NEW WAY OF LIFE

ASSISTED IN MAKING PERSONAL STOCK TAKING

'NON-ALCOHOLIC' THINKING BEGINS (less irrational)

REGULAR NOURISHMENT TAKEN

PHYSICAL OVERHAUL BY DOCTOR

START OF GROUP THERAPY

MEETS RECOVERED ALCOHOLICS WELL AND HAPPY

STOPS TAKING ALCOHOL

TOLD ADDICTION CAN BE ARRESTED

LEARNS ALCOHOLISM IS AN ILLNESS

HONEST DESIRE FOR HELP

REHABILITATION

Adapted from M.M. Glatt. A Guide to Addiction and its Treatment (Lancaster: MTP Press, 1974).

called…call him Stewart, in some bar in Edinburgh whose name I've forgotten. For me it was a noteworthy, if not a troubling, event. Stewart was happily oblivious to my discomfiture – but after all, why on earth not?

I had just conducted his viva voce examination. Since we have strong contacts with the Edinburgh department where Stewart undertook his graduate work, a group of us went out, subsequent to the event, the rite of passage, to a nearby bar. It was an occasion, and a place, it would have been merely churlish to avoid. I looked out at one of those chrome and wood affairs, all painted mirrors and the smell of yesterday's spilt lager mixed with the reek of cheap disinfectant. I have drunk in hundreds of bars like it. The first round wasn't mine. Coffee please, I said. Another coffee, orange juice, Coke, and Stewart's pint of lager followed. Come some social chit-chat, and it was time for a refill. 'Can I get anyone a drink?' said the plausible shade of Mr. Wonderful. Coffees, the juices, Coke…and then another pint for Stewart.

It was strange, simply hearing the words '…and a pint of lager, please' fall from my lips. Usually, in the drinking years, I have aimed at the phrase 'just a mineral water' and in the throes of a near-terminal, jittery hangover, that precise phrase, 'pint of lager', has fallen like a spat-out filling onto the bar.

I didn't feel bad, exactly. I simply felt…removed. What did bother me, though, was picking up the glass. I prayed silently that the barman would pull a clean pint, so that there was no spillage and I didn't have to get this stuff dripped over my fingers. He did, I didn't, but I have never carried a pint with more care for such a short distance. I would have smelt the stain on my hands for hours, however hard I'd washed and scrubbed. As it was, even as I smelt the slightly metallic waft of the top of the hops, I remembered that I had never really liked beer of any description, though in the end, I used it as a cure for the shakes, and as a chaser. Or often enough, as both.

Stewart had his pint, I had a second coffee, and the rest, including friends who knew of my addictions, didn't register, or didn't let on that they did. This was kind of them, and I traded on that kind understanding as a quarter hour later I made my excuses – genuine enough, as it happened – and left for a bus and a fishing-tackle shop somewhere off Princes Street.

And that was it. Just a man buying a pint in a pub in Scotland. You'll probably smile, with a kind of pity, that I'm still so tenderly self-indulgent as to register this smallest of events. And yet I know that in the instants I was carrying that bloody glass back to the table I wasn't just holding some overpriced Scandinavian brew. I was holding a whole world, of addiction and memories, of shame, of rank and inappropriate behaviour. I was holding possibility, and I was carrying danger. Three years back, and there are the howling hallucinations, and a man dressed only in a pair of boxer shorts drinking lager in a bar in Manchester as, heart-breaking and absurd, he was trying to translate Virgil down the beginning of a disastrous and heat-stricken June. Nearly thirty years back, and there's the boy who got drunk on five pints of lager in a pub in York – and then threw up into the dormitory waste-paper-basket. Holding all of this in my right, and steadiest, hand, I'm surprised I could carry the weight. And yet, by some miracle of recovery and renewal, the hand didn't even shake.

64.   31 May 2001

The UK licensing laws are to be changed so that all-day and all-night drinking will be possible. The ostensible reason for this, the government argues, is that there will be less closing-time drunkenness for bar-staff and the police to deal with. There will be no Last Orders, no closing time, no eleven o'clock-swill. Surely, the so-called liberalization of the licensing laws will be done by specific sanction and ratified application (this isn't a blanket measure), but it is now – heavens! – possible to buy a drink all night and all morning at certain places in the city.

The real reason for this change is, naturally, money. Taxes on booze supply the Chancellor with some of his richest revenues. It pays the government to allow people to drink more, more often and more continually.

Of course, the forces of reaction are outraged, but they are outraged for the wrong reasons. Too 'permissive', they say, while out of the other corner of their mouth whispering 'Lock the bastards up'. And yet I somehow doubt whether any one of those voices of reaction has been abstinent for more than a month. Not a small tot in the morning tea? A Bloody Mary while you cook an omelette brunch? Not an early snifter at midday? Not a Pimm's while you're cutting the lawn? Not a wee glass of sherry with the six o'clock news? Not even a night-cap?

This measure will do nothing whatsoever to affect the development or outcomes of alcoholism either for the individual or in the rubbish hinterlands of 'society'. Addicts will get their fix – booze, hard drugs, sex, shopping, power – whatever legislation is in place. It doesn't matter when, theoretically or legally, you are allowed to drink. You'll drink anyway. Think back to Prohibition, and the disastrous underground culture of alcohol. It doesn't matter how expensive a government makes the stuff. Think of Scandinavia, where my friends save up for weeks then blow the lot on a weekend where their hangovers expensively flirt with death.

A true story (and forgive me if you've heard it before): a friend of a friend was in treatment for alcoholism. The clinic was adjacent to a fine 18-hole golf club. Together with a small treatment group – all alcoholics – he arranged for an outside contact to leave whisky miniatures in all the holes of the course each evening, so that he and his pals in non- recovery could nip out and collect them each midnight.

Another story, and this one a commonplace: a man is so concerned about his alcoholism that he arranges to spend the rest of his life on an ice-floe in the Arctic Ocean. Everything is sober, cleanly frozen, and going well, when suddenly he spies an Eskimo hunter walking towards him over the ice. 'No White Man has ever been here,' says the Eskimo, unwrapping a Welcome-gift from his sealskins. The present is, of course, a bottle of traded Scotch.

It's not just that you'll find alcohol, whatever the circumstances or the government legislation. Alcohol will find you. You'll think you're using it. But it is using you.

For the millions of human beings who can drink 'normally' (yes, I know that begs the kind of questions that I can't definitively answer), then the government's liberalization of the licensing laws is a sensible and welcome step, and as a chronic alcoholic, I have no problem with it. But I would urge a second look at the real reason behind the legislation: to repeat, it's about money. The government raises billions, and again more billions, from users of alcohol. And yet it has no easily available and publicly funded treatment centres, no real or cogent policy on the treatment of addictions. NHS doctors, conscious of their status as purse-holders, don't want to treat alcoholics. The few specialist teams of alcohol workers are desperately underfunded. The kind of treatment I eventually, luckily, and life-savingly had is expensive and private, and, for the vast majority of the population, simply unavailable. Surely the positive, humane, and reasonable policy for the government to espouse would be the promotion and enhancement of treatment centres for alcoholism even as it liberalizes the drinking laws? Alcoholics, after all, may have signed their own death warrants, but they have also, via the Chancellor, paid for their own salvation once they finally, critically, and possibly too late, need its teaching.

A Symptom of Something Deeper

I know. I repeat myself. I seem to have been obsessed, in early recovery, with the UK licensing laws, with the accessibility – or otherwise – of ethanol. I was still vitally interested with the drug, alcohol, in all its forms.

As a counterbalance to these repetitions, here are two excerpts from Ken Lincoln and Al Logan Slagle's masterpiece about the present-day structures of American Indian society, The Good Red Road *(San Francisco: Harper & Row, 1987).* The prose is so breathtakingly well-written that it speaks for itself.

Williston Jones lived at Second and Sweetwater, in an alley shack just up from the old whorehouse. When I was a boy, a black pimp used to drive a white Cadillac down in the dirt street called Sweetwater, where Indian girls drank whiskey in teacups with lonely men and disappeared along dimly lit halls. This forbidden part of Alliance was a place of mystery, shadowed by the railroad and Indian 'tent city.'

Williston or 'Willis' went to public school with white kids like myself, here in Alliance eighty miles south of Wounded Knee. Willis was a mixed-breed Sioux Indian from Pine Ridge, just over the South Dakota state line. As kids we hung around ball fields and Indian Creek and the pool hall through the eighth grade... Willis fought all the time. I still remember the rage in his face, an anger burning so deep that kids kept their distance. Even at Indian Creek, where we all swam and fished and smoked driftwood, everyone watched out for Willis. He'd turn on you for no reason. At thirteen I sharpened a metal shoe horn and carried it in my back pocket for protection down the alleys of South Alliance.

But as Willis grew older he got even meaner; he started drinking hard and ditching school. Then he quit Alliance. His anger burned him up. Every fight lodged in his stomach. He wanted to kill something, somebody. His mother died. His father died. His brothers and sisters scattered and died. He was dying, and cheap wine took the ache away at fourteen. Fourteen years old, an alcoholic. It still wasn't legal before 1954 for Indians to drink in public, so he had to steal for his addiction.

He was always fighting. 'Lincoln, I'm gonna cut you up, white bastard,' he menaced in the pool hall. He swung a belt studded with razor blades. Willis went to reform school, later the state penitentiary. Alcohol was his painkiller: symptom, escape, and finally the cause of his despair. Williston made a fist of that knot in his stomach and hid down there, all the while he was drowning.

Twenty-five years later we met again, when I returned with Logan to the northern Plains consulting with alcohol abusers and Indian traditionalists on treatment. For Williston the reservation had been just as bad, or worse, than Alliance. There was less than nothing to do. Not low income, *no* income people, the saying went. Willis had been sleeping in junked cars and working odd jobs for a few dollars to buy white port and Schlitz beer. Summers he slept in the park. I last saw him hunkering on a street corner with T-Bone Wilson, his half-breed drinking buddy.

'I owe you guys something.'

'Yeh, what for?' Willis asked.

'Talking, talking about your drinking. Giving reasons... Mebbe with your help we'll get a halfway house.'

'Hell, that wasn't nothin'.' T-Bone tossed his head. 'We do what we have to. Halfway don't help anyway.'

Willis looked up expectantly. A few dollars would help. He stared across the street at the Sandhillo Bar. A pickup pulled up with a full gun rack. The cowboy spat in the storm drain and went in for a beer. Willis looked straight at me with raw need, nothing but hunger in his eyes. I reached in my back pocket.

'Here's twenty bucks, ten apiece, for…services rendered. But promise me you'll eat something.'

'You bet.' Willis grinned and held out his hands. 'A nice big burger at the Dairy Queen.' They were up off the sidewalk.

'You guys take care, okay?' I had mixed feelings about giving Willis and T- Bone money to buy what was killing them, but they were starving. I knew that, too.

'Sure, we'll take whatever we can. So long, Lincoln.'

Williston hobbled away with pinched-in steps. T-Bone lumbered after him. Williston's toes had frozen off when he was sleeping in wrecked cars several winters back and temperatures dropped far below zero for months. The scars on his leg were deep brown ruts where gangrene had set in a wound.

In 1968 Williston Jones listed the city jail as his home. Some of his friends had used their belts to hang themselves there – four I had known in 1968. Indian girls whispered hoarsely of being raped by cops in solitary cells.

Williston would drink and squat on Main Street near the railroad tracks. Every day the wine scraped his stomach bloody. His liver swelled out under his ribs. His eyes turned yellow and bloodshot. He seldom ate. Most days he drank hard and did nothing but hunker down and fester with rotgut. Some days between binges he laughed and dreamed of making a life, of the 'old ways', of buffalo and Crazy Horse and the *Paha Sapa*, or Black Hills. His visions came lean. Most days he just drifted by, one sickness to the next. He waited on a street corner for the cops to pick him up. It was the only way to go home.

'You'd make a good alcoholism counselor,' I told him that last summer. 'You've been around. You know what it's like being drunk, living on nothing. You talk straight.'

'I got nothin' to hide,' Willis said flatly.

In January temperatures dropped to forty below zero in northwest Nebraska. Indians on the 'res' were huddling around wood-burning stoves. Citizens in Alliance stayed indoors. The schools closed. Williston was hungry and freezing. He went with Harley Poor Horse to scrounge for garbage behind the Safeway market. They found some old barbecued chicken and shared it. A few hours later Williston got sick and vomited. Harley called the city cops. Nurses at the hospital treated Williston for DT's and sent him home to the shack on Sweetwater alley.

The next day he went into a seizure. Williston died in an alley at the age of forty.

There was no autopsy. No inquiry into his death. No family. No mourners. No questions.

'He never did learn anything,' my Lakota brother Mark would later say. 'He lived in the white man's world, and the white man didn't want him in it.

'He was buried in a plain pine box. I always thought of him as my friend, even though he was down and out and no good. When he went to the hospital with convulsions, he'd call me up and say, Mark, will you bring me some cigarettes and candy? I'd bundle my grandson up, and we'd take him what he wanted. Hell, I'd give him wine. Damn alcoholic's got to have it. I've been there.' Mark paused.

'Well, that was the extreme of the Indian – an' he's dead.'
(Reproduced from Lincoln and Logan Slagle (1987), pp.21–23, with permission.)

After breakfast and a pass through the St. Francis Indian Museum, Jay, Logan and Meghan stopped at the alcoholic rehabilitation center near Sinte Gleska Community College. The director, Benjamin Crow, sat in his office looking out on a parking lot paved with mud. He was in his late forties; his round face emitted the exhausted air of someone convalescing from a long illness. Like so many Indian alcoholics, Benjamin was diabetic, his heart permanently damaged by what 'res' drinkers called 'the drug that comes in a pop-top can.' If he had continued to drink, Crow confessed bluntly, he would have died long ago, if not from drinking itself, then probably from some accident, in a car or otherwise.

Meghan...asked him about the Native American Church and traditional religion, whether he thought they provided any ways to conquer the problem. Benjamin had some qualms.

'Alcoholism, the way I know it, is not cured,' Crow stated flatly. He leaned back and looked out on the mud. 'There has to be some other way than non-Indian programs like AA, or church groups, or gover'ment studies. Those are just holding patterns, at best. Got to be tribal an' Ind'in-run. We don't treat people like we got some sort of leper's club runnin' here, draggin' the dead and dyin' into the hospital. We go out to the whole family, not just the ones we get comin' in here.' Meghan nodded her understanding, and he continued: 'But I'd say, too, that Mr. Indian is not always going to make some better way with traditional religion or peyot'. It depends on who he is an' where he lives. Always ask yourself, "Does he do better with it?" We're askin' to find out what works, not just what people think is old-time Ind'in.'

Meghan had a personal interest in solutions to alcoholism; her own Irish-American father was one of millions with 'a drinking problem.'

'Myself and all my co-workers, we're all alcoholics, what you call rehabilitated,' Crow continued. 'We got a certain method of operation to help other alcoholics get some control back over their lives. So we monitor everyone who comes under our care. Meet with each one, every month at his house, to see how he's coming along. The center keeps up a detox clinic, but we only have space for two patients at a time; we got to service twenty settlements with seven counselors.'

'Aren't there state facilities for Indian alcoholics?' Jay asked. He was furiously scribbling notes in the gray-lighted office.

'They treat us as being out of their jurisdiction since we're Indians. Veterans can use the non-Bureau hospitals for vets, but where does that leave Joe Indian or his wife who're not vets? You know, a lot of people come in here needing other kinds of medical attention than just a place to dry out. They're real sick with tuberculosis or diabetes or kidney failure. If they've got no hospital space for them over at the Pine Ridge Public Health Service hospital, an' that's a long way to go, we can only get the doctor here to give librium and put the guy in bed for a while, or else in the drunk tank. Don't cure nothin'. He's back on the streets drinking again in a few hours.'

Jay stopped writing and stared at him.

'I would say that even for Indians living off the reservation you need Indian counselors and staff. They understand because they're Indian themselves. They know all the weaknesses and fears, and all the tricks Indians will pull to stay alcoholic. Any alcoholic makes excuses. You got a better chance of cutting through the smokescreen if you know what his people are like, how they live, and all that. Indians know Indians. This work takes an awful lot of energy, an' Indians are damn smart about hidin' their habits.'

Logan scribbled something, then asked, 'How serious is alcoholism on your reservation?'

'Rosebud alcoholics, beyond just winos like you'd see anyplace, I'll tell you – it's like a drowning epidemic. Seventy-seven percent of all the adults here, and I'm *not* talking to you about occasional drinkers or social drinkers. It's about sixty-five percent *under* the age of eighteen.

'I have been through those Twelve Steps of Alcoholics Anonymous,' he said, patting his still swollen right side. 'For the most part, that is not going to do for Indians, because they're not behaving as Protestant individuals under "one God," and they're nowhere near the "middle" class. The "steps" just don't speak to them – they need Indian concepts, Lakota, even warrior codes to fight their disease. If one family member goes down with it, there's a good chance all the rest do the same. You see a whole family – and you know with Indians that *tiospaye* or "family" is stretching pretty wide – uncles, aunts, cousins, kids – *every*body's going to be sick, right down to the dogs and cats that suck the corks.'

'What keeps everyone so down and out?' Jay frowned. 'Don't they *see* what's happening to them?'

Benjamin clenched and unclenched his fist. He wanted them to know. 'The Indian has got no jobs that are steady, no security, no confidence,' he said in a monotone. 'About all these people got left is being close to each other, however they can. Misery gets to be a bond. They depend on each other for everything, so they get drunk together and *stay* drunk too – help each other to live, some with sharing food, booze, even protection – but *not* letting each other feel the pain of being Indian. Booze washes that down your gut.'

He unbent his arm and opened a clenched hand. 'It's better in their mind not to feel the pain. So booze is like bad medicine, a sort of general anesthesia that's slow suicide.' He got up and leaned on his desk, seeming very tired against the rain and mud visible through the window.

'It would mean a lot if doctors could come together in this thing, with all they've got – cure the basic problem of what alcoholism is for every American, not just Mr. Indian. Then after that maybe we can boil it down to an individual problem. Right now, it's the disease of the whole people that the white man – and being around the white man – brought to the Indian. And the Indian's dyin' as a nation from it. Probably ninety percent of all deaths here are alcohol-related.'

He began to unbend a paperclip with one hand. 'The state and the government fight over him, the whites want what little claims he's got left, land an' minerals an' water an' game, even his holy lands an' cemeteries. Mr. Indian's afraid to make anything of himself, afraid somebody will come and take it again, and he's right! That's the worst thing about talking him out of drinking a painkiller to forget – he's right!

'The vanishing American. Damn! He keeps getting told he's goin' to die out; so what incentive has he got to quit drinking, if it's all lost with the next termination act?'

He stopped, grinned a little. 'So that's the big challenge to the Indian alcoholism counselor – why the counselor should be Indi'n himself. We got to think up things, try to pull in all we can, all kinds of possibilities, to get to that *one* Indian, then his family, then on out. I think we got a chance of making it snowball the *other* way, if we play it right. If being a group can pull us down, why can't we use that to pull us up?' He threw his paperclip, dartlike, out the window into the mud.

Meg had observed AA meetings and attended ALANON, and she asked if it helped here at all. Benjamin knew how AA didn't work for Indians. 'AA wants to get people right with God and fittin' AA's idea of a good person and send 'em home to their communities, you know, to that big white mainstream "under God" beyond the gate.' Crow didn't disguise his reservations. The small-town application of Protestant abstinence just didn't fit. 'I'm sayin' no, we got to figure out a way to deal with the problem, besides getting' Mr. Indian back in the mainstream with God and ever'body decent white. You see, good as everyone's intentions may be, it don't work – it hasn't worked. Look around you. The Indi'n tryin' to go into the white mainstream is either impossible when he's a drunk, or it makes matters worse where he is with other Indi'ns. So naturally the mainstream he thinks about is back home, the *back*water of America, really, of his people's sufferin'. If he goes back to that one, he'll be right back to the bottle. It's a damn drinkin' circle!'

He waved his hands vaguely. 'Look what happens when he dries out. He goes straight home – where else can he go? Someplace where he's goin' to starve because he's an "alky" with no skills? Goes home to stay, or goes home to figure things out, and he gets lonely and guilty and depressed; people get on his back, everybody's hungry, right back where they were, crawlin' inside a bottle. So it's bigger than just wantin' a drink; it's a symptom of somethin' deeper, a pain all around.'

'What if a guy can't help craving alcohol?' Jay posed. 'Could there be a genetic weakness – ?'

'I don't think anybody seriously buys the excuse that Indians have a hereditary weakness for alcohol. So what? It's just one more excuse, just like all the other excuses we've heard for the Indian to give up.' He clasped his chest. 'Say maybe it is so – we got no history of using alcohol, no genetic tolerance, no way to control it socially, and we guzzle the stuff like kids in alleys. *That* is not the answer to the Indian's problem with drinkin'. The real problem is convincing Mr. Indian that *drinkin'* don't answer anything. Period.' He paused and looked down.

'The other night I was talking with this one man in the detox cell, asking him why he was always drunk or hungover. He told me his whole damn family were dying off from cirrhosis, so he felt like giving up. Parents, uncles, cousins, they were all gone. I said, "You're not gonna get the past back that way man, just lose out on your whole present. You got to help yourself. There's people, your own tribe, that will help – but all this self-pity is not getting you anyplace." But what's he got to live for? Think about it.

'In the big picture we're tryin' to start things out from scratch,' Crow said. 'Got to get a program educating all the people about alcohol, starting at the grade school. Little kids watch Mom and Pop and brothers and sisters get drunk and the cats lickin' the empties, so they say, "That's life."

'It's got to be a cure-*all*. That's a big word to show how big the problem is. You got to get them free. No new habits, no substitute drugs – An[t]abuse or librium or even tobacco. We tell people here, "Clean up!"' His face brightened.

'What it's coming down to is this. You *got* to recondition the whole of the people in the way they look at things, especially alcohol, but not just that. In 1954, Eisenhower days, they started letting liquor on the reservations legally to keep Mr. Indian from being a second-class citizen. They'll take away his land and his rights or give him some new "rights" that'll fix him so he's like the rest. Mr. Indian is getting' wise to that,' he noted briskly.

'Now, some tribes, Hopis and people like that, they never let alcohol in. Rosebud did. So you got to tell people that don't remember – drinkin' is *not* part of being Indian. He can still be an Indian without it. They'll sit around and pass the bottle, share every scrap of food they got, like the old days so nobody starves. But that just makes it worse. They all die drunk together.

'You *got* to get at the excuses. You got to step on some government people's feet. You got to keep all the bootleggers, including the respectable ones, from peddling on the reservation. Get to the kids in schools. Catch this disease at its earliest stages, before the person loses his job or whatever life he's making.' He lapsed into what appeared to be a personal revery: 'It's really typical that you'll have some guy, starts out staying under the table on weekends until work on Monday, back in shape Tuesday, jittery Thursday, holds on just barely till Friday, the[n] boom! – drunk as a skunk by six-thirty that night. So get him a job while he's on the wagon, help him change his habits and pay more attention to his kids and wife, and help her. Try to stop him just getting some menial job till he gets paid and then trying to kill himself and his friends on liquor he can buy with that.'

He tossed a paper coffee cup into the trashcan. 'Still, we're all in this together, red man and white. It's the same disease with different symptoms. There's no Indian mumps and no alcoholism that only kills Indians.'

(Reproduced from Lincoln and Logan Slagle (1987) pp. 164–169, with permission.)

June to October 2001

65.   27 June 2001

On Saturday last, Monika and I were married at the Dorpskerk in Amstelveen. The weeks and months of planning – the whole infrastructure of a ceremony involving fifty guests from half a dozen different countries – came to fruition in a weekend that passed in what was not quite a blur of smiling bewilderment.

There were happy moments. What I remember most clearly is the ceremony itself, and the promises we made to each other. I remember the look and feel of Monika's beautiful wedding dress. I remember the hot and stupid tears that were in my throat. And I remember how I could scarcely bear to look at Monika's father out of sheer joy – a joy that was close to responsibility, and the weight of these minor bits of flawed human history, and love, and panic.

Four days on, and I look back on a weekend of great happiness. But we both, Monika and I, have our addicted sides – you mean you haven't noticed? – and what we perhaps remember most keenly are the faces and voices who weren't there.

There were those among our friends who, early on, said that yes of course, they'd be delighted to come. And then, late in the day, they cancelled. They felt bad, or there was a message on e-mail, or they had urgent family commitments. One left us a phone message – sorry I can't be there, work…and so on… This arrived while we were enjoying the reception. And there were others, with more complex histories: those who left insincere and fruitless notes of early congratulation, as if we were some kind of business; those who had been so hurt by my own past and its terrifying actions that they couldn't speak, or couldn't even find, the words of forgiveness and charity and hope. Well, why should they?

And there were those with and among whom I've lived and worked for nearly twenty years, my colleagues. Apart from kind words from two graduate students, and a card from a married couple I'm glad to call friends, not one – not *one* – could apparently be bothered even to send the merest message. Well, again, why should they?

I keep coming up against my own addictions, and they go far beyond alcohol. Remembering 'my own wedding' as a set of owned moments where dislocation and absence lived… What could be more fatally addictive than that? It's like the junkie, the brilliant lecturer, the Nobel Prize winner, who lectures to 250 people in all the pomp and prestige of Stockholm. Every possible honour on, and what does he remember most vividly? Does he remember the 249 people who cheered and clapped with admiration, or the bare one figure that sat with folded hands, unconvinced by both the arguments and the presentation?

You remember that one.

You remember all the ones, the ones who went away, the ones you couldn't reconcile or manipulate or persuade, the ones you hurt. And remembering them, you give them powers – powers that run to self-pity and doubt, anxiety and trouble. You don't remember the present love, the generosity and the surprises of the continual moments. You remember the dark backward of your own lived and busy days, and the hurtling fury of the ones who are no longer there.

And so, in this time of transition, I am learning again that the world is merely the world, with its doubts and pain, its happiness and constructions of hope. I can refuse to give its hauntings any power. There are these moments to live, and they are moments and days of unexpected, and yet somehow known, novelty – days filled with some laughter, some work, and some plans for tomorrow and the summer. About the fractures and hatreds of the past, I have done, I think in all conscience, what I can, but must learn again that some hurts can never be healed. 'You have put a knife into the heart of our friendship,' wrote my closest friend three years ago. *But I am still alive, my dear, but I am still alive*...and can choose to live quietly, properly, and well.

Modesty, conscience, laughter, and a refusal to be deflected into grief: if we can share these things, they don't seem an unreasonable basis for a marriage. As Dankward wrote to us on our wedding day: *There is no way to happiness. Happiness is the way.*

If this is my choice, among all our present and speaking choices, I also begin to know that there are times when, sadly but with purpose, you have to revise the old Christmas card list.

66.   4 July 2001

I have been driving this past week – driving nervously, on the right, looking like any novice every two seconds in the wing mirrors, mindful of errant cyclists, reaching for the gear-shift with my left hand...only to find the driver's door of Monika's Mazda.

The DVLA finally returned my licence, after a great deal of trouble, and after nearly three-and-a-half years of a three-year ban had elapsed.

I wrote in this fractious chronicle, sometime in April last year, that I'd taken this case to a Magistrates' Court in Manchester – and won. The magistrates had no doubt that I was legally entitled to drive, and the ban was lifted – subject to medical reports – fifteen months ago. Therefore I was in the anomalous position of being under no technical disqualification, and yet without a licence. The sticking point was the Medical Section of the DVLA.

I understand that the DVLA's medical advisers have to be satisfied that a driver is fit to operate a ton of metal travelling at high speed. I approve of this caution, and think it is right that the Chief Medical Officer of the DVLA has wide discretionary powers. What I don't understand is why the said Chief Medical Officer withheld my licence when all possible testimonies, all available medical evidence, pointed to the strength and durability of this recovery. Back in June last, for example, I paid a licence fee, and £77, and was subject to the proddings and pokings of a DVLA-appointed doctor. At the same time, I had voluntarily returned to a hospital that had treated me in 1998, where I had asked for blood readings to be taken and forwarded to my GP. I had consulted my GP. I have no reason to believe that any of this evidence was anything but positive. The key problem, at that time, was that I had not been dry for a year, and this is one of the diagnostics available to the Chief Medical Officer when assessing one's fitness to drive.

Nevertheless, I was informed by phone last summer – one of those bloody awful, lengthy, put-you-on-hold forever messages – that I was legally entitled to drive. A week later, and a letter arrived stating that I wasn't entitled to drive. (I hadn't been a year sober.) It was the first of many contradictions to emanate from the DVLA.

Through the autumn, I marshalled evidence – from hospitals, from my doctor, from the university. My solicitor was baffled. Everyone was baffled. But of course, it wasn't their problem. In February, when the ban had technically elapsed, I expected to hear from the DVLA ('You will be contacted soon before the expiry of the period of disqualification...'). I did not.

I wrote again, phoned, faxed. I pointed out that I had already undergone all the medical tests with which I'd been asked to comply. I'd filled in the same damn forms at least four times, claiming truly, in black and white, that I suffered from a medical condition and that its name was 'alcoholism'. I received further, and contradictory, notices from the DVLA, and one rather threatening letter that claimed, wrongly, that I had failed to contact them or inform them of my actions. At this point, I called in a barrister friend, a man also, and blessedly, in recovery. The result of his intervention was that I once again attended the clinic of yet another DVLA-appointed doctor, and paid another £77. Meanwhile, my barrister friend was tearing out his hair in frustration. 'They're rude, arrogant so-and-sos, Chris,' he said. Rude and arrogant I had come to expect. Ignorance I had not.

However, a week ago and the phone rang. The good news was that the DVLA had granted my licence. The bad news – I had wearily expected this – was that they had sent out the wrong forms. Nevertheless, as of last Tuesday I am free.

I look back to the night of the ban, the terminal sorrow, the near coma, the sheer blind grief. I know I could have killed you. I could have killed your children. It is right that I should have been severely punished. I served out my community service, I paid my fines. Yet this frustration and blockage I didn't expect, and found hard to live with. I know: if I hadn't committed the offence, I wouldn't have been in this position. Yet I couldn't have tried harder, with both words and actions, to live out the meaning of the one word, Sorry.

Society is entitled to punish the anti-social behaviour of its drunks and addicts. We have rights, within a society, according to our way of living the responsibilities that accompany the rights. Yet I think the law should recognize that those making a sustained effort to recover their lives are taking on powerful extra responsibilities. In this context, society's representatives might be content to aid and assist those efforts.

Still, I lived with the frustration. We won the case.

67.   9 July 2001

I'm about to make a research and writing plan for the period 2001–02. I've made such plans every year for almost as long as I can remember. Yet I look back to last year's plan, find that the schedule was impossibly ambitious, and know, uncomfortably, that all the plans I've made have been full of irrational and magic thinking. Take last year's plan. No sane or well-balanced human could have achieved what I told myself I would achieve – a couple of books, new books of poems, several international conferences, learning a handful of major European languages… This plan, even assuming it was possible and useful, would take five years, let alone one. And there, squashed in the top right-hand corner of my chart (yes, we ran to a spread-sheet of Mr. Wonderful's god-forsaken ambitions), there's a column called 'Personal'. In my own *Personal* column I've listed 'Sobriety, Solvency, Fitness, Rest and Recuperation, Driving Licence'. These take less than one eighth of the column inches devoted elsewhere to the work I was to have completed since July last. In the *Work* columns there's the daily grind of words, papers, language analysis, poetry. In the *Personal* column there's a forgotten, crushed life. It's as if this is a graphic illustration of the relative importance I attach to working, as opposed to living. All these years, and I have thought that if I could work enough, develop a world-class reputation in, oh, just a mere two or three different fields, then this would make me loved, or more accurately, loveable. And all this time, I neglected the difficult and vital arts of living. And what are these? Connectedness, choice, listening, laughter, re-creation – among others. My chart tells me that these have been insignificant compared to ambition, words, the hiss of Success, Success.

I face this now in the context of this new life, this new marriage. If I get that new job, if I take on that new project, if I stand there prating to a world-gathered audience like a serious clown in my lecturer's waistcoat with all the prizes and the honours, then yes, of course, Monika will love me and we'll be happy forever, amen.

It's magic thinking. It's arrogant thinking. It lacks balance, as you'll doubtless have noticed, but it also, unforgivably, lacks intelligence, and therefore lacks clarity. How can I be so arrogant as to assume that Monika would love me for reasons X, Y, and Z? How could I be so insecure in myself and my own strange and particular gifts to think that my humanity could be slave to the patina of the bauble that is reputation? How could I allow myself to think like this?

Because I'm an addict, is why. Because I'm an alcoholic, whose addictions have gathered like waves, and broken on the shoreline made of smashed glass, down all the years of ambition and apology.

It's time for some realistic thinking. Like any human being, I am limitless, but I must know my own boundaries. Without recovery, for example, there would be no words, no work. It is, it has to be, recovery first, second, and third. And then family, and friendship, laughter and renewal. And then, and only then, work. I will not spread myself, I refuse to spread myself, across the columns of ambitions like a smear of crazy hope, only to find my driven, disappointing life crammed like neglect into a top right-hand corner. After all, recovery has its moment, and its moment is only today. Live that span of 24 hours as well as you can, and tomorrow will become clearer and more possible. (Or, in the meta-language of recovery, 'Keep it in the day.') Allow space for relaxation without guilt, and without fear. Make time for recovery, for honest words, for honest laughter. Look after yourself, so that you don't get hungry, angry, lonely, tired. Live for the joy of it, and the work will follow as surely as a tide.

I look behind me to where the research and writing plan for 2000–01 lies on the living room table. Multi-tasking? For heaven's sake. This was magni-tasking, and all of its ambitions are a useless shore of ground-up glass. Did it make me happy, any of it? Did it enhance this fragile and new life, this fragile and new recovery? No. All of these magic ambitions were merely aiming to please, and it's time that stopped. I can't buy recovery from good opinion, I can't even buy it from human love, it can't be won like a degree or an honour. It merely has to be lived, as well and as peacefully as possible, stranded on the beneficent island of today. And I know that perhaps I will have the courage never to make another 'research and writing plan', or pin it up on the cork-board so that it functions like a continual spur to guilt and reproach. A modest list, perhaps, and the love and spontaneity of today. These will have to be enough. I don't want to go back to the death-or-glory days, because the result would be death, and my last squalid look at human life would be at the stains on the carpet.

A 'Research and Writing Plan'? I have just written it.

68.   18 July 2001

I was thinking again about drinking habits. As I try, with different, indifferent success, to try and understand my former habits so that I can shake them, I come up against the recent, the not-so-recent, and the entirely old. It seems to me that you can adjust the habits most realistically if you lose the most recent habits first, working through until you come to the old, ingrained, and therefore, hard-to-eradicate patterns. In this sense, I speculate that drinking habits are not quite the same thing as alcoholism. Alcoholism may be something innate; it may be nature, not nurture. But drinking *habits*, as distinct from the arguably congenital 'disease' of alcoholism, are certainly nurture. *Habits* are to the underlying structure of addiction what a performance of Mozart is to the score on which it's based. Performances vary, within certain limits; the score itself is a more or less permanent given, a constant.

In this sense drinking habits can be likened to one's learning of languages. It's well known that language use is part nature – we're apparently hard-wired to learn languages, and to do so as children – and part nurture. If you learn languages within the chronological and genetic window for language-learning, you are invariably fluent however many languages you are exposed to. This helps to explain why children brought up in bi- or tri-lingual households speak both or all languages without any trace of an accent. If, on the other hand, you've begun to learn a language 'late' – after the age of thirteen or so – you will always be less than totally fluent, and you will almost always speak that second or third language with an accent. Your competence in that language will never be 'native-like'.

So the linguistic habits you learn last are the first you'll lose. Say you learn German at night-school at the age of forty-three, having learnt French at 'A' Level. You may in fact be a fairly competent reader and speaker of present-day German, but if that German is the last language you've forced yourself to learn, that competence will be the first you'll lose if your exposure to German-as-a-foreign-language doesn't continue. On the other hand, you'll retain much of the French you studied at school, even though you've been exposed to French less recently than German, and maybe haven't used it for years. And you will never, until the day you die, lose competence in your native language, even if you don't use it for thirty or forty years: it was the first to come, and will be the last to leave, as you become dust, and words become ash.

What has this to do with alcoholism? The drinking habits you learn last are the first, and the easiest, to lose. In this case it was vodka, or vodka-and-Lucozade, or vodka-and-just-about-anything. I would drink vodka in the morning to still the shakes, and drink it at night because I was too weary and ill to think beyond that clear and biddable poison. But the vodka, and the habits that went with it, I have found quite easy to lose. The vodka was a disastrous latecomer, and its habits came with it. The vodka and its habit were the first to be jettisoned.

Behind that, and there was an earlier habit of a few beers, and/or a bottle of wine (or two) on Friday and Saturday nights. This habit has been harder to unlearn, possibly, and precisely, because it was prior. Friday night comes, and there's still a voice in my head that's saying, 'Okay, Chris: let's party.' The voice is all the more loud and insistent if it's been a difficult and tiring week: 'Okay, Chris: let's party. You've deserved it, for heaven's sake...' As I walk past the Amsterdam bars, the sidewalk cafes, on a Friday night, this is what I hear…until I head for coffee and another meeting. It has been possible to cope with this old habit, but it's more deep-rooted because I learnt it earlier than the vodka.

Behind this, and there's another habit, more deep-rooted still. I go back to my first serious drink/drunk, that disastrous night in Keighley when my mother was taken into hospital. And there I was, fifteen or sixteen years old, and drunk. I was buying off the pain, trying to fix the disaster, aiming for peace, and nostalgia, and finding trouble and misery. Nevertheless, that habit – of fixing, of drinking on pain – was established there and then, as if it had been waiting to happen all along. Perhaps I was an alcoholic before I ever acquired the habits of alcoholism, but whatever the case, I know that the habit of drinking on pain (even on minor inconvenience) has stayed with me always, and always will.

I don't know whether the 'last to be learnt, first to go' idea has ever figured in treatment strategies. I don't know how it could. But the general tenet seems to hold for my direct experience, and thinking this through has helped me to understand my own addiction with more rigour…and more compassion.

69.   24 August 2001

There are times when I despair of alcoholics who think they suffer from a 'disease'. Suffering from a disease seems so much less reprehensible than suffering from selfishness and weakness, whose alcohol '-ism' abbreviates *I, Self, Me*. I've heard it dozens of times – the prideful alcoholic in months or years of recovery who confesses to a roomful of fellow drunks that he or she 'suffers from the disease of alcoholism'. That belief makes it easier to live with the disgusting truths of former drinking: *It wasn't me, officer, it was the disease*. The often-made and equally often self-serving analogy is with cancer.

I have come back to this problem of definition thousands of times during the thinking of the past few years. 'If it's a disease, it's a disease like no other, because you have choices…' That's one strand of my thinking. Another is: 'Well, yes, it has all the aetiology of a disease – but you can recover.' Another is: 'I am suffering from this disease, but what can I do about it? Poor me. And by the way, make mine a double.'

The truth is that I don't know whether alcoholism is a disease in the commonly understood sense. No one does. And even if we did, there'd still be the problem of whether the disease was inherited or acquired. Working that out would then translate into difficult private and public laws – not least, if addiction is partly genetic, the problem of whether or not to allow oneself to have children.

It seems to me that a more useful working analogy is with computer viruses. I offer this analogical restatement as a kind of obsessed addendum – as something that is trying to be both patient and painstaking with the truth of this condition.

It's a fact that computers 'catch' viruses. It doesn't matter if the computer comes from the shop already loaded with the virus (in which case the computer would be 'born' with it), or whether the computer acquires the virus later (in a rogue e-mail, say). However it picks up the virus, whether it's been natured or nastily nurtured, quickly or slowly the computer will become disabled.

Let's think about this for a moment. If a computer acquires a virus, the hardware is left, for the moment, pretty much intact: the computer *looks* the same, you can still switch it on, it will still – usually – run through all or most of its set-up routines. It will check its sub-systems against its main operating system, and the two systems will still be more or less working synchronously. It may even scan for viruses, while failing to detect the virus that has already infected it. Yet somewhere, deep inside the electronics, something is amiss. Some software has been infected (it could be the e-mail program that hosted the virus in the first place), and slowly, more and more of the software's operation becomes skewed. This is what unchecked viruses do: their purpose is to replicate. They can therefore be progressive, and fatal.

Drinkers in early alcoholism seem to me like pieces of human hardware that have been infected: they may look the same, they may run through their set-up routines as normal, they may work hard, long, productively, and imaginatively, but somewhere, deep in the human program, there's the addiction virus, and its purpose is to replicate. It begins, undetected, in a piece of evening software – the cocktail-party, the social drinking – and that's okay: society encourages everyone to *enjoy* having that same virus, even to share it, because governments make billions from precisely that dubious enjoyment. But what's not encouraged, what can't be predicted, what can't be legislated on by societies or individuals, is how the virus spreads. It spreads into sick mornings, into self-abuse, into hurt and wreckage; it spreads into unpaid bills, vomit on the carpet, divorce. It spreads into real diseases and real doctors. It spreads into everything I've lived. More bits of software are infected, and though the human computer may still just about look the same, the synchrony between the operating system and its component parts no longer exists. The thing – the entity that was once a sum of functioning parts – is sick.

The thing is sick. If it's a computer, it needs a radical diagnostic, and perhaps, in extreme cases, the operating system has to be reinstalled. If it's an alcoholic, it needs detoxification, and critically, it needs its human systems reinstalling after the detox. This means after-care: the cleansing, the lifelong process that is the commitment to learning recovery, the willingness to vigilance. It makes sense to me, and it makes a deeper sense when I think of what I wrote in the last *Wonderful* piece. When the human systems are progressively reinstalled, what it might pay to check out is first, the replacement of recently acquired drinking *habits* (as distinct from the acquired sickness, considered *in toto*), and next, the replacement of addictive software that was running earlier.

Thinking in this way helps me to avoid – that is, I usually avoid – the perilous self-pity that sometimes comes when I allow myself to believe that I suffer from the 'disease' of alcoholism. However it happened, I did become sick – really, physically sick, as well as mentally unstable – and I know the extent to which my hard drive, as it were, became progressively infected with the virus. True, what counts, both in my own life and in society's terms, is how the happening is handled next, but that handling also depends on finding accurate terms of reference, not the unreliable metaphors and meta-language the world likes to employ around the term 'disease'. Analogizing alcoholism with computer viruses might be a useful place to start in all our recoveries, even as we remember that computers do crash terminally, and that millions of alcoholics are never diagnosed, nor ever recover.

70.   28 September 2001

When the car caught fire on the last day of our honeymoon it proved to be one of those occasions that addicts certainly need and, less certainly, love. The drama: what a human location for constructed adequacies. The sirens, the spectators. The threat of an impending court case somewhere in Greece, with proceedings in a language I don't quite understand... Amen, *kyrie*, and pass the ammunition, in this case the slugs of vodka. Shock spreads its humours into aftermath and self-pity. Why us? Why me? Why now?

It wasn't the moment of crisis that triggered it. It was the time just afterwards, sitting, vaguely and knowingly shaking, in a bar on the Liston, in the centre of Corfu Town. The air was still acrid, the unsmiling, shocked witnesses were dispersing, the shade was hot with unforgiving, and Monika was visibly trembling.

My fault, I thought, my fault... Though it wasn't my fault, nor was it ours or anyone's. How like an addict to blame themselves for a random and dangerous accident. My cowardice, I thought: why couldn't I have put the bloody thing out, instead of standing and filling buckets from a horse pump while enthusiastic Greek car-park attendants hurled water at the conflagration? Monika intervened at this point of maudlin: what did you expect to do, stand on the bonnet and piss on the bloody engine? The money, I thought – feeling honour-bound to pay for terminal damage to a 12-year-old and under-insured Fiat Tipo whose stained and firestruck shell was at that moment being trailered to a nearby garage. A drink, I thought: bring me a drink, any drink, but preferably a large brandy, a steadier, a stiffener, a belter, a loosener, a muscle relaxant, a snifter, a cocktail, a pick-me-up...

Every instinct of every addict is selfish. I, Self, Me. This was a psychological cameo. To my credit, my first thought was of Monika – get out of the bloody car, get away, miles away, let me deal with it – but my second was of how badly I needed a drink, not only during those moments of powerlessness and crisis, but critically, after them. I stared at my cut hands and went moody. I ordered a coffee. I stirred in three goes of sugar. At this point I wasn't thinking of Monika, or the kind people whose car we'd so disastrously borrowed, or the useless spectators who could quite easily have been hurt if the wretched car had exploded in the heat. I was thinking purely of myself, and my instincts to raise something poisonous to my parched and awful mouth. And as I thought only of myself, I thrashed myself for uselessness, for carelessness, for middle-age, for – and why not? – for everything.

I'm writing about this retrospectively because I live with those moments still, as I allow them to instruct me. I think, often, that I am beginning to be cured. Perhaps, say the addicted jurymen of myself who judge me moment by moment, perhaps those awful years of crisis and hurt were just you, Chris, trying to cope with *a hard time*. Wouldn't anyone have done the same? (they ask, wheedling slightly). You'd lost so much, it was a miracle you survived, you were managing your grief, it was natural, it was merely *a hard time* and it's over now, go on, it's alright, it's safe, you can pick up a glass of wine, for heaven's sake…

Poisonous whisperings. And yet I know, deep within the analyses of my own knowing, that I am an addicted and addictive soul, whose first instincts are to Fix. The crises can come and go, the times of truth and untruth, the days of enduring strength, the brutal and quiet instants of patient heroism at the office desk – and Oh, I am a hero, I am Mr. Wonderful, and thank you, Chris, for all your support, we think the world of you. But what the world doesn't see are the incessant hours of self-questioning, the hesitant understanding, the doubt and the lived addiction buried uncomfortably in this increasingly plausible and specious, professional, married, middle-aged Self. I just want to Fix, to fix up the bad feelings, to make them go away, to buy time, over a bottle with bubbles in it, for the illusions of their leaving. That is my reality, and my deepest understanding. That is What I Do, it's the programme that kicks in whenever it can, which is often, and then always, and then everywhere.

Somewhere in the not so distant past an old car is burning, and the Greek afternoon is bitterly rancid with oil and flame. Memory itself can sometimes become like an illness. And yet I can choose, from this only perspective of sober freedom: I can choose that the sickness of remembering will not be allowed to hurt me, or anyone I love. Instead, deprived of its power, it can become some kind of fellow pilgrim.

71.   3 October 2001

'A drunk son-of-a-bitch is still a son-of-a-bitch sober.'

(Commonplace, reported from an Al-Anon meeting)

It's time to bring these – What are they, I keep asking? Journal entries? Jottings? – these scraps of witness to some kind of close. I had thought, naturally, that I would write not only the World's Greatest And Most Shattering Book About Alcoholism, but also that I would do so in exactly 100 short essays. '100'. Exactly. A number drawn from Dante's beautiful and exacting cosmology, as manifest in the *Divine Comedy*. A round, perfect, precise, addictive number.

As it is, I have said to myself, and to whomsoever might be listening, pretty much what I could have said, and what I needed to say as I attempt to explain – if only to that Self – some of the metaphysics of this condition. Last weekend, and late last night, I looked over some of these cuttings, these conceptual parings from the crooked heart, and inserted page numbers while correcting the worst typos. I have edited very little. Editing would destroy the contemporaneity and the truth: I can't live recovery by retrospective action any more than a river could learn to flow backwards. And besides, editing these pieces would be an invitation to the lure of half-truth, of making the words seem tidier, more elegant, more astute than they were, or ever could be. The words were not particularly astute, and if I had aimed for stylistic elegance I would have written very differently. If there is any truth here it lies in the authenticity of self-observation, aided, perhaps, by adequate persistence and tonal consistency. The act of that observation has also meant humour, and a small measure of difficult pity for the strange creature who lives among his strange, generated landscapes on the cognitive island of today.

There are certain themes that recur here, and more tellingly, certain images that recur. One of these is the image of the empty railway track somewhere in a fog-bound, desolate Eastern Europe.

I was thinking about this image recently. Early recovery, for me, does feel like that. You wake up, come round, lurch into consciousness, and instead of the betraying warmth of the bar, the bottle, and the voices in both, there is nothing and no one. There's just you – or so you think – and a railway track, empty. There's fog smeared everywhere across the day, rolling into the distance and into the huge and endless birch forest on either side of the railway line. No one is coming. No bird sings. You pick yourself up, and in the utter absence of anything better to do, you start walking, stumbling along the gravel, your mouth tasting like iron.

Then I thought, rather suddenly, about how memory hurts. In early recovery, memories are often, if not usually, drinking memories. They are loaded with loss, sexual disaster, disease, shame, guilt. They're like cages full of wild animals – and of course, you step into the memory-cage because you know how to be cut apart and mauled again. That is your territory; it is also your characteristic behaviour. You are medicating yourself, expiating, explaining, by continual punishment. It's what you know how to do. It's terrible, but you don't yet realize how terrible it is.

Somewhere else, a figure is walking along a railway track, deep in an empty forest in (it may be) Poland. He is configured by loss, and shame, and memory, but he's walking, and that's better than the fact of death. After a few minutes, another figure looms out of the mist, and walks alongside the first. They recognize each other from some nowhere bottle in the nowhere, no-name past. 'What, are you here?' They just keep walking, together, loaded with their memories. Still no bird sings, and they don't speak much. But walking together is, somehow, better than walking alone. And an hour later, a third figure comes walking out of the forest. They walk along the railway track, the three together, each bowed with their different shames, their respective, awful memories. But then again, at this point in the apparently pointless journey, the fog starts to lift, and each one definitely hears the same bird singing, deep in the branches of the forest. As pace follows pace, mile follows mile, more faces and voices join them, and they're walking together, all of them with their different pasts, their idiocies and guilts, their particular accents, their individuated losses, their capacities. And soon, walking together, and sharing the journey, they come to the small, bright knot of a town, and a station. There is hot coffee, and a choice of new destinations.

There are their memories, the wild beasts ranging about, the hooded, clawed birds. The faces they loved, bruised and hurt. The torn mouths of insults, the rage. The resentments and the self-pity. The overflowing ashtray. Vomit and black-out, and the words they've forgotten. But as these chosen, unchosen, temporary faces gather over coffee, pausing at a point somewhere in the journey they had to make, each looks around for his or her memories and finds that those memories have lost the power to tear today apart. It's not – it is surely not – that the past has transfigured. It is not even that these ones recovered from yesterday and fog have consciously changed, while they walked, into some miracle of strength and presence. They are all recognizable as what they were before. Yet, somehow, their memories also are present, but have lost their power. Nowhere in their walking Now, over the hot coffee and the tentative laughter, are the omnipotent isolations of the drunk and the fixer, the grandiosity, the rambling, self-pitying monologues. As the memories lose their power, the ego loses its capacity to interest or to charm.

Still, the memories haven't disappeared, and will never, quite, disappear. But this is the act of recovery, the act of mere walking, into the first fog, towards a destination that has been a reported source of hope to a few million others. It is trust, and consolation, and company. It's the acknowledgement of a shared journey. There – in the knot of three, or four, or forty, all walking – there also, always, are the razors of memory and the squalid hurts. Yet deprived of their power in the chosen act of recovery, the memories have themselves become not even scars, not even bruises. They have become companions.

72.   9 October 2001

And this coincidence – not quite frail, but certainly travelling – was nearly done. I ask myself for a provisional summary, and find nothing but today, 9 October 2001, a date of no particular value were it not for the fact that the world – what Bush and Blair like to call 'the civilized world' – has again gone crazy, to the extent that parts of it are again at war. My own face hangs over the notes – on the train, in the office – much as it has always done. Where am I? Am I in my diminished ambitions? Am I in the overhead locker on the KLM flights between Manchester and Amsterdam? Am I in the strategy documents and the committee minutes? Am I in the doctor's notes, the bank account, the credit statement?

I am nowhere but here, and that's the pity but it's also the hope. The pity is in the recovering, non-recovered addict. Clean of alcohol, there's yet all the other addictive patterning – the using, the vanity, the cigarettes, sugar, coffee; the raw manipulations. How much has this changed? True, I no longer engage, tearfully and furiously, with those drunken mono-logues passing the awful midnights. I'm cleansing myself of fantasy. Then again, by cleansing myself of fantasy I'm also, it seems, cleansing myself of creativity. Sometimes I feel both stale and small. Curiously, colleagues at work have sometimes remarked that I am 'smaller', by which they seem to mean that I've lost weight, though I guess they might also mean that I am a conceptually less vivid presence within the Faculty – assuming that the Faculty noticed the presence in the first place. Less...vivid? That would be true, too. 'Chris used to be a big guy,' said one, 'a broad, heavy-set sort of chap. I wouldn't have liked to have met him on a dark night...'

Well, well. It's I that have bruised.

And the hope? The hope seems to be in however many months of recovery this is, today – something like twenty-two months, give or take a few days. A Second Birthday stares at me from the end of December, though I try not to think of it because it's too far ahead, and in any case, what does an alcoholic do with the idea of a celebration?

And today? Today's not particularly great, nor is it dire, apart from the people who bomb each other on the other sides of the world; except for the vagrants, the refugees, the starving, the dispossessed, the con-fused, the grieving, and the lost. So many lost people, so many languages and tongues, so many driven hurts, and so much fear. I try to remind myself that I can't fix up even that fraction of the world's problems I can see, and tell myself only that I can find a remote, tiny, yet productive echo of those troubles in myself. Those echoes can be attended to, and their disquiet eased, today. But about the wider noise I can do nothing, whether I stand on the barricades and ask 'Why war?', or write Disgusted-from-Greenfield letters to the local papers. I'm sometimes appalled by my own enforced quietism, this apparent lack of action, the inertia, the terrible scepticism. However, that is how I am, today, and it's where I am – still alive, still questioning, still trying to remember some easing politeness, and trying not to forget to laugh, particularly at myself, Chris McCully, another short-lived fragment of a frail travelling coinci-dence.

Elsewhere, in the infrastructure of this life and journey, the circum-stantial events seem positive. There's a new, if precarious, financial security, and the times when I had to live on a 99p supermarket chicken for three days (and share it with guests) seem, today, to be over. A recent check by an interested and interesting banker yielded nothing but positive results, though it will take another couple of years, perhaps more, to re-establish financial liquidity. (Then again, 'total liquidity' might not be a good thing for a professional alcoholic.) Likewise, my physical health is good: I have scars in unfortunately intimate places; I get tired far too easily, and the consumption of sugar is abnormal; for the first year of recovery I suffered from flu germ after germ, because the immune system was still not completely recovered from its hammering by vodka; and I still have a numb big toe, the residue of peripheral neuropathy. But in general, I have rarely felt better, and sleep is an indescribable blessing.

Sleep. '...Nature's soft nurse...' Yes, I sleep, and sleep normally, or at least, rather better than the dying King Henry IV. While I sleep alone, during the commuting weeks, I still keep the radio turned to the World Service, and – pathetic, touching – still like to see, if possible, a crack of light somewhere beyond the door, though I tell myself I'm not afraid of the world, nor of the dark.

What I am afraid of is, I suppose, my memory – not the memories within the memory, but the memory of waking up, sweating, dis-eased, and shaking, during the years of vodka, telephones, and loss. I still find it more than difficult to revisit those jagged remembrances, though I can bear them if I have to, and as I wrote recently, many of those memories have become a form of companion, rather than a species of nightmare.

Then there's work. I have my job, and I'm learning to think of this as 'merely' a job, rather than the proud vocation I once imagined university work to be. The truth in this context seems to be that even as this univer-sity valued me sufficiently to put up the money for final treatment of my alcoholism, it also valued – and rather more – my driven, addictive capacity to work. The fact that I can no longer afford to work in such a driven, endless, addictive way has confused many people. I'm consider-ing, in fact, whether to give up this work, or at least, try to find another job outside the UK, and if possible, closer to my new home in Amster-dam. I have been here – in the same university department – too long.

This said, it's frustrating to know that I have to make the necessary changes slowly and carefully. My instincts are still for the Grand Renunciation, the stuff-your-pension speechifying. What a bore I am to myself sometimes.

More important than the job, though still imaginatively less real, are my family, and friends. I've worked hard on trying to stay properly connected with them, though I dare say that, swamped by what I imagine to be the value of My, My, My work and worries, I've sometimes let them down. I often remind myself to work harder on being less self-absorbed. The fact that I need these reminders is an indication of just how self-absorbed I can be. But you will forgive me, I hope, if I write less now of the family, and nothing more of Monika. I do so because I'm trying somehow, however clumsily, to protect them. And I also do this because it's hard to type when your eyes slowly dance.

More important than my family is recovery, and the activity that goes with it. I still begin every day in life with some form of reading and reflection, and each day ends with retrospection. I wouldn't skip doing this; nor have I. I hated it at first. It seemed worthy, pious, boring, and useless. In a relatively short space of time it became a reminder, a corrective, a lifeline. Since I do a great deal of this reading – and even, more recently, this thinking – in Dutch, it improves my Dutch, too. And now and again, I still attend recovery meetings, of various forms and types. I guess that I'm one of the world's least committed and most sceptical recovering drunks, and those whose lives and habits circle around AA will forgive me when I say that the AA meetings I've attended have ranged from the unspeakably awful to the absolutely revelatory. From abjection to revelation, there are just a lot of sick people present, banging on about the drinking gestures of the unreliable, hurtful past. These people are, in fact, precisely like me, and I'm proud to be a part, however haphazard, of that liberal, recovering, and (mostly) good-humoured constituency. I've found more truth and human construction around the tables of recovering alcoholics than I've found in the small back rooms of political meetings or the panelled spaces of university councils – each filled, it may be, with men and women whom the world accounts wise. What does the world know?

Today is just today, and its pain, laughter, trouble. It can't be pressed into a different imaginative shape, it resists annexation, it can move neither more slowly nor more quickly, however much and however passionately you wish it different. Its need, its humour, and its forgiveness will leak into tomorrow, and I, Chris McCully, will be part of those things, too, and they will pass in turn – as I will, eventually. And today, really I don't know if and when I shall have my next drink: I only know, and can only promise, that it will not be at any time between now and nightfall.

On that provisional note of fragility and transience I will end, simply saying that despite these labours I am trying to learn to be happy, and that I feel very much better. Yet I am not now, nor ever will be, cured.

'Crate Britain – Shock report warns we're nation of boozers' from The Sun (UK daily tabloid), Friday 13 June 2003

By Jacqui Thornton, Sun Health Editor

BRITAIN WAS LAST night branded a nation of boozers in danger of drinking ourselves to death.

Addiction charity Turning Point found more than 3.8 million people are hooked on alcohol – 800,000 of them women.

That's six times the number addicted to hard drugs.

Booze also kills 13 people every day – three times more than Class A narcotics including heroin.

Turning Point carried out a survey amongst a section of its 69,000 patients in England and Wales.

Vodka

The study found that the average length of time patients had been dependent on booze was 14 years.

Many of those quizzed sank a bottle of spirits every day, though one was on three or four bottles of vodka.

That's 1,000 units in the week, compared with the recommended 28 for a man.

Chief Executive Lord Victor Adebowale called for the Government to end its 'neglect' of alcoholics and give them as much help as drug addicts.

Whitehall has earmarked £573 million in 2005 for drug treatment – but spends just £95 million a year on alcoholism. Due to lack of cash, six in ten problem drinkers have treatment delayed for up to 18 months – by which time it can be too late.

Turning Point wants alcoholics needing care to have an assessment in two weeks and to be put in detox for a month.

When drinkers do get treated, it has spin-off benefits to the NHS and courts, the study claims. It found a person went into hospital suffering from alcohol-related problems every seven minutes.

Heavy drinking causes about three per cent of all new cancer cases, 8,000 every year. It also increases the risk of dying from strokes, cirrhosis of the liver and damage to the brain and nervous system.

The cost to the NHS is £3 billion a year, almost an eighth of the total hospitals budget. Those dependent on alcohol were also eight times more likely to appear in court, with it [alcohol dependency] being involved in almost half of all domestic violence incidents. Ex-boozers getting help include jobless Mick, 56, from Acton, West London who used to down 20 cans of strong cider every day.

He now has two months of a six months detox course to go at a Turning Point rehab centre.

Mick said: 'I told myself I could handle it, but in truth I didn't care if I was shaven or had clean clothes. At breakfast I'd have some cans, then be down the off-licence at opening time.'

Mick, who turned to booze three years ago after being forced to give up work through stress, said: 'One day a lad aged 29 in the same house died through drink and drugs.

'That made me question what I was doing. If I had carried on I would be dead by now.'

(Reproduced from The Sun, *Friday 13 June 2003, with permission.)*

APPENDIX 2

News of a relapse

In July 2003 I was sent a report culled from *BBC News online* (14 July). The report contained news of a post-liver-transplant George Best, someone whose recovery interested me very much. Since I have been unable to track down the copyright holder of this material, I supply a paraphrase here, together with a brief commentary.

- George Best and a 31-year-old man were arrested in Reigate on suspicion of assault causing actual bodily harm after a pub brawl. The two men were later released without charge.

- According to his wife and another witness close to George Best, Mr. Best seemed to be going about with a new group of friends who were not 'helping him'.

- His wife is said to have been furiously angry with the pub for serving George.

- Tommy Docherty is reported to have said how saddened he was. After George Best received his transplant, Mr. Docherty thought that George had alcoholism 'cracked'. Mr. Docherty added that George Best was the only person who could help George Best.

- George Best's doctor, Professor Roger Williams, pointed out how dangerous it would be if Mr. Best continued drinking, but also said that 'occasional lapses' were common with people who had the condition of alcoholism.

And that was it. To any non-alcoholic outsider, George Best's continued drinking, as this was reported in July 2003, looks like insanity. To me, it is analogous to what happens to thousands, perhaps millions, of alcoholics...and to their families. It is analogous – although I was mercifully spared both the liver transplant, and the public spotlight – to what happened to me. That is, alcoholic drinking seems to be a kind of programmed behaviour. Changing the programming is many times more difficult than, say, stopping an oil-tanker dead in mid-Atlantic. The addictive pro-gramming respects nothing, not even the people, or even the replaced organs, that are helping to renew the life of the alcoholic. Of course it looks like insanity, but inside the alcoholic a remorseless logic is working itself out. Drinking is what you do, because drinking is what you are. And alcoholic drinking will take what is left of you away, forever.

As George Best's doctor pointed out, relapse is common. From an increasing personal experience and understanding of others' recovery, and of my own, I suggest that it takes a *minimum* of three years to 'stop drinking' – that is, to renew one's life after acknowledging that you are drinking alcoholically. That minimum would also have to be sustained by honest and continual contact with other recover-ing alcoholics. And even then, relapse will be common, as the remorseless logic of addiction keeps trying to reassert itself.

Tommy Docherty got it partly right. The only person who can help George Best is George. There are no rescuers, and no more excuses. Together with the rest of us, George's recovery really begins not with a liver transplant, but with surrender. 'I am completely defeated by the fatal logic of the addiction that's working inside me and making me up. I am chaos. Without recovery, I am going to die.'

But alcoholism is never 'cracked'. George can never crack it, and no more can I. All I can do, today, is to keep on choosing to recover. And because his story moves me so much, I wish George Best the same kind – and the same extent – of the luck, the hope, and the love that has followed me into this present recovery.

APPENDIX 3

'Alcoholism, genetics, and National Socialism' Chris McCully with Monika Schmid

SOME TIME IN June 2003, CBMcC caught a glimpse of a news report on the BBC1 evening bulletin, in which it was claimed that scientists had found, or were on the threshold of finding, 'the alcoholism gene'. I looked on the BBC website the following day for a text of the report, but although I found plenty of interesting material there on genetics, I found nothing specifically about the previous night's report.

I began to ask myself questions about what legal, political, and social issues would arise if indeed it were true that scientists had identified 'the alcoholism gene'. Unfortunately, one hasn't to go very far to discover what one society did with, and to, alcoholics once it made the assumption that chronic alcoholism was genetically transmitted. That society is the Germany of the 1930s and 1940s. It's worth pointing out that what happened to many alcoholics, and to their families, under the Nazi regime is in many respects simply the logical consequence of ideas that had been current in many parts of Europe and the United States for decades before the National Socialists ever came to power in Germany. That is, the Nazi doctors and scientists usually didn't consider themselves as doing anything *wrong*. Indeed, if they thought about it at all, they might well have considered – on the evidence, they *did* consider – that they were engaging in a medically (behaviourally) logical, and therefore acceptable, form of social Darwinism.

As always, it is history, or a version of history, which helps us to learn lessons that are both terrible and generous. The lessons are generous because they are quite freely available to anyone who might care to take an informed interest. They are terrible insofar as they teach once again that 'society' – most characteristically, a self-styled ethnic grouping within that society – typically adopts an 'all or nothing' approach to its ethical problems. This shows very clearly in Nazi medical thinking about alcoholism: if there was a *genetic* component in alcoholism (and here the Nazi scientists were backing what was at that time no more than a brilliant hunch), alcoholism was *always*, and *wholly*, genetically transmitted. People being people, and society being composed of those same people, there is always the temptation to engage in the crude reductionism involved in 'all or nothing' thinking. That temptation is particularly acute when reductionism becomes explicitly politicized; that is, where reductionism is ideologically favourable to a ruling or dominant class – as happened in 1930s Germany.

'We know better,' we say. We know about the distinctive, but inter-related roles played by genotype and phenotype. We know about the complementarities, the reciprocity, of Nature and Nurture. Yes, we know much better now... But do we?

Robert Proctor, in his book *Racial Hygiene: Medicine Under the Nazis* (Cambridge, MA: Harvard University Press, 1988), gives a wonderfully detailed picture of how it was that the assumption of 'genetic transmission' coloured Nazi medicine. A particularly valuable part of Proctor's text is devoted to the medical and philosophical backgrounds that allowed such an assumption to become ideologically expedient in Nazi Germany. Proctor makes it clear, for instance, that ideas about the genetic transmission of disease had been widely explored during the decades spanning the turn of the nineteenth into the twentieth century[1]:

> The publication of Charles Darwin's *Origin of Species* in 1859 represents a watershed in the history of biological determinism in general and scientific racism in particular...

> The impact of Darwin's theory was enormous. Scholars in both Europe and America, excited by the prospect of founding a science of man on biological principles, began to apply the principle of natural selection to the science and ethics of human society...

> The German eugenics, or racial hygiene, movement emerged in the late nineteenth century... In 1895, in the founding document of what came to be known as racial hygiene, Alfred Ploetz warned against the various kinds of social 'counterselection' (such as bloody war, revolution, welfare for the sick or inferior) that lead to racial degeneration. If only the fit are to survive, Ploetz argued, then such counterselective forces should be avoided. He listed ways this might be achieved. War and revolution should be avoided wherever possible, and support for the poor should be given only to those past child-bearing age. Inbreeding and procreation by the very young should be discouraged, and people should be protected from agents such as alcohol, venereal disease, or anything else that might damage the human germ plasm.

---

1   Extracts excerpted and reprinted by permission of the publisher from *Racial Hygiene: Medicine under the Nazis* by Robert N. Proctor, Cambridge, Mass.: Harvard University Press. Copyright © 1986 by the President and Fellows of Harvard College.

But most of all, Ploetz warned against medical care for 'the weak', for this allows those individuals to survive and reproduce who otherwise, without the intervention of doctors, would never have survived... Traditional medical care thus helps the individual but endangers the race: Ploetz called for a new kind of hygiene – a racial hygiene (*Rassenhygiene* – Ploetz coined this term) that would consider not just the good of the individual but also the good of the race. (pp.13–14, 15)

Once the idea of 'purity of the breed', or 'the good of the race', is introduced into human medical ethics, then clearly it is possible for a society to 'select' *unfit* individuals. And, lest we are tempted to see such selection as a specifically German phenomenon of this period –

It was in the United States that theory was first turned into practice in this sphere. In 1907 Indiana passed the first laws allowing sterilization of the mentally ill and criminally insane; by the late 1920s twenty-eight American states and one Canadian province had followed suit, enacting legislation that resulted in the sterilization of some 15,000 individuals before 1930 – many of them against their will and most while incarcerated in homes for the mentally ill. By 1939 more than 30,000 people in twenty-nine American states had been sterilized on eugenic grounds; nearly half the operations (12,941) were carried out in California. (ibid., p.97)

Sterilization was illegal in Germany until the passing of the Sterilization Law in 1933. This sanctioned the compulsory sterilization of individuals on 'eugenic grounds':

The new law allowed for the sterilization only of (supposedly) 'homozygous' carriers of genetic disease; sterilization of 'recessive' carriers was forbidden and remained punishable as a criminal offense. (This presupposed, of course, that the various indications for which one could be sterilized – feeble-mindedness, schizophrenia, alcoholism, and so on – were single-gene traits that followed the simple rules of Mendelian genetics; today we know that such a notion is virtually meaningless.) (ibid., pp.101–102) [Then why did the BBC report, in June 2003, the discovery, or imminent discovery, of a single 'alcoholism gene'? – McC]

Under normal circumstances it was doctors who would refer individuals for sterilization, but family members could also volunteer brothers, sisters, fathers, and mothers to the medical profession for sterilization. Indeed, so pervasive – one might also, were the phrase in this context not so repulsive, say 'so attractive' – was the new social Darwinism that individuals volunteered *themselves* for sterilization 'for the good of the race'.

Sterilization, however, is expensive. It costs time, in particular, and time, to a Nazi doctor, is money. Medical documents from the period 1934–1936 make it

clear that practitioners in many cases felt that the use of public funds for the treatment of those suffering from an 'incurable disease' amounted merely to 'dissipation'
(a somewhat unfortunate term). Funds therefore were to be reserved for 'healthy'
(racially pure, congenitally undamaged) Germans. Considerable savings were to be
made (it was argued) if funds were withdrawn from the 'treatment' of those with
congenital diseases…such as, for example, the disease of being an alcoholic, the
disease of feeble-mindedness, or the disease of being a Jew.

Sterilization became 'disinfection'.

> Such problems did not remain in the realm of theory. After the war, docu-
> ments presenting detailed calculations of the 'savings' achieved through the
> euthanasia operation were found in a safe in the castle at Hartheim (one of six
> euthanasia institutions equipped with gas chambers). Euthanasia officials
> calculated that the 'disinfection' (murder) of 70,273 individuals in the course
> of the operation had resulted in savings of the following food items (in kilo-
> grams):
> Bread 4,781,339.72kg
> Marmalade 239,067.02kg
> (ibid., pp.183–184)

As the above quote begins to make clear, if voluntary or even compulsory sterilization had started to prove costly in terms of the available time of medical practitioners, then what was the sensible, eugenically proper alternative? It was 'disinfection'
– liquidation.

It will always be impossible to know exactly how many alcoholics went,
together with schizophrenics, gypsies, Jews, and other 'a-socials', into the gas
chambers. But some earlier records are available, particularly as these relate to the
sterilizations undertaken in the first year of the Sterilization Law (1933–34). It is
perhaps important to point out here that those sterilized included not only alcoholics, or those with Huntington's chorea, but those suffering from deafness, or
epilepsy, manic depression, or those unfit for military service. Recurring, in the
context of those referred for sterilization, are also terms such as *Störer* ('those who
create a disturbance') or *Gauner* ('crooks') or *Vagabunden* ('gypsies'). In other words,
it was ideologically desirable to reinterpret almost any kind of 'social deviance' as
'genetic defect' (Heyll 1997).

In Düsseldorf alone, in the period 1933–34, and based on some 2000 cases,
alcoholism is represented with 3.7 per cent among the total 'applications' for sterilization, but with over 4 per cent of the *actual* sterilizations. Sterilization took place in
73 per cent of all 'cases' of alcoholism referred for sterilization. (The numbers are
therefore 58 alcoholics sterilized, from 78 applications for sterilization.) In the
Düsseldorf statistics for this period, and with reference only to sterilization, alcoholism shows a higher incidence of *actual* sterilization than in any other 'congenital'

disease referred for 'treatment'. Thus in cases of simple-mindedness, schizophrenia, and manic depressive illness, 68 per cent of referred cases were actually sterilized, while in real terms those sterilized for epilepsy and deafness are 50 (against 58 alcoholics); for physical handicap, 45; for Huntington's chorea, 36; for blindness, 24 (Esch 1997).

And so, if we ask what a human society does with the knowledge that 'alcoholism is genetic', we don't have very far to look for an answer:

> [R]esentments towards social deviance found their approval as apparently justified opposition towards 'diseased hereditary material' (*krankhaftes Erbgut*). The possibility to apply the term 'hereditary disease' almost arbitrarily furthermore made it possible to extend those sectors of society that were considered *erblich belastet* (hereditarily impaired) further and further...
> (Heyll 1997, p.324)

To this feeble-minded reductionism, to this dangerous determinism, we would want to put a final question. Human genetic material is both durable and, as we know, adaptive. Over the millennia of human history and pre-history – a space of time during which the human gene pool has continually adapted for 'fitness' – what *advantages* have been conferred on human society *because of* the existence of genetic material whose nurture is called 'alcoholism'?

Some reading

What follows is a list of some of the titles I have found most useful, and other works which, in many different ways, went into the making of the present book.

AA World Services (1975) *Living Sober.* New York: AA World Services.
Booklet including practical suggestions on how to handle difficult personal and social situations while in recovery.

AA World Services (1976) *Alcoholics Anonymous* (3rd edn). New York: AA World Services.
The 'Big Book of AA'. A small, pocket-sized edition is also produced by AA, and is an indispensable travelling companion, small – and discreet – enough to fit into a pocket or bag. This travelling text is only available for the 2nd edition of the Big Book.

Esch, Michael G. (1997) 'Die Umsetzung "des Gesetzes zur Verhütung erbkranken Nachwuchses" in Düsseldorf und die Rolle der Medizinischen Akademie.' In Michael G. Esch *et al.* (eds.) *Die Medizinische Akademie Düsseldorf im Nationalsozialismus* (pp.199–227). Essen: Klartext.

Forstater, Mark (2000) *The Spiritual Teachings of Marcus Aurelius.* London: Hodder and Stoughton.
Grandly titled but readable little introduction to Stoic thought and practice.

Gorski, Terence T. (1989) *Understanding the Twelve Steps.* New York and London: Simon and Schuster.
Concise and useful guide to AA's Twelve Step programme.

Heyll, Uwe (1997) 'Friedrich Panse und die psychiatrische Erbforschung.' In Michael G. Esch *et al.* (eds.) *Die Medizinische Akademie Düsseldorf im Nationalsozialismus* (pp.318–340). Essen: Klartext.

Hulskramer, George (ed. and trans.) (2000) *Grenzeloos Inzicht.* Haarlem: Altamira-Becht.
Dutch translations of meditative, largely Buddhist, texts.

Kellermann, Joseph L. (1969) *Alcoholism: A Merry-go-round Named Denial.* [Pamphlet]. Published for Al-Anon Family Groups UK and Eire, 61 Great Dover Street, London SE1 4YF.
Largely aimed at Al-Anon members, but useful reading for alcoholics.

Kinney, Jean and Gwen Leaton (1995) *Loosening the Grip: A Handbook of Alcohol Information* (5th edn). St. Louis and London: Mosby-Year Book Inc.
Indispensable and comprehensive.

Lincoln, Kenneth, with Al Logan Slagle (1987) *The Good Red Road: Passages into Native America.* San Francisco: Harper and Row.

Miller, Alice (1981) *The Drama of the Gifted Child.* New York: Basic Books Inc. *Translated from German by Ruth Ward. Also translated as* The Drama of Being a Child, *and originally published as* Prisoners of Childhood.
The psychology of childhood dependence. Brilliant.

McCully, C. (2002) *The Country of Perhaps.* Manchester: Carcanet Press.

Nakken, Craig (1996) *The Addictive Personality* (2nd edn). Center City, MN: Hazelden.
Informative and useful guide to how alcoholism is often embedded in other forms of addictive personality traits and behaviours. One of the best and most insightful books I've ever read on addiction.

Proctor, Robert N. (1986) *Racial Hygiene: Medicine Under the Nazis.* Cambridge, MA: Harvard University Press.

Rinpoche, Sogyal (1992) *The Tibetan Book of Living and Dying* (edited by Patrick Gaffney and Andrew Harvey). London and Sydney: Rider.

Tudge, Colin (2002) *In Mendel's Footnotes.* London: Vintage.
Popular introduction to the work of Gregor Mendel, and to the subsequent science of genetics (including some of the legal and social problems posed by the central findings of the science). Readable and informative.

Index